Can Islam Be French?

Princeton Studies in Muslim Politics

DALE F. EICKELMAN AND AUGUSTUS RICHARD NORTON, EDITORS

Can Islam Be French?

PLURALISM AND PRAGMATISM IN A SECULARIST STATE

John R. Bowen

PRINCETON UNIVERSITY PRESS

PRINCETON AND OXFORD

Third printing, and first paperback printing, 2012
Paperback ISBN 978-0-691-15249-3

The Library of Congress has cataloged the cloth edition of this book as follows

Bowen, John Richard, 1951–
    Can Islam be French? : pluralism and pragmatism in a secularist state / John R. Bowen.
        p. cm. — (Princeton studies in Muslim politics)
    Includes bibliographical references and index.
    ISBN 978-0-691-13283-9 (hardcover : alk. paper) 1. Muslims—France. 2. Islam—
France. 3. Islam and politics—France. I. Title.
    DC34.5.M87B68 2009
    305.6'970944—dc22   2009004645

British Library Cataloging-in-Publication Data is available

This book has been composed in Sabon

Printed on acid-free paper. ∞

Printed in the United States of America

10 9 8 7 6 5 4 3

To Vicki, Jeff, and Greg

Contents

Acknowledgments

I HAVE BEEN WORKING in France since 2000 and have developed close working relationships, and friendships, with many colleagues. Among those from whose example, writings, or comments I have benefited in writing this book are Valérie Amiraux, Jean Baubérot, Christophe Bertossi, Martin van Bruinessen, Jocelyne Cesari, Jacques Commaille, Jan Willem Duyvendak, Claire de Galembert, David Gellner, Ralph Grillo, Nacira Guénif-Souilamas, Christophe Jaffrelot, Baber Johansen, Riva Kastoryano, Gilles Kepel, Farhad Khosrokhavar, Jack Knight, Michèle Lamont, Marie McAndrew, Ian McMullen, Françoise Lorcerie, Tariq Modood, Françoise and Joël Monéger, Olivier Roy, Patrick Simon, Patrick Weil, Jean-Paul Willaime, and Malika Zeghal. Younger scholars and students often provide the most important new insights, and in my case they include Alexandre Caeiro, Yolande Jansen, and Marcel Maussen. For his critical and encouraging eye, I thank Fred Appel at Princeton University Press and his colleagues Natalie Baan and Marjorie Pannell, who expertly steered the book through production and copy editing. It is from those engaged in teaching Islam that I have learned the most; many are mentioned in the book, but here I must underscore my personal gratitude to Hichem El Arafa, Saïd Branine, Chokri Hammrouni, Larbi Kechat, Dhaou Meskine, and Samia Touati for guiding my way to a better understanding of their knowledge and their challenges.

As before, I must single out Martine and Robert Bentaboulet, whose continued hospitality, lively discussions, and convivial repasts have made my time in Paris more like "real fieldwork"—for, as many in anthropology know, fieldwork is as much about discovering new friendships as it is about discovering new truths.

But if one holds down a day job and a day life, long-term fieldwork of the sort pursued here requires frequent travel. For making my trips financially possible I thank Washington University and the benefactors of my chair, Georgia Dunbar-Van Cleve and her late husband, Bill Van Cleve, along with generous support from the Carnegie Corporation; for making them humanly possible I thank my family, to whom the book is dedicated.

PART ONE

Trajectories

CHAPTER ONE

Islam and the Republic

MY TITLE, of course, rests on an indefensible premise. Islam cannot be exclusively French any more than it can be American or Egyptian, because its claims are universal. Although inflected and shaped by national or regional values, Islam, like Catholicism and Judaism, rests on traditions that cross political boundaries.

Let me try another way to understand the question: Can Islam become a generally accepted part of the French social landscape? Of course, it will not have the background status of Catholicism anytime soon—Parisians may not notice a cross or a church; they certainly notice a headscarf or a minaret. But could it become accepted—more or less grudgingly, more or less intuitively—as one among many normal components of the normal social world? Quick off the mark there are signs that suggest yes, perhaps, and others that indicate no, maybe not.

Among the positive signs: A 2006 survey found that French people as a whole think Islam can fit into France. When asked if there is a conflict between being a devout Muslim and living in a modern society, 74 percent of all French people said no, there was not. Only about half as many other Europeans or Americans deny such a conflict. Indeed, French people are more positive about modern Islam than are people in Indonesia, Jordan, or Egypt! This positive answer may be related to an equally hopeful finding of the survey: French Muslims are about as likely to emphasize their national identity over their religious one as are U.S. Christians—and they are much more likely to do so than are other European Muslims.[1] So, at least when talking to pollsters, goodly numbers of French Muslims and non-Muslims seem to think that Islam could be French.

But increasingly, public figures criticize some Muslims as harboring values incompatible with French citizenship, even if they neither break laws nor contravene norms of public behavior. Two incidents from 2008: A court approved a request to annul a marriage on grounds that the wife had lied to the husband about something he judged essential to their marriage. The judgment was in accord with French jurisprudence, but because the "something" was the wife's virginity and the couple was Muslim, public figures denounced Muslims who harbored "archaic" notions about women, and the annulment eventually was overturned. At about the same time, the government successfully kept a married woman with children from obtaining French citizenship because she wore a face covering and stayed at home, proof that her "radical religion" had prevented her from "assimilating" French values.

And consider what Parisians read. I dropped into the Virgin Megastore in Saint-Denis, tucked in behind the famous cathedral and in a largely Muslim corner of town. Free for the taking was the store's magazine, with a picture of a naked woman on the cover and with "pleasure" as the issue's theme. When I entered the store I saw books on Islam, the Qur'an, and how to pray; we were in the month of Ramadan. But the table holding new, small-format books placed near the cash register featured thirteen titles, ten of which approached Islam and Muslims from quite a different point of view. *Dishonored* and *Mutilated* each concern violence by Muslim men against Muslim women. *Sultana* describes the horrible life of a Saudi princess. Both *The Sold Ones* and *The Fatiha* (referring to the first verse of the Qur'an, recited at a marriage) treat forced marriages. *Muslim But Free* is Irshad Manji's story; *Disfigured* is Rania al-Baz's, each about Muslim misogyny. *Gang-Rape Hell* tells of violence against women in the largely Muslim, poor outer cities of Paris. *Souad, Burned Alive* and *Latya, Her Face Stolen* complete the picture. (I do not count no. 11, a translation of *Reading Lolita in Teheran*, which suggests that without Nabokov, the Persians might have found themselves bereft of literature.)[2]

Things are not that different on the North American side of the Atlantic, from where Irshad Manji comes and where another denouncer of Islam from within, Ayaan Hirsi Ali (*Submission*; *The Caged Virgin*), sometimes lives, and where books on Islam's threat to Europe have taken off: "they're asleep; we're next," we, over here, are warned in *While Europe Slept*, *Eurabia*, and the latest, *They Must Be Stopped*.

Now, in the so-called "public sphere" dominated by such books and their sensationalist televised counterparts (Fox News, *Envoyé Spécial*), very seldom do we hear from Muslims who are *not* in the business of denouncing their own kind—save the well-intentioned but not very effective pleas that "Islam is a religion of peace," as if that were a satisfying response to *Disfigured* and *Submission* and unceasing reports of terrorism training. ("Whom do you believe, me or your own eyes?") Left largely to the side—either out of their own prudence or out of the "public sphere's" decision that their voices are less interesting—is a broad middle group of Muslims who do *not* wish to renounce the possibility of just war (yes, *jihâd*) and *do* wish to remain true to Islam's norms (yes, *sharî'a*), and who *do* tune in to scholarly opinions (yes, *fatwâs*)—and who, all the while, live ordinary, nonterrorizing lives. They do so at the same time that many of their Catholic fellow citizens subscribe to doctrines of the just war, wish to enter heaven, and listen to what the pope has to say (as do, mutatis mutandis, their Jewish and Baptist and Mormon neighbors).

It is a subset of *these* Muslims to whom I have been listening in France: scholars and educators and public figures who are trying to configure a set of teachings and norms and institutions that will anchor Islam in France, for now but especially for the next generation, and without renouncing the traditions of Islam. Theirs is the question that I intend in this book's title: Can Islam become a workable reality for Muslims who wish to live fulfilling social *and* religious lives in France? This book concerns some of their answers to that question.

In an earlier book, in some ways a companion to this one, I explored the ideas and anxieties of some non-Muslim French men and women about the visible presence of Islam on their soil. I did so largely through one particular lens, the conflicts over the wearing of Islamic scarves in public schools, but I touched on a broader array of issues, from racism (also aimed at non-Muslim people of color) to the shape of the urban built environment.[3] That study posed the question of whether Muslims who wish to publicly practice their religion can make their way in French society without having to pretend to be something other than Muslims. Can they become *citoyens à part entière* rather than *citoyens entièrement à part*, "complete citizens" of France rather than "citizens completely on the sidelines"?[4] Particularly thorny are the issues implied by the phrase "pretend to be something other than Muslims." How far will the French state go in requiring not just obedience to the law and correct public comportment, but assimilation to a particular set of (post-) Christian practices and values?

Although in the final chapter I return to those issues, throughout most of this book I focus on the Islamic side of the same issue: what forms of Islamic ideas and institutions will enable those Muslims wishing to practice their religion to do so fully and freely in France? I explore the development of mosques and of Islamic schools and institutes and, simultaneously, the Islamic reasoning that subtends and suffuses these institutions as it answers such questions as the following: What should an Islamic secondary school look like in a secularist society? How does one teach Islam in a way that remains connected with global deliberations *and also* provides guides for French living? What should mosques do? Should a marriage be conducted in a religious manner or at city hall? May I borrow money at interest from a bank to buy my home?

As in my previous books on France and on Indonesia, I set out to practice an "anthropology of public reasoning." The "anthropology" part of that phrase means that I look whenever possible at ongoing interactions in social life: at how a teacher reasons or an imam persuades or a city official justifies his actions. I bring in written texts when these enter into social life, when they are used in teaching or read widely, but I begin from social interactions in mosques, schools, public meetings, and

Internet exchanges. The "public reasoning" part means that I highlight the ways in which people deliberate and debate in these public settings. It is in these practices of deliberation—justifying one's beliefs and seeking areas of agreement—rather than in a static notion of an achieved consensus that I find hope for pluralistic forms of civic integration.[5]

A critical component of the anthropology of public reasoning is the study of justifications: on what grounds do speakers advance one position rather than another? What kinds of argument do they pursue, and how are these received? In the Islamic context these questions often turn on sources of authority: which past authorities or scriptural texts are cited? Does an argument emphasize the distinctive demands placed on Muslims in France, the universal character of God's call to walk along the straight path, or both? Through these questions I wish to highlight the specific forms taken by Islamic reasoning in these particular French social contexts.

This attention to Islamic justifications should, I believe, extend current social science analyses of how people in different societies justify their positions on policy issues. Some of these analyses have discerned distinct sociomoral conceptions of worth or value that underlie specific acts of justification and that, in weighted combinations, form national (or subnational) "repertoires of evaluation." Parisians and New Yorkers may both recognize that material success, social solidarity, and personal morality are legitimate bases for judging the actions of others, but the two groups will assign different weights to these three values.[6] Repertoires, therefore, can be mapped onto particular territories.

The problem faced in this book is a bit different. Muslims who are engaged in deliberating about Islam in France must navigate between two spatially distinct realms of justification: a transnational one, based on the norms and traditions of Islam, and a national one, based on the civic values of France. The repertoires of evaluation at use in these two realms are not differentially weighted versions of each other but refer to entirely different foundations: God in the one case, the Republic in the other. Each repertoire is a distinct assembly of norms and values that delimits acceptable from unacceptable ways of explaining and justifying actions.

In much of this book, I focus on a handful of individuals, Islamic public actors who find themselves at the intersection of these two realms as they teach and deliberate about how best to create Islamic institutions in France. As *Islamic* actors, they find themselves engaged in exchanges with scholars who live in Syria, Senegal, Turkey, or Egypt, some of whom post articles on Web sites, have their books translated into French (and other languages), and appear in public discussions in Paris, Lyon, or Lille. Each of those scholars commands his own type of authority—the professor at an established Islamic university, the scholar who commands an impressive range of scriptural texts, or the inspirational leader of a Sufi order—usually at a level far beyond that of any Islamic public actor living in France. As French Islamic actors formulate their own opinions, they must keep in mind the commentaries and judgments that might be delivered by those transnational authorities—and as we shall see, sometimes those authorities deliver quite negative judgments on certain opinions developed in France.

At the same time, these Islamic actors live in France and must respond to the experiences and exigencies of life in that country. On the one hand, they must craft their opinions to the lives of French Muslims, whose questions concern how to live in a secular society: how to worship, work, or marry in the absence of Islamic institutions. On the other hand, they must try and adapt what they say and do to French norms and understandings about religion and social life, lest they be attacked as insufficiently secularist or as overly communalist.

Now, if those French understandings were clear and unambiguous, this task might not be so difficult, but France contains a tension, if not a contradiction, between its Republican political model and the way religion-minded citizens organize their lives. In the ideal world of Republican France, everyone develops similar values and orientations by participating in public institutions, starting from their education in state schools. This direct, sustained contact between the state and the individual underwrites the dual capacity to live together and to deliberate in rational fashion, because everyone lives and reasons starting from the same first principles. On this view, intermediate institutions such as voluntary associations, private schools, and religious practices are to be discouraged, lest they nourish divergent values and create social divisions. Jean-Jacques Rousseau, perhaps the emblematic figure of this philosophy, affirmed the ultimate identity of citizens' interests in the general will, to be expressed through the state and reproduced through its institutions.

But Rousseau also upheld the rights of citizens to form voluntary associations in order to carry out their diverse interests. When in the first few years of the twentieth century the state got out of the business of subsidizing religions, it intended to turn religious life over to private associations of French citizens, who would then, in turn, leave schooling to the state. The Catholic Church resisted these measures, and a series of compromises led to new laws extending governmental support to religious buildings and permitting religious private schools—even financing them if they taught the national curriculum. These compromises never fully satisfied those who saw religious institutions as compromising Republican unity. Struggles for women's rights during the 1960s and 1970s were waged against a Church unwilling to allow freedom of control over women's bodies. State support to religious schools continued to excite passions on both sides well into the 1980s.

When, beginning in the 1980s, Muslims sought to follow the example of other religions by forming religious associations, building houses of worship, and seeking state funding for religious schools, they encountered a double source of resistance and suspicion: as one more religious body threatening Republican unity, and as one element in a global movement threatening the West. Were they trying to resist integrating into the rest of French society? Did they harbor values distinct from those held by others in France? To some degree these questions imply a reluctance to acknowledge the degree of religion-based associative life already basic to France, but they also point to the special difficulties faced by Islamic public actors in finding a stable equilibrium between the French rules of the game and a respect for Islamic norms.[7]

Above, I narrowed the book's title question to, What can Muslims do to create a workable Islamic reality in France? And yet even in this reduced form the question opens up two more specific sets of queries: given the transnational nature of Islamic public reasoning, how far can or should French Muslims adapt the norms and institutions of Islam to local norms and institutions? And how far will they be allowed to follow a Republican path that is itself internally contradictory?

Neither question is limited to France. From Morocco and Nigeria to Pakistan and Indonesia, we find Muslims wrestling with how to adapt Islamic texts and traditions to local, contemporary ways of life. The issue is posed most profoundly for matters of gender equality, religious pluralism, and the right to choose to leave Islam.[8] In Indonesia, for example (where I have worked for many years), some scholars have contrasted what they see as an overly Arabic-cultural and patriarchal bias in Islamic legal teachings to the more gender-equal nature of Indonesian life, and they have drawn on that contrast to develop a new code of Islamic law for Indonesia.

The second question, concerning the "fit" between Islamic traditions, on the one hand, and national norms and values on the other, arises most sharply in Europe and North America only because Muslims are relatively recent immigrants to these lands. The same questions once were asked of Catholics and Jews, and each time they emerge, they bring to the fore contradictions within each national political tradition. In the United States, for example, this contradiction lies between the formal claim to divorce matters of state from matters of faith and the less formal but often more powerful "commonsense" view that the country was based on a Protestant way of life, later expanded to a "Christian" one and (sometimes) today to a "Judeo-Christian" one. The positive challenge to each country is to make more precise the background conditions of life in a country, so as to make clear what is required of new arrivals and therefore what is also required of people who have lived there longer. What precisely *is* the role of religion in U.S. public life? What precisely *are* "British values?" What *should be* the shared way of life of all who make their home in France? The relatively new presence of Muslim residents could provide an opportunity to revisit and perhaps to expand the meanings of living together in all these countries rather than remain an irritating reminder that such meanings are a bit cloudy.

If, as I suggest, the questions I have posed are by no means limited to one country, why focus on France? I find that in France, the general dilemmas and tensions I discussed above stand in particularly clear relief, because of two distinctive features of the French experience. First, Muslims have had a longer and deeper experience in France than anywhere else in Western Europe.[9] They came to work in France earlier and in greater numbers than did South Asians in Britain (the next deepest Muslim-European presence), and the Algerians among them eventually became citizens of France rather than merely imperial subjects. Most Muslims arriving in France came from countries where large numbers of people spoke French to some degree, a feature that contrasts sharply with the histories of Muslims' arrival in the Netherlands, Germany, or the Scandinavian countries. Not that this familiarity was peaceful: strikes, repression, and the brutal Algerian War characterized the long years of colonial rule, and the riots of late 2005 showed the world how little a part of French society many of the children and grandchildren of those immigrants now feel. But these have been conflicts and struggles occurring within a postcolonial Francophone space with a long history to its name.

Second, to continue the contrast with Britain, if Muslims from northern and western Africa have been in France longer than Muslims from South Asia have been in Britain, they nonetheless had a harder time gaining religious recognition. While their British counterparts formed local associations to promote halâl foods and Islamic curricula in local schools and to build places of worship, French Muslims were encountering strong legal and cultural resistance to these forms of local lobbying. British multiculturalism provided smoother pathways to creating Islamic institutions than did French traditions of secularism, and British localism allowed Muslims to make advances with local school boards and councils, while in France it took the much slower creation of national organizations to advance these agendas—and at that, slowly.[10]

The French specificity thus cuts both ways: a longer familiarity but a sharper set of obstacles in the way of Muslims seeking to create an Islamic way of life. Muslim religious innovators in France have been pushed harder and farther to find ways to simultaneously satisfy Islamic and Western ways of life than have their counterparts in Britain, Germany, Italy, or, for that matter, the United States. Some of the French Muslim innovators today are looking for patches of convergence, if not explicit agreement: areas where at least some versions of Islamic norms overlap with at least some notions of French (or more broadly European and North American) ones. Some of these overlaps are on matters of legal interpretation—ways to see a civil marriage as already Islamic and to enforce an Islamic marriage contract in civil court. Others are overlaps achieved through tacit accommodations and through nuanced ways of speaking—how an Islamic biology teacher approaches evolution while wearing a headscarf, or how a municipal official finds a way to help build a mosque while proclaiming secularist principles. The results are, I believe, of general interest if they suggest pathways toward accommodation and innovation that do not sacrifice either accountability to secularist principles or faithfulness to the message of Islam.

Much, of course, has been written about Muslims in France, and even more about Muslims in Europe and in the West. Emblematic of work on France is the title of a 1997 publication, "Is Islam Dissolvable in the Republic?" Answers differ, but the question remains a common touchstone for most French students of French Islam: Can Muslims divest themselves of their older identities and habits such that they resemble others in France? Can Muslims coexist with others? Can they integrate, or assimilate? Can Islam become more like (privatized forms of) European Christianity?

Some of the more interesting among these studies, most of them in political science or sociology, construct typologies of Muslims' orientations toward the wider societies: Muslims are Republican, communalistic, or somewhere in between.[11] Others, with more immediate policy issues in mind, phrase the issue in quasi-quantitative terms: How far have Muslims managed to assimilate, or integrate?[12] Some draw insightfully on in-depth interviews to highlight specific questions: How do some Muslim women use their choices of dress to negotiate space for themselves vis-à-vis their families or vis-à-vis the religious traditions out of which they come? How do Muslims experience prison in religious terms?[13]

Still others stress that Muslims inevitably will become more like Europeans as they create privatized and individualistic versions of their religion.[14] Hence the intense interest among some officials, journalists, and academics in estimating *how* religious they (still) are, manifested in polls asking "Muslims" (usually identified by last names) about regularity of worship, mosque attendance, and fasting, in order to sort respondents into categories of practitioners, mere believers, or neither.[15]

My starting point is a different one from that of most of these works: less "how are Muslims fitting in with France" than "in France, what do certain Muslim public actors propose to make of Islam?" My interest is from *within* the religious tradition, and in particular from the broad set of concerns that we can call "normative" and that stretch from matters of worship and service to God (*ibâdât*) to matters of relations among humans (*muʿâmalât*). But as my object is public reasoning and its social contexts rather than ideas per se, I want to see how some Muslims explain, persuade, and offer opinions to other Muslims, or, to use the analytical terms introduced above, I want to see how they develop and communicate new repertoires of evaluation within the Islamic realm.[16]

I begin by explaining how the historical trajectories of Muslims in France have shaped their strategies of adaptation and innovation. I refer to "Muslims" in the sense of "sociological Muslims," that is, people whose background and traditions form part of the long history of Muslim civilization, regardless of whether they worship regularly or what they believe. It is very important not to ascribe a uniformity of religious observance to Muslims, and most "sociological Muslims" in France do not take active roles in debates about Islam. But most of them consider themselves to be Muslims, and they are seen as such by others around them. I do, for that reason, retain "Muslim" as a socially relevant characteristic applying to a broad category of French residents. But it does not mean that all Muslims always highlight that dimension of their identity in their everyday lives.

In subsequent chapters I narrow my focus to Islam and to what I call Islamic public actors, that is, men and women who engage in public activity with respect to Islamic concerns. In part two, I examine how some of these Muslims have developed mosques, schools, and institutes through which they convey certain ideas about Islamic knowledge and how it should be understood in contemporary France.

I start with a handful of mosques and their social and political environments. I do so because the creation of mosques has been a key concern of Islamic public actors, particularly since the early 1980s, and because some mosques have become centers for broader social activities. Although I discuss all the major Muslim populations in France, including Muslims who came from northern and western Africa, Turkey, and the Comoro Islands, most of what I write in this volume concerns first and foremost scholars and public figures from North Africa (the *Maghreb*)—Tunisia, Algeria, and Morocco. Muslims from the Maghreb make up the great majority of French Muslims, and it is they who have tackled the problems posed above in the most direct and public way. As I describe in detail below, Turkish and West African trajectories have differed from those of North Africa in ways that are relevant to the study of Islamic public reasoning. Turks have focused on creating their own mosques and schools, most of which remain tightly linked to parties and movements in Turkey. West Africans show a more diverse array of patterns, in which Sufi orders tied to West African teachers predominate. Both populations look toward authorities in their homelands to a greater degree than do North Africans, and therefore have taken a less predominant role in debates about what to make of Islam in France. (They also are relatively more recent immigrants to France.) But if the questions posed by the title of this book have been taken up most enthusiastically by North African Muslims, the answers and institutions that follow from them will sooner or later shape thoughts and actions of all those in France who seek to live by what they see as Islamic norms and values.

Across three chapters, I consider how some Islamic public actors have created Islamic teaching environments in France. I begin with the director of one of France's major Islamic institutes and his response to the challenge of teaching about Islam in a Western European country, then explore the contours of the Islamic educational field in France, and finally look at an early effort to teach the French national school curriculum in an Islamic private school. Here pedagogy is at the fore: do certain ways of teaching suggest certain attitudes toward religious knowledge and toward civic knowledge?

In part three, I turn from spaces to debates and focus on a small set of questions arising from everyday dilemmas facing Muslims living in France (and, with some differences, elsewhere in Europe and North America). In each of two discussions, I analyze the shape of reasoning and debate in specific public spaces, and the constitution of a socially embedded realm of justification. The first considers the issue of whether one should take out interest-bearing bank loans to purchase a home. The debate takes us toward a longstanding question: Should Muslims living in "non-Muslim lands" be exempt from certain rules? These debates have been continuingly transnational, and I consider some of the spheres in which they have occurred, including mosques, schools, and the Internet. The second discussion brings up the question of how to properly marry and divorce. These debates include interrogations among Muslims about the Islamic validity of civil marriages and parallel debates among French jurists about whether to recognize Islamic forms of marriage and divorce. With this discussion, I move toward asking whether it is possible to create a convergence of norms and practices *across* these distinct realms of justification.

These issues, and others not explored here in detail (ensuring halâl quality, carrying out sacrifice, limiting the wearing of religious dress), involve dialectical movements between institutional constraints and normative arguments. They all potentially involve Muslims and non-Muslims—even the debates over bank interest, although currently involving Muslims alone, could very soon involve non-Muslim financial institutions, as they have in Britain and the United States. Although these debates start from concrete issues, they also bring up longstanding issues in Islamic reasoning: Should norms differ by region, or change over time, and if so, to what extent? How far may scholars move from the specific injunctions given in scripture to general principles that can be inferred from scripture? These last two questions structure much of the debates considered here, as they do in much of the world, as Muslims living in Asia, Africa, the Middle East and lands of more recent settlement in Europe and North America engage in global deliberation, and sometimes sheer confrontation, on how Muslims ought to adapt to new social exigencies.

I examine closely two lines of response to these broad normative questions, each possessing a long Islamic lineage. The first suggests that Islamic norms should be inflected across differing social settings, such that Muslims living in one place would be exempted from rules that otherwise would apply. The second, to which I devote more attention, urges Muslims to evaluate their normative statements over and against what they see as the overall "objectives of God's revelations," the *maqâsid ash-sharî'a*. Those who advocate this "maqâsid approach" draw on a long tradition of thinking about the interest and welfare (*maslaha*) of Muslims.[17] But they also encounter objections from several quarters, both within France and beyond its borders. Some scholars, mainly in centers of Islamic learning, emphasize the importance of remaining within longstanding methods of legal reasoning and accuse those pursuing maqâsid reasoning of departing from those methods. Others, both ordinary Muslims and the scholars to whom they listen (many in Saudi Arabia and the Gulf states), insist on keeping to the letter of the revealed texts. Of course, many who advocate justifications based on maqâsid also pay close attention to the study of scripture and to one or more older legal traditions (the *madhhabs*), and the controversies have to do with priority and emphasis.

The maqâsid approach continues to grow and develop in several directions: toward social engagement in broad, interfaith causes, toward pedagogical refinements, and toward daily advice to Muslims dispensed in mosques and institutes. Its emphasis on adapting norms to broader religious goals makes it particularly useful to Muslims caught in the twin dilemmas of religious accountability and secularist acceptability. In fact, many of the diverse approaches within Islam that are emerging in France, and across Europe, share a tendency to justify both normative innovation and resistance to such innovation on grounds that I call *socially pragmatic*. Whether an Islamic actor advocates reasoning on the basis of one or more legal traditions, or in terms of the objectives of the Qur'an, or in terms of principles derived from scripture, he or she often justifies the choice of style of reasoning in terms of the resulting benefit for Muslims. I examine the major objections to this form of reasoning, as well as its possibilities for adapting Islamic norms to French social conditions.

I end by returning to the question posed by the book's title, but now noting that for many non-Muslims in France, the critical issues may be less matters of secularism and public space than the perception that Muslims represent an undesirable source of value-pluralism. The spaces marked as Islamic provide young Muslims social and moral foundations for civic engagement, but they also produce anxiety among those in France who fear that some Muslims have not adopted, and may not adopt, "French values."

Across these chapters, I trace real and potential pathways of convergence in normative reasoning from the two directions of French social and legal norms and from Islamic ones. But the convergence will depend on the acceptance of a certain measure of social pragmatism from both sides. Islam is more likely to "be French"—that is, to be a fully accepted feature of the French socioreligious landscape—when both Muslims and non-Muslims have developed convincing reasons to accept pragmatic forms of justification, ones that accept the social welfare of all as a good reason to support a policy, and that accept a pluralism of values as perfectly coherent with appropriate understandings of French secularity.

CHAPTER TWO

Fashioning the French Islamic Landscape

THE ENTRY OF ISLAM into France's public space touched two sharp nerves that had long run through the nation's history of contentious politics: the tensions generated by waves of immigration, and the thin, sometimes frayed thread of religious toleration. In one sense Islam was nothing new, in another it was wholly different, and its entry brought back into public consciousness fights and fissures that previously and otherwise could be more easily forgotten: colonial repressions, modern anti-Semitism, and the struggles between Catholics and Republicans.[1]

France as a whole was shaped by immigration, and most of it was from elsewhere in Europe. Some in France thought that the Poles and Italians were too Catholic for France, and the Jews not patriotic enough.[2] But the arrival of many Muslims after the Second World War did signal something new: a dramatic transformation in the religious topography of France wherein Islam no longer marked the boundaries of "Europe" but was growing in its center.

This shift had been taking place for some time. When Charles the Hammer stopped the Moorish armies pushing north from Spain, or when Saint Louis sent Crusaders against the Saracens who had taken the Holy Land, Islam came to define the edge of Christendom as the dangerously close monotheistic cousin waiting on the periphery. But when France invaded Algeria in the 1830s and eventually took control of much of northern and western Africa, it brought a mass of Muslims under its rule and, when they were needed to work or to fight, onto its metropolitan soil. Islam itself became an instrument in France's dealing with Muslim rulers, with temporary Muslim workers, and with competing European powers. France billed itself as a "great Muslim power" with a population that included French citizens and Muslim subjects. Islam had become an *internal* periphery, a product of this colonial division of imperial France.[3]

By the mid-twentieth century, Muslims in the colonies had won independence and other Muslims had settled in France, now not as temporary workers but as permanent residents and citizens of France. Eventually, many of these new residents presented themselves in the public eye as Muslims: not as workers or North Africans or postcolonials but as practitioners of a new *French* religion. The idea that Islam would take its place alongside Catholicism, Protestantism, and Judaism as a recognized religion, with services in public places, and schools, and special ways of marrying and burying—all this was very new for those French men and women who were either more or less Catholic, Protestant, or Jewish, or who had thought that religion was on its way out of public life altogether.

So now France would have to sigh and step back and form commissions to decide how best to "integrate" Muslims and their Islam, how to make Islam something visible to and thus controllable by the state, tolerable to non-Muslims, and oriented toward Paris rather than toward Algiers or Riyadh. Perhaps an Islam of faith and properly circumscribed devotions could be French, but an Islam of schools, mosques, and people whose everyday demeanor marked themselves off from others and who sought religious knowledge outside the country—that was a different story, one that was harder to square with those stories of Charles the Hammer and Saint Louis, and with the more recent stories of Jules Ferry and laïcité and the combat with the Catholic Church.

MIGRATION PATHWAYS

Let us look more closely at how the French history of colonial rule and Muslim migration has shaped Islam in France today. Most Muslims living today in France either came from, or trace their origins to, former French territories in northern or western Africa. Their stories are deeply interwoven both with the creation of the French Empire and with the demand for labor on French metropolitan soil. Out of these two histories has developed a particular set of locations and dispositions that distinguish the French Islamic landscape from others in neighboring parts of Europe.

Algerians were the first to come in large numbers to France, and they and their descendants still make up the largest population of Muslims. France began its control of this part of North Africa in 1830, encouraged European settlement, and by the 1870s had made Algeria into a part of France itself, rather than a protectorate or a colony.[4] During the first half of the twentieth century the French government and private companies brought Algerian men to metropolitan France whenever unskilled labor was needed. During the Great War they were imported to replace French factory workers called up for active duty, and to serve in the military themselves. Labor migration continued during the interwar years, but it was the rebuilding of France after the Second World War that led to the most massive efforts to encourage labor immigration, much of it, again, from Algeria. As political repression and economic hardship increased in Algeria, particularly during the Algerian War (1954–62), families increasingly came to settle in France. They continued to do so until the global recession of 1973–74, when France suspended labor immigration, leaving close to 900,000 Algerians in France. Algerians have stayed: today they are the least likely immigrant group to return to their natal land—one-half as likely as Tunisians, one-tenth as likely as Portuguese.[5]

By the 1960s, Algerians had been joined by other North Africans in hostels and in housing projects throughout France: in Lyon and its suburbs, in the fast-growing eastern region of Alsace and Mosel, across the broad northern arc of industrial cities around Lille and adjoining Roubaix, and in the cities and suburbs of Marseille and Paris. The Moroccans and Tunisians who joined them largely arrived after their counties had won their independence, although some had worked in France during the colonial period. By 1974, 260,000 Moroccans and 140,000 Tunisians lived in France, with students and professionals adding to early streams of industrial workers.[6]

These North African Muslims arriving in France included speakers of Berber languages and a range of Arabic dialects, but they shared the use of Arabic in religious life, common North African religious traditions, and an allegiance to the Mâlikî legal school of Sunni Islam. They thus were able to worship together in the prayer spaces in their apartments or in mosques. Despite a lingering spirit of competition, particularly between Algerians and Moroccans, and the occasional dispute over mosque leadership across ethnic boundaries, the common heritage has meant that this largest group of Muslims in France has far fewer internal cleavages than is the case for Muslims in Britain, the Netherlands, or Germany.[7]

West Africans also came to France as laborers and soldiers, but most came later and retained stronger prior religious ties than did North Africans. Large-scale immigration from Mali, Senegal, and Mauritania began only after these countries had won independence and had signed formal labor agreements.[8] Many Muslims from these countries preserved strong ties to their Sufi religious leaders and today welcome those leaders to centers in Paris or Marseille. Many West Africans are not Muslim, and in the French public eye the West Africans are not as closely identified with Islam as are the "Arabs." But as the more recent arrivals, they are less likely than North Africans to be legal residents and to have permanent employment, and they are more likely to live in crowded quarters and, for cultural reasons, to live in polygamous families. Increasingly it is these Muslims rather than North Africans who are targeted by the larger society as insufficiently adapted to France, and whose problems and actions are most often framed in racial terms.[9]

Among major Muslim immigrant populations, only the Turks came from a country with no historical ties to France, and they have developed the most ethnic-specific set of religious institutions. Workers came from Turkey on labor agreements beginning in 1969, and settled in Paris or in eastern France; by the late 1990s there were about 350,000 people from Turkey, including Turks and Kurds, in France.[10] Few spoke French, and most relied on preexisting ties to find work, to agree on marriage partners for their children, and to shape their religious lives.[11] They are much more likely than are North Africans to marry someone from their country of origin, and much less likely to speak French to their children.[12]

Muslims from overseas French territories also make up important communities: by 2005, about 193,000 Muslims with their origins in Mayotte and 70,000 with origins in the Reunion Islands lived in metropolitan France.[13] In addition, violence and political turmoil have brought asylum seekers to France from Bosnia, Lebanon, Iran, Pakistan, Iraq, and elsewhere.

Because of the staggered time frames of immigration, some immigrant groups have much deeper roots in France than do others. Algerian immigrants are three times as likely as other Muslim immigrants to have arrived very young and therefore to speak fluent French. They also have a deeper history of engagement with France than even this statistic suggests, because many adults who arrived in France from Algeria were born in Algeria when it was part of France, and all Algerians *were* French until 1962. At the other end of the spectrum are the West Africans, who are the most likely to have arrived in France as adults.[14]

Contemporary immigration streams have by and large continued these historical patterns. In 2004–5 there were 4.9 million people living in France who had been born elsewhere (40 percent of whom had taken French nationality). Some 1.5 million of the total had come from North Africa, including 677,000 from Algeria, 619,000 from Morocco, and 220,000 from Tunisia. Another 225,000 were from Turkey, 67,000 from Senegal, and 56,000 from Mali. (Portugal, Spain, and Italy were the other large sources of immigrants.) Between one-fifth and one-third of each of the Muslim-majority country groups had acquired French nationality.[15] These Muslims live mainly in city centers or peripheral ring cities in the regions of Paris, Lyon, Marseille, Lille, and Alsace. Paris proper is 10–15 percent Muslim, Marseille 25 percent, and Roubaix, near Lille, 50 percent.

This history of immigration, determined largely by colonial control and labor recruitment, thus gave a very specific profile to Muslims in France. The large majority of Muslims trace ties to three northern African countries, and they share broad patterns of language, culture, and religious affiliation, along with a relatively long-term familiarity with France. The two populations next in size remain more tied to religious organizations in their countries of origin: West African Muslims to specific teachers and mosques in Mali or Senegal, and Muslims from Turkey through one of two competing transnational organizations. This profile in turn has shaped public deliberations in France: the most visible Islamic public actors in deliberations and activities in France come from a North African background and share a common religious frame of reference. These features have made it easier for them to form national umbrella organizations and to work across country boundaries than would otherwise have been the case (and than is the case elsewhere in Europe). Put another way, the fissions and quarrels that do surface among public actors have been due more to competition between individuals (and sometimes between mosques) than to differences in religious ideas and histories or in background language and culture.

Residence and Boundaries

Where Muslims have settled also has shaped how they interact and think about identity and interests. In the 1950s the state built hostels and low-rent apartments for single workers near factories and away from city centers, a decision that was intended to neutralize Algerian nationalist recruiting drives as well as tightly link immigration to specific labor needs. France also began to build "moderate income residences" (*habitations à loyer modéré*), the now infamous HLMs that have come to stand for peri-urban decay and violence. Low-income families gained access only slowly to these projects, but when they did they heartily welcomed the opportunity to live in clean, new apartments with indoor plumbing. Following the modernist style of the day, projects were built as separated islands of 500 or more apartments, often far from public transportation.[16] By the 1990s, the average project in the Paris region held about 9,000 residents; the very largest, Val-Fouré in Mantes-la-Jolie, has held as many as 28,000 people in 7,600 apartments.[17]

Eventually, as factories closed down and the more upwardly mobile families moved away, the projects became unemployment traps rather than starting points on the escalator to success. People in the outer cities generally have high unemployment rates, but the official numbers understate the realities faced by youth in the projects. A town may have a 20 percent unemployment rate, twice the national average, but for younger residents the rate may be 30 percent, and for those who left school and throng the projects the rate may be 50 or 60 percent.

It is the children who grew up in the projects who burst onto the front pages of newspapers throughout the world in the November 2005 riots. They are likely to be young people of color: about 18 percent of all people in France live in HLMs, but 50 percent of North African immigrants, 37 percent of other African immigrants, and 36 percent of Turkish immigrants live in these projects.[18] Dark skin color makes already poor chances at employment even worse. A 2005 report on employment is one of the rare studies in France to have examined the difference that ethnicity makes. The authors conclude that having a North African background makes you two and a half times more likely to be unemployed than if you are (or, more important, if you look and sound) "native French," controlling for level of education, and that this difference has changed little in fifteen years.[19]

But at the same time, and somewhat counterintuitively, the low-cost housing projects have served to counteract ethnic self-segregation even as they have reinforced social and economic segregation. If you apply to an HLM company you end up wherever the housing office sees fit to put you. As a result, blacks, North Africans, and "native" French live in the same buildings. Although in some housing projects the majority of residents are immigrants, French citizens make up a majority of all HLM residents, as well as a majority of residents of the so-called "dangerous" suburbs. (The boys and young men who were arrested during the riots of late 2005 included "French with roots" [Français de souche], "blacks" of West African ancestry, and "northern Africans" [maghrébins], with parents from Algeria, Morocco, or Tunisia.) Mixing has its limits, though: young people observe ethnic boundaries, particularly between blacks and North Africans. You date across those lines at your own risk, and in 2005 one black-brown relationship led to a conflict and a killing, and prompted the Interior Minister at the time, Nicolas Sarkozy, to make unfavorable remarks about the residents that some say heightened social tensions.

There are some bright spots in the poor ring cities where institutions and associations thrive, but also gloomy spots where they do not. Within the département of Seine-Saint-Denis, where the 2005 riots were concentrated, the cities of Saint-Denis and Clichy-sous-Bois at first glance seem similar: high unemployment rates, subsidized housing, foreign residents, and poor schools. Saint-Denis, however, has a bustling market center with easy access by subway or train to the center of Paris, a campus of the University of Paris, private Islamic schools and associations, and the Basilica, a major tourist attraction. Clichy-sous-Bois (where the riots began) has few such advantages: isolated housing projects, few cafes, no educational institutions beyond the mediocre public schools, and difficult access by public transport.[20]

These projects are not, then, ethnic enclaves, nor are they museums to the past; they are populated by recent immigrants as well as the descendants of older ones, because immigration continued, even after the 1974 halting of most labor migration.[21] The sense of exclusion some of them feel is based on a sometimes volatile combination of economic stagnation or decline, on the one hand, and ethnic or racial discrimination on the other. The latter is apparent on all fronts: in seeking jobs and housing, in treatment by the police and other state agents, and in everyday attitudes exhibited by others in France. These are not young Muslims wishing to separate themselves from France but young citizens of diverse origins wishing to fully join it.

Immigration trajectories and settlement patterns thus have created a population of immigrants and their children and grandchildren less seg-regated by ethnic identities and religious tendencies than in some other European countries and whose rage, when it breaks through, comes from anger at denial of equality within France, not from a desire to create a separate Islamic existence. But Islam has provided an increasingly impor-tant sense of identity and attachment for many of these French men and women: if it is not an Islam of separation, in what ways is it an Islam of France?

RELIGION RISING

By the 1980s, the children of North African immigrants were seeking equality and respect as new members of the French political community, as had European immigrants before them. They called themselves the *Beurs*, a term that comes from the slang transformation of *Arabes*. No longer thinking of themselves only as Algerians, Moroccans, or Tunisians, they had developed a sense of sharing a North African identity, in large part through their everyday interactions with others.[22] But above all they wished to obtain social and economic equality. And whereas in the 1960s and 1970s their parents (meaning usually their fathers) may have par-ticipated in trade union associations intended to ameliorate their living or working conditions, the new generation sought more public and civic ways to achieve equal rights and recognition as French citizens.[23] Many of them formed local associations concerned with sports, after-school tutor-ing, or Berber-language radio. In the early 1980s some of these associations organized marches to protest the treatment of the "second generation," most notably in the 1983 March for Equality, quickly dubbed the "Beurs' March," in which 10,000 people participated. But the bitter legacy of the Algerian War, the long-term suspicion of Islam, and the visible difference that "native French" thought they saw between themselves and these new strangers remained as obstacles to acceptance and equality.[24]

At this point the Beur generation took two divergent paths. Some of the movement's leaders followed the route of previous immigrant groups and joined the Socialist party, where they campaigned for color-blind equality, notably in the organization SOS-Racisme founded in 1984 by Harlem Désir. (Another organization, France-Plus, emphasized "integra-tion.") Others, less hopeful that standard socialism-plus-unions could

close the identity gap with the French, looked for new sources of meaning. Some of these men and women thought that Islam would offer an
identity that would distinguish them both from their parents and from
the native French society that did not seem to want them. They attended
lectures sponsored by nascent French Islamic organizations and read
books newly translated into French. They thought they had found a new
way toward living in France.

The growing sense that "true Islam" could provide a third possibility
for constructing a subjective identity, beyond the undesirable "North African" and the unattainable "French," also led some Muslims in the late
1980s to demand that they be allowed to practice their religion in a public way, by building mosques, carrying out collective rituals, and dress-
ing in an Islamic way. These public actors were largely of North African
origin or heritage and also included some French converts to Islam—as I
noted earlier, Turks and West Africans were more likely to focus inward
on their own communities, or to look beyond the boundaries of France
to their countries of reference.

Lyon was once again the starting point for the new associations. The
Union des Jeunes Musulmans (UJM, Young Muslims' Union)—originally
with "of Lyon" added—was founded in 1987 to demand that France recognize the right of Muslims to "live our spirituality in the open and not
in a reclusive way in the private sphere."[25] The union was created in reaction to the nonreligious character of the Beur movement. As one of its
founders said, "We were the radicals; we did not fear crying out 'Allahu
Akbar' at our demonstrations."[26] The movement started its own bookstore, Tawhid (an expansion of the Tawhid cultural association, founded
the year before the UJM), which began publishing the writings and lectures of the Swiss scholar Tariq Ramadan.[27] The UJM and Tawhid developed links to regional associations elsewhere in France and distributed its
publications through bookstores and at national or regional meetings of
like-minded associations. These from-the-ground-up organizing activities
also developed links to antiracism and antiglobalization movements.[28]

At about the same time, other groups began developing projects to
construct "cathedral mosques"—usually meaning a large building with
a minaret—in Lyon and Marseille. These demands were not always welcomed by other French residents, and the resentment over economic competition that had fueled the Far Right in the 1970s now was reinforced
by resentment over visible cultural difference, an unalterable newness on
putatively ancient French soil. Many in France saw large mosques as incompatible with the French built landscape, and late that summer one
mayor even bulldozed buildings used by Muslims for prayer.[29] Others
were offended by the sight of Muslims praying in the street on feast days,
when the available buildings did not suffice.

But above all it was the appearance of three schoolgirls in headscarves in September 1989 that revved up collective anxiety. Elsewhere I have examined at length the mixture of political philosophy, media-fueled fears, and political opportunism that made a few headscarves into a problem claimed by a few left-leaning intellectuals to constitute "the Munich of the Republic," meaning a threat to France comparable to the Allies' capitulation to Nazi demands.[30] The girls' actions symbolized something new: publicly claiming an identity as a Muslim in the "temple of the Republic," the school.

The new attention to these girls stimulated a series of sociological studies of French Muslim women's life choices.[31] Some of the scarf-wearing girls interviewed by these sociologists emphasized the distinction between the traditions of their parents and the "true Islam" they now were discovering on their own. "I became a practicing Muslim thanks to France," said one young woman, "for it provides structures so that we might learn Arabic and our religion. I am glad to have come to know my religion, true Islam, because, 'back there,' it is too traditional and troublesome."[32] Others spoke in very different ways about their past, considering their Muslim identities to be part of identities as Moroccan or Algerian, and some resented the lectures they received from some Muslims about how they should change and how their decision not to wear a headscarf meant they were not Muslim. Some born in France nonetheless called themselves "Algerians who live in France" and used "the French" to refer to non-Muslims.[33] Others said they maintained a private Islam, that whether or not they prayed regularly, they refrained from marking themselves off publicly as Muslim men or women.[34] Many of them began to seek out a new kind of Islamic pedagogy, a way to study religion that would go beyond the simple inheriting of a tradition from Morocco or Algeria. They attended talks at mosques or in lecture halls by new, younger Muslims who spoke French as their first language, as well as lectures by preachers from Egypt and Syria who came to the annual gatherings of Muslims at Le Bourget, north of Paris. They bought books and cassettes, and when the first Islamic institutes opened, some of them signed up.

By the late 1980s, then, some younger Muslims who were either born in France or came to study or to work sought a more systematic basis for their religious practices and beliefs. They did not abandon other identities, of course: Muslims did and do continue to think of themselves in multiple, complex, and contextually sensitive ways, just as non-Muslims do. But some among them became more likely to think about Islam in a way that did not intrinsically link religion to the traditions of a particular country of origin, and to look for guides outside their immediate circle of family and friends. This shift in thinking created a demand for new teachers, schools, books, lectures, and forums of all kinds about Islam.

Those who began to teach them included both slightly older Muslim men and women born in France but more often Muslims who had been born elsewhere, who had grown up with some religious education, and who now found a new set of opportunities to spread an understanding of Islam. Some had served as imams or teachers in Muslim-majority countries; others had been trained in secular subjects and engaged in a kind of Islamic pedagogical bricolage to construct a suitable way of teaching their new students.

These characteristics would favor the emergence of Islamic institutions that presented Islam in French and with respect to problems that surfaced in France, because the new students would be young French women and men from diverse origins. But these institutions would also take account of global debates and deliberations about Islam, both because students would have access to a world of Web information and because their teachers were trained in a broad array of Islamic schools and universities. The challenge for both then would be, how to build an Islamic knowledge that would be legitimate in transnational terms and also pertinent to the situation in France.

Authorities

Who are the people who have stepped into these roles as religious authorities for French Muslims? Because the traditional Islamic institutions that define specific authorities are virtually absent from Europe, it is difficult to use the Islamic vocabulary of *muftis*, *'ulamâ*, and *faqîhs* (juris consults, scholars, and jurists). I prefer to speak of different types of Islamic public actors, each with specific claims to legitimacy and specific bases in social institutions, particularly religious schools, mosques, and Islamic associations.[35]

Among these several types of authorities, teachers usually work in private Islamic schools or institutes, offering classes on weekends and evenings for Muslims who wish to learn more about their heritage. Those who occupy the principal positions at these schools usually also contribute to public discussions about Islam, for example by writing for magazines or speaking at gatherings. Sometimes they are experts on Islamic jurisprudence, and sometimes they have taught themselves its elements. They are evaluated by younger Muslims more in terms of their abilities to plausibly represent themselves as learned in Islamic matters than in terms of their formal training. In any case, few or perhaps none have the kind and level of training that would earn them a position as a jurist or expert in a Muslim-majority country.[36] In the 2000s, some of them are developing plans to teach at a higher level of knowledge in order to train future scholars and teachers.[37]

Mosque officials may be called *imams*, a term that in the European context often means the person in charge of a mosque, who may or may not lead collective prayer. (Sometimes *recteur* is used to refer to the administrative head of the mosque.) Those who are in charge of the two largest cathedral mosques in Paris and Lyon have the ear of the state and the French media. They speak in very Republican ways. Several other leaders of major mosques in Paris, Marseille, and elsewhere have remained somewhat outside the state's orbit and have large and stable followings. These leaders usually have an array of associated activities: classes, neighborhood associations, women's groups. Many other imams come and go in the smaller mosques, sometimes seizing the right to give Friday sermons for a matter of months, or longer. In what sometimes resembles a market for imams, groups of mosque-goers champion one or another of these (usually young) men; some of these imams may have brought "Salafi" ideas from Saudi Arabia to France.[38] Because mosques now have become the basic electoral unit for the national Islamic representative body, the control of mosques has taken on some degree of political importance.

Finally, there are leaders of local associations and leaders of the national federations. The legitimacy of the latter in the eyes of the state rests on the number of followers or affiliated mosques they can claim; their legitimacy in the eyes of those followers has to do with their ability to show themselves as having a political voice in France and to present an attractive version of Islam. Among the most important are the Union des Organisations Islamiques de France (UOIF, Union of French Islamic Organizations); the "Great Mosque" of Paris, controlled by Algeria; a shifting confederation of mosques allied with Morocco; and two competing groupings of Turkish mosques.

Outside of these institutionally based Islamic authorities in France are independent speakers (such as the Swiss-born Tariq Ramadan), networks of students and activists, and the many Islamic scholars and public figures in Muslim-majority countries, accessible through the Internet but also through books and lectures in France. I will refer to a number of these people in the following chapters.

STATE RESPONSES

As Islamic visibility grew in the 1980s, state and municipal authorities began to respond to new demands, often in experimental ways or by drawing on colonial experience.[39] But the colonial administration of Muslims itself had operated on the basis of unresolved questions concerning the citizenship of Muslims and the role of the French state in controlling Islam, and particularly so in the case of Algeria. From the 1830s on, Algeria was considered to be an extension of France and its residents were considered to be full national subjects. And yet successive generations of French administrators worked to ensure that Muslim residents would not have the same political or legal rights as other residents. As part of France, Algeria was to experience the separation of religion and state, yet Muslims largely remained under a separate legal regime that included elements of Islamic law, and the state continued to regulate Algerian imams and mosques.[40]

This ambiguity in French colonial policy toward Islam and toward French Muslims has left its traces in most recent policies, making the "French rules of the game" difficult to pin down. Islamic institutions remain a matter of both domestic and foreign policy. When in the 1920s France built the Great Mosque of Paris, it did so as a state project, developed through private associations (to avoid violating the 1905 law on secularity) and with active participation from Morocco and Tunisia. Today, Algeria appoints its director, but the French state seeks funds for its maintenance from foreign states. Periods of crisis over the presence of Islamic headscarves in public schools came when French public intellectuals became simultaneously anxious about global political Islam and the state of domestic cohesion.[41]

Anxieties about security and integration underlie the series of state efforts to manage Islam. Models were available in bodies that consult with the state regarding matters affecting Catholics, Protestants, and Jews, and after a series of efforts, in 2002–3 the Interior Minister, Nicolas Sarkozy, brought together the leaders of the main Islamic federations to form the French Council for the Muslim Religion (Conseil Français du Culte Musulman, CFCM; hereafter the Islamic Council).[42] Sarkozy directed that the first president be the head of the Paris Mosque, Dalil Boubakeur. The Paris Mosque had long been a favored partner of the state, and it leads one of the major networks of mosques and Islamic cultural associations. When competing for seats on the council the mosque could claim some degree of allegiance from Algerians, who represent the largest number of Muslims in France, and from some other Muslims who mistrusted other, more "religion-minded" Muslim organizations.[43]

Although Sarkozy created the Islamic Council in his role as Interior Minister, he consulted representatives of those foreign states that had large numbers of Muslim nationals resident in France. Moreover, although the council was supposed to provide an alternative to foreign interference in French Islam, it in fact has had the opposite effect. The Algerian, Moroccan, and Turkish consulates saw the 2003, 2005, and 2008 council elections as opportunities to ratchet up control over "their" constituents by promoting slates associated with each of the home countries, and they did indeed mobilize these residents of France to vote for "their" slate.

The state later was to draw on council leaders to negotiate with terrorists in Iraq who had taken two French reporters hostage.[44] Its creation may have given Sarkozy a stronger bargaining position when, in 2003, he consulted the director of Cairo's al-Azhar University to see if the ban on Islamic headscarves in schools could be seen as Islamically correct. (The Egyptian scholar responded that Islam recognized the right of the French state to pass such a law.)[45]

If the state's governance of Islam has retained something of the colonial-era ambiguities—Is it foreign or domestic? Does the state regulate its institutions or consider them private?—the state has firmly adopted rhetoric and policies of domestication. Successive prime ministers have proposed schemes to give imams more training in French institutions and values and to make available, through a French foundation, funds that might in part come from overseas sources. As Interior Minister Michèle Alliot-Marie said on July 6, 2007, echoing her predecessors, her ministry was committed "to build and control a French Islam" (*de construire et de maîtriser un islam français*),[46] even as the state plied its own transnational political trade regarding Islam. Islam remains a security problem in the eyes of many in government. Deportation, harassment, delays in renewing residency permits—these weapons remain available to the state when it needs to deal with recalcitrant imams, those who speak in a way that is judged to be inconsistent with French values.

At the same time, many Muslims do not see the borders between France and the rest of the world as bearing religious significance. Muslim scholars teach obedience to the state's laws, but Muslims seek religious guidance wherever they find it—"even in China," as the Prophet Muhammad is supposed to have said, and certainly from sheikhs of personal renown or at celebrated institutions in the Middle East and North Africa. The notion that Islam should be taught by Frenchmen in France, a notion that has entered the realm of bureaucratic common sense, is an attempt to cut those very pathways to seeking knowledge globally that many Muslims see as intrinsic to Islam.

Where to Sacrifice?

Underneath these high-profile policy measures, the state and municipalities have found themselves responding in practical ways to Muslim demands. In a halting and experimental fashion, government agencies have tried to create institutions that would meet legitimate demands made by Muslims yet remain within politically acceptable boundaries. The deep entanglement of the French government with religious concerns provides the somewhat counterintuitive and essential context for what follows in this book.

Let me illustrate this entanglement with two practical challenges that have effects on normative thinking: arranging for the massive distribution of properly slaughtered meat on the Feast of Sacrifice, and providing space for congregational prayer.

On the tenth day of the "month of pilgrimage" (*dhul al-hijjah*), Muslims celebrate the Feast of Sacrifice (*Îd al-adhâ*), also called the "great feast" (*Îd al-kabîr*) and, vernacularly in France, the "sheep festival" (*fête du mouton*). In the Qur'an (37: 83–113), God describes the prophet Abraham's trials, first when his people turned against him for smiting the idols they worshipped, and immediately thereafter when God ordered him to sacrifice his son. God provided a substitute victim in the form of a ram, and blessed Abraham's descendants. The Prophet Muhammad urged his followers to sacrifice an animal on this day (or one of the two following days) in the tradition of Abraham; he also urged that they distribute some of the meat to the poor. In those regions of Africa from which most Muslims have come to France, the sacrifice is a deeply embedded, family-focused ritual.

Although carrying out the sacrifice is feasible in rural societies, or if sheep, goats, or other animals are in plentiful supply on nearby farms or ranches, it is a logistical nightmare in large urban centers such as greater Paris, and in particular since the early 1980s, when slaughterhouses were moved into rural areas. A few Muslims slaughtered sheep in their apartments or in parking areas, neighbors complained, and the state stepped in, asking mayors to try and find a way for Muslims to carry out the sacrifice appropriately. A series of experiments followed throughout the 1980s, 1990s, and into the early 2000s, most involving cooperation among city authorities (who provided space), private entrepreneurs (who provided sheep), and mosques (which provided certified sacrificers). No solution lasted, particularly after campaigns by the Far Right and by Bridget Bardot to end all animal sacrifice.[47] As of 2009, the most likely longlasting solution is a set of partnerships involving the state, the larger mosques, and the major supermarket chains.

The officials overseeing these operations have seen their task as one of facilitating Muslims' tasks, but some also think that Muslims should adapt to modern French norms. The head of veterinary services for the Seine-Saint-Denis department, which has many Muslims but no slaughterhouses, drew on his twenty years of service in Africa to argue that even though he tried to arrange things for Muslims to sacrifice, they needed to change their ways of thinking. In 2004 he told me, "Many of these Muslims have no idea how to slaughter an animal, they grew up in an urban environment, but they continue to want to do that. I consider it to be a festival, a tradition, and not part of religion. The young don't give a damn about Abraham's act; it is much more about identity than religion.

I am now a convinced atheist but I had a Catholic upbringing and I know that communion is a sacrifice; but we can transcend that; the Protestants rethought that, for example. All religions have to evolve, and the Muslims need to do that in order to adapt to France."

This official's attitude, one of sympathetic disdain, combines his experience in Muslim-majority countries, his sense that therefore he has a pretty good idea of what is and is not Islamic, and his conviction that Muslims simply have not yet understood what would be involved in providing sacrificial animals to all. His attitude was not unusual. Just before the Feast of Sacrifice that occurred in February 2003, the subprefect of Mantes-la-Jolie, the site of one of France's largest mosques, issued a statement "reminding" officials (including Muslims on the Islamic Council), that "the Muslim religion authorizes sacrifice over the three days," and that instead of sacrificing, Muslims were permitted to send money to "their countries of origin," implying that all Muslims were immigrants. Many Muslim leaders objected to the Interior Ministry that this statement was out of order, and the minister, Nicolas Sarkozy, denied that any state officers would usurp the prerogatives of religious authorities. And yet Sarkozy had written to Muslim leaders a week earlier asking them to "remind the faithful that that ritual sacrifice is part of tradition and not among the obligations pronounced by your religion."[48]

As the state took on the task of arranging for the sacrifice, then, it also sometimes succumbed to the temptation of entering into Islamic debates about what is or is not required of Muslims—and, as we shall see later on, the practical difficulties of sacrifice have also led some Muslims to reconsider their obligations.

Where to Pray?

French officials also have reacted to Muslims' demands for prayer space, as well as taking initiatives to create politically symbolic mosques. It is worth recalling that mosques were built in southern France as early as the eighth century (in Roussillon), and that Muslims have prayed on French soil at various time ever since. When the state brought large numbers of African Muslims to France during the Second World War, they also built temporary mosques at military camps, as did some companies employing Muslim workers. But these efforts were sporadic, and aside from the construction of the Paris Mosque in the 1920s, the state did little to create permanent places for Muslims to worship.[49]

In the mid-1970s, however, men living in workers' hostels in the Paris region went on strike to protest rent hikes and the constant intrusion of hostel employees in their daily lives. At the same time, workers at the

Renault factory at Billancourt outside Paris went on strike over wages and job security. Included among their demands was having space to pray on the factory grounds, and they won that demand—largely because the factory owners and hostel managers saw it as a relatively inexpensive way to quiet down the workers at a moment when French industry was under considerable economic pressures.[50] The men who ran the hostels often had been state employees in the colonies, and it was natural for them to transfer the colonial notion of Islam as social control to post-colonial life in France.

These Muslim workers now had their own social spaces, islands of meaning and spiritual order in lives increasingly full of economic and social stress.[51] In the hostels, residents decorated the prayer spaces with rugs on floors and often on walls, and took charge of assigning the tasks of imam (in the sense of prayer leader) to the more knowledgeable among them.[52] Often it was people from the same country or ethnic group who took over the care of a particular space, and it was (and is) not unusual to find two prayer spaces in one housing complex, with one used by North Africans and the other by West Africans. Eventually most of these prayer rooms became affiliated with a Muslim association that depended on either the Algerian, Moroccan, or Turkish state, or with a group that was opposed to the regime in power in one of these states, or with a transnational Sufi order. Many of the associations then became part of the larger federations of mosques described earlier, and thereby part of the broad Islamic Council structure in partnership with the Interior Ministry.

Between 1970 and 1985 the number of prayer rooms in France jumped from about 100 to about 500, largely as the result of the responses to the strikes. Some 80 percent of the hostels had prayer rooms. Catholic priests also had made prayer space available in several churches or in build-ings no longer used for services.[53] By that time, new political processes were under way that once again multiplied the number of prayer rooms, but now beyond the limits of workers' hostels. In October 1981, under the new Mitterrand government, Parliament had passed a law that made it much easier for noncitizens to create associations for social or cul-tural purposes. The state-sponsored Social Action Fund (Fonds d'Action Sociale, FAS), which once had focused on creating new housing for Alge-rian workers as a way of countering nationalist activities, now began to disburse subsidies to immigrants' social and cultural associations, funds that many Muslims were able to combine with their own limited monies to convert one or more first-floor apartments into prayer spaces. Their newly registered "cultural associations" often provided Arabic classes and after-school tutoring, as well as places to worship. Sometimes an imam was able to procure a municipal salary as an after-hours tutor and coach for the children.[54] These cultural associations were largely responsible for the second major increase in the number of prayer spaces in France: from about 500 in 1985 to 1,279 by 1992 and to about 1,600 by 2003, in effect tripling the number of prayer rooms in eighteen years.[55]

Until the early 1980s, most of the larger structures used for congregational prayers, and thus called mosques, were located in large warehouses, houses, or apartment buildings. Things changed in 1980, when the mayor of Mantes-la-Jolie, northwest of Paris, decided to support the efforts of an Islamic association to build a dome-and-minaret mosque, and again a few years later in Évry, south of Paris, when the right to construct what came to be called a "cathedral mosque" was granted to a group of Moroccan Muslims as part of an overall urban plan. In the early 2000s, Nicolas Sarkozy as Interior Minister let it be known to his prefects that Muslims' efforts to build mosque-looking mosques were to be supported. Since that time, some mosque associations have worked in partnership with municipal authorities.[56] Their stumbling blocks have been less often purely financial than political, and on both sides: ambivalence in the mayor's office about risking attacks from the Far Right for aiding Muslims, and difficulties among Muslim groups in agreeing on a mosque project.[57]

Marseille illustrates the imbrication of religious and political debates over projects to build a large-scale mosque. Discussions about building a city mosque for North Africans in Marseille began in the 1930s, not long after the inauguration of the Paris Mosque.[58] But serious discussions about building a central mosque came in the late 1980s, when the general idea emerged in France that creating "cathedral mosques" in each city would provide a visible (and easily monitored) place for Muslims to worship. Although the initial plan was shelved in the face of Far-Right opposition, it resurfaced in the late 1990s, and again after the attacks of September 11, 2001. It is worth noting that support for this idea grew along with anxiety over political Islam at home and abroad. The two tendencies might seem contradictory: one promotes Islam in public space, the other combats it. But in fact they grow out of the specific historical policy of the French state toward religions: support religion by facilitating worship in properly built houses of worship but strictly control any "leakage" of religion into those domains where Republican unity requires secularism, of which the primary concern remains with the schools.[59]

Subsequent debates in Marseille have turned on a conflict between two conceptions of what a mosque should be in France: Should it be the visible symbol of Islamic culture or the practical neighborhood prayer space? The Paris Mosque argued that Marseille should have an Islamic cultural center that also would contain a mosque. Mayor Jean-Claude Gaudin supported this plan on the grounds that it would underscore Marseille's position as France's window onto the Mediterranean world. Precisely because this conception of "Islam as culture" dominated the early city plans for a cathedral mosque, some Muslim leaders argued against building such a mosque, seeing it as a vestige of colonial-administered Islam, and argued instead that worship was best done in mosques placed throughout the city, in districts where Muslims lived. The conception of the mosque as a place for worship eventually won out, but so did the idea of a single main mosque for the city. This combined outcome came about largely because several Islamic associations came together to create a new, unified mosque association (and their representatives won the 2005 elections for the Marseille region's delegates to the national Islamic Council). In July 2006, the mayor signed a contract with this new association. The city agreed to lease land for a new citywide mosque for ninety-nine years at an annual rent of 300 euros, and the association promised to keep the proportion of foreign donations to "20–30 percent" of the total cost.

The mayor long had hesitated to take this step for fear that any cooperation with Muslims would be seized on by the Far Right in local elections. And, indeed, Far-Right groups immediately sued to stop the mosque project on grounds that the nominal lease constituted a hidden direct subsidy to the mosque in violation of the 1905 law separating religions from the state. In April 2007 they won their case before an administrative court, which annulled the contract. In July 2007 the city responded by signing a new contract, this one with a lease of fifty years and an annual rent of 24,000 euros.[60]

Most mosque creating taking place in France today resembles the Marseille experience in that local Muslims raise money and attempt to enter into partnerships with municipal authorities, who sometimes, perhaps out of electoral calculations, support these projects. The fear of foreign control of mosques has been overplayed in France, notes the person most centrally placed in the Interior Ministry's Islam desk over the past decade, Bernard Godard: "The generosity of the faithful long has been a major part of a process, one that some people thought was the result of miraculous manna sent from the East."[61]

Distinctive Features

At this point we can tentatively identify certain distinctive features of the French Islamic landscape. First is the active role played by the state and by certain municipalities in seeking to organize religious life for Muslims, usually in response to a perceived problem: bloody sacrifice in public, disorganized prayer spaces, or electoral pressures. Although governments throughout Europe engage in the governance of religion in one way or another, France is striking for the coexistence of explicit and legally enshrined secularism, on the one hand, and equally vigorous state and municipal engagement with representatives of religious groups, on the other. Other European states generally allow a greater public role for religion and play less of a direct role in regulating religion than France, even where they grant recognition to religious groups (as in Belgium and Germany). I have discussed this tense coexistence elsewhere, but it should be reiterated here as a key dimension of the opportunity structure faced by the Islamic public actors we meet in subsequent chapters.

Second is the dominance of North Africa as the public and political Islamic reference in France. France's long colonial engagement in and with North Africa leads many non-Muslims in France to think of people from a North African background as the prototypical Muslims. To some extent the state also treats Islamic issues as concerning first and foremost people from this region. The demographic and political dominance of North Africans reinforces this tendency.

Third, despite some degree of country rivalry and some degree of tension between Arabic and Berber speakers, differences across Muslims of North African background are less acute and explicit than are those dividing major Muslim populations elsewhere in Europe. Muslims who moved from Pakistan, India, and Bangladesh settled in Britain in such a way as to reproduce not only ethnic difference but also those between villages or lineages. Furthermore, strongly felt theological or juridical oppositions among Islamic religious institutions in South Asia often were reproduced in Britain, most notably between various offshoots of the Deoband school and those tracing Sufi-oriented Barelvi backgrounds. Elsewhere divisions are more often among two or more distinct immigrant populations: in northern Belgium and the Netherlands between Moroccans and Turks, for example. No one group is in a position to dominate the landscape, nor do any groups have the long historical ties that North Africans have to France.

We must be careful not overstate the case: Tunisians may think of their traditions as superior to those of Moroccans; Moroccans and Algerians may fight for mosque leadership; and, certainly, racial tensions emerge between North and West Africans. But France's sociohistorical Islamic landscape (migration trajectories, colonial history), together with its formal opportunity structure (the state's active role) favors the emergence of institutions and forms of reasoning that are capable of subsuming differences of ethnic, national, or religious background. And, as we have seen, such was the type of institution that younger Muslims were demanding in the 1980s and 1990s. What has emerged in response?

PART TWO

Spaces

CHAPTER THREE

Mosques Facing Outward

MOSQUES BECOME IMPORTANT in this landscape, and not only for religious reasons. Mosques and their smaller cousins, prayer houses, have
become important spatial nodes around which Muslims work to shape
the Islamic presence in France. They do so in ways that start from congregational prayer but extend to teaching, social services, and political
representation. Three brief portraits of mosques will give us a better idea
of the range of ways in which mosques "face outward" as starting points
for social networks and political struggles and, in doing so, cross lines of
ethnic origins and normative traditions.

In the first case, we see an out-of-the-way "apartment mosque" in a
poor outer city of Paris, Clichy-sous-Bois, thrust into national promi-
nence at the outbreak of the 2005 riots. The case shows the state's ambivalence toward Islamic public actors: they are just citizens, perhaps, but at
times they are expected to participate in the governance and appeasement
of "their" people. The Tawhid Center in Saint-Denis, our second case,
provides prayer space but also illustrates how younger Muslims have
created from-the-ground-up social networks to develop knowledge and
faith. Finally, the main mosque of Lyon, one of France's few cathedral
mosques, points to the polyvalent role of major mosques as providers of
services, from sacrificing animals to dispensing aid to the poor.[1]

These examples also point to the ways in which France's distinctive
landscape shapes the ways Islamic public actors innovate in institutional
and conceptual terms: allied with mayors and ministers, charged with
achieving certain social ends, mosque leaders can no more fold in on
"their community" than they can think of their institutions as "only"
religious.

IN THE UNRULY SUBURBS (CLICHY-SOUS-BOIS)

Many of the mosques that make the news once were inconspicuous, if
not invisible. The world learned of the mosques in Clichy-sous-Bois, east
of Paris, when riots began in late October 2005. After years of endur-
ing repeated and often rough police stops and searches, Clichy residents
reacted angrily to the death of two young men pursued by the police.
The deaths sparked angry, destructive rampages in some (but not all) of

Paris's poor ring cities and in other parts of France. On the first anniversary of these deaths, October 27, 2006, the imam of one of Clichy's two mosques, Dhaou Meskine, gave a prayer underneath the electrical transformers where they had died. The newspaper *Libération* carried an audio recording of the prayer on its Web site: "May the youth of the neighborhood live in peace, and pursue education," he intoned.

In fact, the suburb has two mosques, both carved out of apartments in low-income housing projects. The "upper Clichy" mosque had a tear gas canister lobbed into the prayer space at a moment when men had gathered to pray. Dhaou Meskine presides over Friday worship at the "lower Clichy" mosque, to which the riots quickly spread in the first days after the youths' deaths. We will meet him again in chapter six, because he also leads the first Islamic secondary school in France, at Aubervilliers, several suburbs west of Clichy-sous-Bois along the "red belt" of working-class, former industrial suburbs on the outskirts of Paris.

Dhaou left his native Tunisia when conditions for politically engaged Islamic leaders became difficult, and spent his time in Saudi Arabia and France. In 1984, the Clichy mosque's leaders invited him to become their imam, to give sermons, to lead prayers, and to advise on theological matters. As he recalled in 2006, the mosque's leaders had chosen him in part because they were divided into Algerian and Moroccan camps, and thought that a Tunisian imam could be neutral.

I visited the mosque with Dhaou in April 2006, during the period of celebration of the Prophet Muhammad's birth. He met me at his school, in the splendid crimson robes and cap he wears on his outsize frame for the Friday prayers. We drove in the large van that he uses to take pupils on outings, and crossed through the suburbs along the northern border of Paris to Clichy. We had some extra time, so he showed me the city, which consists mainly of HLM projects built in the 1970s. "They look like matchboxes," he commented. "There is misery in those; if you live on the sixth story and the elevators have been out of order for months and your wife is pregnant. . . ."

We parked next to the housing projects that contain his mosque. We could see a long dark stain where a car had been burned the previous fall. "The municipality is only slowly removing the burned cars." We entered the building and immediately came to a set of three apartments that the residents had refashioned to form prayer space. To the right, you enter a long row of three rooms: the room in the middle is a kitchen and the rooms on either side serve as men's prayer spaces. Dhaou delivers his sermon and leads the prayer in the farther room. To the left, you enter a separate apartment that serves as the women's prayer space. Loudspeakers enable everyone to follow the prayers. The kitchen is used more for mosque administration than for cooking; a board had been placed

Figure 3.1 Dhaou Meskine ready to leave for prayers, Aubervilliers, 2006

between what would have been the stove and the counter to serve as a desk. The man in charge was busy on the phone trying to have a leak repaired. The leak was in the middle of the back room, and caused water to steadily drip down onto the middle of the floor. Chairs had been set around it to keep people from praying under the water.

Figure 3.2 Apartment building with mosque, Clichy-sous-Bois

In each of the three prayer rooms, rows of tape were laid down at an angle across the room to indicate the lines along which men or women should stand while at prayer. In the main room, the seat from where the sermon is delivered, the *mimbar*, is placed so as to show the direction of Mecca. Dhaou stood in front of it rather than climbing on top to speak. On the wall a plaque featured eight clocks that could be set to indicate times in different cities. None of them were set, but an electronic clock told Paris time.

At the proper moment, Dhaou rose and grasped the staff lying next to the mimbar and delivered a fifteen-minute sermon in Arabic on the Prophet Muhammad and his life. He then sat, rose again, and, after delivering a benediction in Arabic, added a very short French version. He stressed that they should all look for the middle way, between those who condemn the celebration of the Prophet's life and those who would treat it as a religious feast day, an *Îd*. It is simply a time for recalling Muhammad's life, he explained. "This year has been a particularly difficult one for Muslims, and we can profit from recalling the conditions Muhammad faced, and by consulting his biography." He then gave examples of how Muhammad had kept calm in the face of threats, and offered solutions to racism by uniting peoples from all different origins: "Anyone who does not love any one of God's prophets is not a Muslim, according to the Prophet." He explained that we should not humiliate others, but the economy and politics of the world do so: "When we push poor countries into debt by charging interest on loans, they cannot then build schools or mosques or wells, so they have famine and war. Muhammad offered the solution to this problem by abolishing interest and this revelation is appropriate for the entire world today."

He later explained to me that he sizes up his audience: here, most understand Arabic, so he spends most of his time talking in that language; if the congregation has more French-only speakers, then he will give more time to the second sermon. Many older people long opposed the idea of giving a sermon in any language but Arabic until Larbi Kechat, the imam at the Adda'wa mosque in Paris's nineteenth arrondissement, began the practice. "But why speak if the people do not understand what you say?" explained Dhaou. "Most of the young people, in my mosque and elsewhere, do not understand Arabic, and there are people from many different countries—there are forty nationalities in Aubervilliers!" Because this day coincided with the Prophet's birthday, he took his message from the occasion, but on other days he speaks of general ethical matters: helping one another or, his own specialty, the importance of educating children.

After the prayer most people slowly filed out, though some remained to make additional individual prayers. A series of men approached Dhaou to ask him questions. One man from Mali wanted to know if he could marry a woman religiously without performing a civil ceremony, and Dhaou said categorically no, he must not, because what if they were to divorce? "They want to do this because they do not want to have anything to do with the state," he told me afterward. Another man wanted to bring his grandchildren to France from Algeria and wanted to know what Dhaou thought. "It depends on their schooling: would it be better there or here?" he responded, and sent the man away to think it over.

On the return journey we drove by a plot of land on which the Clichy mosque committee plans to build a new mosque. One of the few bits of vacant land left in Clichy, the weedy plot sits next to a large shed, but it is near the marketplace and is well served by bus lines. Three architectural drawings of the proposed mosque decorate the hallway in the apartment. By 2008 the mosque association had convinced the municipalities to sell them the land outright rather than leasing it. They raised about half a million euros from local families and business people, enough to pay for the land and begin the structural work. With another 2 million they can complete the exterior construction, and invite people to donate or work on the interior, and they will be encouraged to do so because the mosque won't be finished: "If they took a bank loan and built it then it would be very hard to get people to contribute to the project, because the mosque already would be done."

The Clichy mosque project is one of a number of efforts pursued by Muslim associations together with municipalities. The nearby town of Bobigny granted a long-term lease to association in 2006; both Corbeil and Creteil have similar arrangements. As we saw in the previous chapters, leases of land to mosque associations in some other cities have been challenged in court by Far Right groups. Aubervilliers, where Dhaou has his school and which has a large Muslim population, has no structures built to be mosques; prayers are held in what once were factories, each holding 600–800 worshippers. By contrast, the new Clichy mosque is projected to accommodate 4,000 people.

On that day in 2006, Dhaou discussed the riots of the previous fall:

> In the twenty-one years I was imam in the lower Clichy mosque, there never was any trouble in the building. When the riots started, the young men in the mosque association got out and talked to others and were able to calm things down. It was only after that, when the politicians said impolitic things, when Sarkozy thanked the police for their good work rather than lamenting the deaths, and the police claimed they did not run after the boys, that these lies made everyone angry and the riots started up again. But then we calmed things down, and the disturbances moved to upper Clichy, and the police used tear gas, and then claimed that kids had done it. The rioters [*casseurs*, lit. "breakers"] were young people who were not part of anything. They were without hope. They came knocking, a little too hard, true, at the door of the Republic, asking, "Where is the Equality? Where is the Fraternity?"

Most places in France where Muslims pray during the week or on Fridays resemble the Clichy mosque in that they are fashioned out of spaces originally designed for other uses: apartments, residences, warehouses, or shops. According to a 2005 government report, of the 1,685 "mosques" across France, only twenty could hold more than 1,000 people, and an additional fifty-four could hold between 500 and 1,000. The vast majority of the rest were simply these converted rooms in residences or older commercial buildings, reworked to make prayer possible.[2]

Most mosques are run by committees of people who live nearby. These mosque committees, usually legally registered as associations, then engage someone to lead congregational prayers and deliver sermons. This man, the *imam*, is not necessarily the director (often called *recteur*) of the mosque; the director may be simply one person on the mosque committee and may change from time to time, or it may be the person who found the funding and led the process of building or fixing up the mosque, and who may be a charismatic leader. Sometimes the imam is also the director.

The riots of late 2005 brought to the fore the question of the broader, extrareligious roles and responsibilities of the mosques and their directors and imams. The state sees mosque directors as necessary allies in the drive to control Muslims, but then the very perception of cooptation risks depriving mosque leaders of their legitimacy with "the base." The Interior Ministry's Bureau of Religions tries to involve directors of the larger mosques directly in the national Islamic Council. Small mosques may be part of federations, such as the UOIF, the FNMF, or the Paris Mosque constellation, and in such cases it is the federation that deals with the state. But a number of mosque directors choose to remain outside the Islamic Council.

The state expects even these "independent imams" to keep order. The secret police (the Renseignements Généraux, RG) made it clear after the riots that imams were supposed to work through the mosques to keep youth from rioting. Several city administrations that felt "let down" by "their" imams let it be known that they would be less forthcoming with aid for mosque projects in the future. But if independent imams did indeed "keep order," they were seen as dangerous for the very fact that they worked outside the state sphere. Dhaou Meskine and Larbi Kechat in Paris, or Mamadou Daffé in Toulouse and other younger imams elsewhere, are perceived as at least irksome, and perhaps dangerous, because they are not under state control. After Dhaou's role in keeping riots from rekindling in Clichy he was told by someone in the prefecture that this action was not appreciated. The prefect of the département of Seine-Saint-Denis, Jean-François Cordet, deplored the fact that "*les barbus* ["the bearded ones"] took over local administration" and that they made their influence evident each time there was a civil disturbance in their neighborhood.[3]

In 2005, the Interior Ministry tried to mobilize the new national structure to control the disturbances, asking Islamic Council president Dalil Boubakeur to visit the Clichy mosque on November 1—where he received a cold welcome, his car was hit by "projectiles," and he left quickly.[4] For its part, the UOIF issued what it called a fatwa against rioting. On November 6, 2005, the fatwa body of the UOIF declared that "it is strictly forbidden for any Muslim looking to receive divine grace and satisfaction to take part in any action that blindly strikes out at public or private goods or that could threaten life." It went on to say that "any Muslim living in France, citizen or guest of France, has the right to demand respect for his person, dignity, and convictions, and to act for greater equality and social justice. But such action, whether taken in spontaneous or coordinated fashion, should not violate the teachings just mentioned or the law that regulates life together."[5]

The fatwa elicited predictable objections on the part of the UOIF's rivals in the field of Islamic political deliberations. Boubakeur, head of the Paris Mosque, accused the UOIF of implying that the rioters were destroying property for religious reasons, objections echoed by a major Muslim Web site, oumma.com, which went further to claim that the fatwa "brought to mind a sinister period when the authorities tried to use the official Muslim clergy (sheikhs or dependent imams) to suppress people in revolt," that France was not Saudi Arabia or Tunisia, and that the UOIF was playing the role of "CRS of French Islam," referring to the security police, the Compagnie Républicaine de Sécurité, best known (and perhaps unfairly maligned) for their crowd-control duties.[6]

If these reactions were somewhat predictable—Boubakeur and the UOIF miss few opportunities to blast each other's initiatives, and oumma .com is no friend of the state-led Islamic Council—they did point up the assumptions of the fatwa, that the rioters, generally assumed to have little involvement in religion (not even the secret police said that Islam or "Islamists" had anything to do with the riots), would respond to a religious argument, and that the riots were carried out by people who were, in the UOIF's words, "acting for greater equality and social justice" but who had gone too far.

INSIDE THE NETWORKS (SAINT-DENIS)

Some mosques are more than mainly-on-Friday prayer spaces. One multifunctional Islamic center is found on a peaceful side street in Saint-Denis, the community just north of Paris best known for its cathedral. A few moments' walk from the cathedral, a bit farther from the Paris soccer stadium, the low building that houses the Centre Tawhid is tucked away on a side street. Tawhid refers to God's unity and was the name chosen by the young Muslims in Lyon who in the late 1980s formed a cultural center and a bookstore, both linked to the Union of Young Muslims (UJM). Around 1990, some of those same young Muslims formed a Lyon-based working group called the French Muslims' Collective (Collectif des Musulmans de France) in order to organize activities that might promote an understanding of Islam.[7]

The Lyon Tawhid Center and the collective both expanded, and the Saint-Denis Tawhid Center is part of that broader universe, though a fiercely independent part. The building holds a bookstore and a series of small rooms that serve as a mosque. Aside from Qur'ans and some hadith collections, most books are in French, and include works by European Muslim writers (Tariq Ramadan and his brother Hani prominent among them), translations of Saudi theologians and Moroccan historians, and the latest French-language works on Islam by non-Muslim scholars. Ablutions may be performed in two small washrooms to the side. At prayer times during the day everyone inside helps roll out the plastic carpeting on which regulars and passersby alike will pray. The bookstore's proprietor, Abdelkadir, closes the front door, and business does not resume until after prayers.

To the far left as you enter is an area that can be used for small discussions and meetings, and as of 2008 it was used by people working for the halâl certification company AVS (À Votre Service, "At Your Service"). Indeed, I often heard the prayer rooms referred to as the "AVS mosque." The AVS offices proper are in another building just behind the center, and Tariq Ramadan has at times kept his Paris office next door. The Paris-region branch of the collective meets in the building. At one time a major Islamic institute (now called CERSI) also was housed in the building in the areas used for prayer, and two blocks away was the publisher of a glossy Islamic magazine. By 2006 some of the women and men active at the Tawhid Center had started a Malcolm X Center in the suburb of Fontenay, which holds talks on foreign affairs. Iran, Iraq, and globalization are prominent among the topics.

Although each of these activities—halâl certifying, bookselling, praying, lecturing, teaching—are independent, a certain spirit unites them: that of a younger set of Islamic leaders, mostly not born in France but well educated in French, making their Islamic lives through a range of independent entrepreneurial activities. AVS employs the imam of the center; the bookstore extends the center's intellectual life, and the collective organizes the lectures and seminars and courses that take place there or in larger buildings elsewhere in Saint-Denis. In the early 2000s the same core people entered into a coalition with six other Paris-region Islamic associations called the Inter Associatif Musulman Francilien, to sponsor larger lectures, always in French and often including non-Muslim speakers, on topics from schooling to Islamic theology.[8] Many of them also participate in the transversal (and transnational) association called Muslim Presence (Présence Musulmane), which focuses on the teaching and activities of Tariq Ramadan and has an active Canadian branch.

We are in a different world from the mosque in Clichy-sous-Bois, which is but a leaky union of apartments with a board across the kitchen counter for an office and where Arabic goes farther than French. The Tawhid Center world is a French-speaking node in a complex and shifting global network of communication.

I often would stop by the center, and one Friday in May 2001, I arrived just before the prayer services to see the imam, Fouad Imarraine. Fouad, a short, pleasant man, showed up at about 1:40 p.m., donned a gown, and promptly went to the mosque part of the building, beckoning me to follow with the others. Worshippers included older men from North Africa as well as young ones from Mali and Senegal, and Europeans. Fouad

Figure 3.3 Saint-Denis street scene, 2006

delivered his twenty-minute sermon entirely in French but for the obligatory short Qur'anic citations. He began with part of the second verse of
the Qur'an, al-Baqarah. The verse begins with the letters Alif, Lam, Min,
and after reciting the verse (in Arabic), Fouad said that by beginning in
this way, with letters, God was pointing to writing, and directing us to
read and then to use our knowledge for the good of society. Muslims
gained knowledge as their civilization spread and as they came into contact with different people, he explained. Each generation has the responsibility to convey knowledge to the next one, but in keeping with their
knowledge and their environment. He challenged his audience (as good
sermon-givers do in many religions): "What have we in Saint-Denis done
in *our* relationship to knowledge?" On another occasion, Fouad sized up
his audience and gave a small part of the sermon in conversational Arabic before switching to French for the duration, and on that occasion his
theme was the gift, *sadaqah*, rather than knowledge. "We should think
of everything we do as a sadaqah, even kind words—and even something
we do for a non-Muslim, as long as we do it for God's sake."

When we next talked, in October 2003, Fouad was no longer regularly
giving the Friday sermons, because much of his time was taken up with
his job at AVS and with the collective. He saw his work as helping to train

the next generation of leaders. In any case, most imams do not last long, and "most people go to a mosque because it is a convenient place to pray, not because they want to hear a particular person give the sermon," so it does not really matter who gives them. He explained to me that mosques either ask imams to work on a voluntary basis or ask the Moroccan consulate or the Paris Mosque to send (and pay for) an imam. Only three mosques in the Paris region pay their imams, he said. "The Saudis send no one, because they know nothing of France. In any case, people are less interested than before in going elsewhere to study Islam. They see people who went to Saudi Arabia or to Egypt for study and who returned after a few months because they did not like the local way of teaching, or because they could not fit well in the society. They also see that there are very few openings for imams, and that is true also for people who have graduated here."

Fuad's comments echo a general problem for Muslims in Europe: that the centers of learning in the Arabic-speaking world are insufficiently attuned to European realities, but that Europe offers neither high-level training in Islam nor adequately well-paid positions for graduates of the centers that exist.[9] Since 1992, the UOIF has run a program designed to train imams and chaplains near the town of Château-Chinon in Burgundy, and in 1999 it opened a branch in Saint-Denis, ten minutes' walk from the Tawhid Center. The Paris Mosque also has such a program, and a number of other institutes, although they emphasize teaching knowledge and not preparing people for the profession of imam, also say that some of their students work in mosques leading prayers. But it is hardly a way to find steady, well-paying employment. Fouad commented, "I know three people who finished the imam course at the IESH [the UOIF's program], and only one is looking for work as an imam. Most people who attend these courses do not really intend to work as imams; they are responding to an internal need to learn more. Especially now, they know that it would be very unlikely that they would find work as an imam."

Fouad himself did study Islam in France, beginning at the Sorbonne in 1984. He had come to France with his parents from Morocco when he was very young and grew up in the Parisian suburb of Fontenay. He was one of the first children of immigrants to study Islam at the Sorbonne, and the teachers gave him strange looks; they wondered why he was there, and the teachers from North Africa assumed that he must know all about Islam already. "That was when I realized that those who taught Islam knew nothing about Muslims in France. This still is the case." He then studied at the institute now called CERSI that is profiled in the next chapter.

Fouad's sermons resemble those given by Dhaou in that they stress moral duties. It is not surprising that when a research team commissioned by governmental agencies studied the content of Friday sermons across France, they found that nearly all of them took a "moralizing" tone and rarely spoke of politics. The study examined sermons delivered over a two year period in 1999–2001 (after September 11 but before the invasion of Afghanistan) in twenty-three mosques throughout France. Nearly all were delivered in Arabic, sometimes with a French translation, and a clear majority of the sermon-givers were from Morocco. A separate 2001 study had estimated the Moroccan imams at 40 percent of the total, but that study considered only nationality, not origins, and some of the Moroccan imams in the sermon study had taken French nationality. Rare was the imam born in France.[10]

The nature of Islamic teaching and worship in France remains global: people who have grown up speaking Arabic and studied in well-known Islamic universities or, for Sufis, people who have come from the sacred centers of the order are more highly valued than men and women whose education has been entirely in France. The North American phenomenon of native-born Muslims spending long years in Islamic centers abroad is not yet widespread in France (or elsewhere in Europe), in part for economic reasons (North American Muslims have more resources than do their European counterparts) and in part because the conception of how the political borders intersect and interact with the spiritual borders is different. For a French Muslim born in France, an imam or teacher coming from Rabat, Dakar, or Ankara to teach or to lead prayers carries with him generations of knowledge and legitimacy.

Furthermore, France receives a constant flow of students and educated workers from these counties, and often these men (and sometimes women) become, either completely or in their spare time, teachers and leaders in Islam. Some of these Muslims teach themselves something of what they would need for their new roles. It has been possible for them to do this to some extent because, although their educations were in medicine or literature or politics, they had grown up with Islam, knew the Qur'an, and usually had learned enough Islamic sciences to furnish a starting point for leading prayers and giving sermons. Elsewhere in France these leaders include Mamadou Daffé, a research scientist in pharmacology and also the imam of the al-Houceine mosque in the Mirail district of Toulouse. A student from Mali, he studied Arabic and Islam on his own in order to be able to serve the Muslim community.[11] Larbi Kechat, described below, learned to give sermons only after he had taken on a leadership role in Paris.

The collective and other associations carry out much of the work of organizing lectures, giving courses, and promoting study groups for young Muslims. They attract less attention than do the more highly structured groups participating in the Islamic Council or the cathedral mosques and their directors. The imams and directors and bureaucrats who compete for positions on the Islamic Council receive press coverage because they are part of national politics—as also do "problem" imams who say impolite or uncivil things and thus are quickly denounced by the "national imams," and sometimes deported.

By contrast, French Islamic associations such as the collective are like other French associations: they are strongly anchored in cities or even neighborhoods, and enter only warily and provisionally into large-scale federations. Often the names change and the actors remain in place. They enter into coalitions with one another to accomplish particular goals, and then withdraw and form new coalitions. None of this manner of coalescing and separating is "Islamic"; it is just how local-level associative political life works in France. The Lyon-based Union of Young Muslims (UJM), for example, indicates its family of loosely connected organizations through the links featured on its Web site (ujm.fr), which in late 2008 included Tariq Ramadan's Web page, the Tawhid publisher, several Islamic Web sites (the scholarly La Maison de l'Islam and the more news-oriented oumma.com and Saphirnet), the sites of other regional Muslim associations in Grenoble and the Loire valley, the Paris Tawhid Center, the Collective of French Muslims, and the halâl food inspection service AVS.

I first met one of the collective's leaders, Karim Azouz, in October 2005. Karim explained that the collective was a loose confederation of regional groups that depend on frequent reunions to keep their "visions" aligned. They pursue social and political goals in collaboration with other movements, such as the Schools for All coalition formed to fight the ban on headscarves in schools, the antiglobalization European Social Forum, and the movement called Les Indigènes de la République. "These activities are important because that is how we make our presence known to everyone in the society," Karim explained. They also collaborate with other Islamic collectivities: "We wish to create a French Islam that will be free of control by either the French state or foreign states," a concept which he contrasted with that of the Islamic Council.[12] Not everyone is part of these discussions: they talk with Présence et Spiritualité Musulmanes associated with the Moroccan Islamic movement leader Abdessalam Yassine, the Turkish Millî Görüs, and various North African collectives—"but not the Tabligh, not the Salafis; what would that have produced?"

They also meet for internal study of the teachings of Islam, "to shape an Islam for here, France," and in particular regarding the status of women, and relations to non-Muslims.

[JB: What are your main references?]

Qaradâwî has a fine intuition within the Arabo-Muslim world, but he is too attentive to echoes within that world, and so he carries out a discourse of "an Islam for minorities." We do not agree with that; we have to create a way of being part of one world living together, part of the majority, where we come to a position of working with others because of our reflections on Islam, but with something positive in addition, which is our religion and values, so we work on antiglobalization issues and global warming, together with the Greens.

In taking this position, Karim echoes Tariq Ramadan's argument that one can find all the universal values one needs for today's political concerns—gender equality, bioethics, environmental concern—in Islam. Because his explanations also reminded me of other teachers I had heard in courses offered around Paris, I asked him whether they emphasized the idea that the objectives of the Qur'an, the *maqâsid* in Arabic, should be made the primary basis for interpretation. "That is very important; we just spent two days training our members, showing them how to think through these positions in Islamic terms, using [the fourteenth-century theologian] al-Shâtibî and others; we had people who knew these authors explain them. *Maqâsid* gives us a way to illuminate *fiqh* [jurisprudence]; the future is through the study of the *fiqh mu'âmalât* [jurisprudence on social relations]. We see nothing to change in *ibâdât* [worship and service to God]: prayer remains as before." He stressed the importance of teaching Muslims why broad-based positions have a basis in Islam: "This way, our militants know how it is that we arrive at positions on global warming through the objective [*maqâsid*] of protecting the planet."

For Karim, Muslims trying to formulate an Islam for France suffer under "a double handicap: those born here have no knowledge of the Islamic bases for knowledge, whereas those who do have that knowledge were all born elsewhere and do not know this society." Even at the best Islamic institutes in France, the teachers do not extend and apply Islam to problems of French society. Karim was quite critical of CERSI, the institute we will see in the next chapter: "Students leave the classes without knowing how to relate their Islamic knowledge to changing society. It is like university students in Third World countries." He sees the answer as requiring more, not less, involvement of universities elsewhere in the world: "We must create the demand in France so that the Muslim scholars elsewhere who do have this knowledge about Islamic jurisprudence will respond to our problems. One of my friends said it is as with marketing, you have to create the demand for the product before anyone will create the product."

Today the collective has branches in several cities in the south, and a strong presence in the regions around Lyon, Lille, and Paris. The cofounders of the UJM, Yamin Makri and Abdelaziz Châmbi, continue to play central roles in the collective. Each of the regional councils (Lyon, Lille, Paris, the South) consists of members of different local associations, for example the student associations in each city. "We let the associations in each city know when we are going to work on a problem, and then we let them decide whether to organize demonstrations or other actions. But in some cases we require that they participate, as in the case of opposition to the law on scarves in schools; all the associations were represented at the demonstration in February 2004, and many of our members also belong to Schools for All. We say if they do not choose to participate, what sense does it make for them to be in the Collective?" Each year the associations gather in Lyon for a national meeting, when they can revisit the participation of each association, but each local group guards its independence. Muslims have learned both sides of the French political paradox: the very unifying force of the state engenders and strengthens the resolve of associations to remain independent from it.[13]

Muslim women take on leadership roles in many associations. For many years the three Ghezal sisters, Hayat, Hanane, and Soumicha, have organized lectures and debates around Paris, and in the early 2000s they formed the Collectif Hamidullah (named after a Muslim scholar and teacher active in Paris through the 1980s), dedicated to preserving collective memory concerning Muslim scholars in France. As an Algerian woman active in organizing local debates explained to me in 2005, "Women always have been involved but now they are becoming more so, for two reasons. First, they have more education now and can take on new roles; second, their headscarves keep them from finding jobs elsewhere. You see many women in the mosque offices or schools for this reason."

Some associations revolve around social programs and are not exclusively Islamic in focus. The Schools for All association is one such example (and also includes many female leaders): although Muslim women and men were central to its activities, many non-Muslim social activists were equally involved. Among the associations that work for the interests of immigrants such as the MIB (Mouvement de l'Immigration et des Banlieues) in Paris, DiverCité in Lyon, and les Motivé-e-s in Toulouse. Some may enter into alliances with self-styled "Muslim lists" in municipal electoral campaigns, or demonstrations against expelling immigrants, or other causes. They are not Islamic but often include close ties with Muslim associations—less true for MIB, more so for DiverCité, for example.[14]

THE WORK OF AN EVERYDAY IMAM (LYON)

In April 2006, I took the two-hour high-speed train to Lyon, where a ride on the city subway and ten minutes' walk took me to the city's main mosque. Considered one of the cathedral mosques of France, the all-white, imposing structure sits in a part of town with new buildings and

Figure 3.4 The Great Mosque of Lyon

near the army hospital. Officially inaugurated in 1994 in the presence of Interior Minister Charles Pasqua, the mosque received a personal gift from King Fahd of Saudi Arabia and additional money from the Gulf states, Turkey, Tunisia, and other sources.[15] The main prayer area boasts an elaborate chandelier, an overlooking balcony is reserved for women, and an immense basement provides rooms for the Arabic courses the mosque offers on nights and weekends for adults and children.

The mosque is closely associated in the public eye with its director, Kamel Kabtane, who presides over the mosque association. In the domain of Islamic politics Kabtane has associated his mosque with the Paris Mosque, because both he and the Paris Mosque director have Algerian origins, but he is one of the more independent actors on the national scene. He receives foreign dignitaries and argues for the rights of women to wear headscarves, but he also offered his association's services to calm things down during the late 2005 riots. He is a "notable" who guards his independence but maintains his ties with the municipal authorities and is opposed to the entry of Salafis into France. When in 2002 the head of the Lyon-region school district argued with some teachers over the question of headscarves, he suggested that Kabtane be consulted as an authority on the matter. (They refused, saying that such a step would violate the principles of laïcité.) President Chirac received him among very few

Muslims on the annual occasion for religious leaders of France to present their good wishes to the president.[16] Once head of the regional Islamic Council (CRCM Rhône-Alpes), he lost that office in June 2005. He has a Jewish mother and Catholic wife, and says, "I sum up all humanity!"

The few large cathedral mosques already built in France—Paris, Lyon, Lille, Évry, Mantes-la-Jolie, and a few others—take on a wide array of religious and social functions. They attract large numbers of worshippers, particularly on the two major feast days of the year, and these days test their physical limits. The Îd al-Kabîr, or Feast of Sacrifice, falls during the period of the pilgrimage to Mecca, and worshippers gather for morning congregational worship before finding an animal to sacrifice in remembrance of Abraham's willingness to sacrifice his son. At the close of the fasting month of Ramadan comes the Îd al-Fitr and, once again, a major congregational prayer. For both events the Lyon mosque tries to accommodate around 10,000 worshippers by placing people throughout the basement and setting up tents outside. Even during the nights of Ramadan as many as 6,000 people show up for the optional nighttime prayers.

The mosque also is one of three in France that can license ritual sacrificers to prepare halâl meat, and they draw on their connections with the Corbas slaughterhouse, located south of the city, to solve the difficult problem of finding enough animals for local families to sacrifice on the Feast of Sacrifice. They buy 700–800 sheep and take orders up to one month ahead of time. Each person who has put in an order then comes to the slaughterhouse himself the day before the feast day, finds his sheep, and is given a time to come and pick it up, killed and dressed, the following day. The sacrificer works with a list of names and the corresponding number of a sheep, and when he kills each one he is supposed to say Bismillah and then the name of the owner, to communicate the intent of the owner to sacrifice the sheep in the name of God. The mosque employs a veterinarian who oversees sacrifice in surrounding abattoirs and who estimates that 30–40 percent of the meat prepared in their département is done so under the mosque's auspices.

Lyon and other large mosques try to meet a wide range of Muslims' needs, from marrying couples and arranging burials to providing classes in Arabic and Islamic knowledge; some mosques seek to train future imams as well. A mosque's "everyday imam" can be called at a moment's notice to attend to an emergency. When I was in another cathedral mosque, that at Évry, talking with their imam, a call came in from someone who had had a death recently, to ask what services the mosque provided. The imam immediately arranged for a man already in the caller's area to perform the washing and to lead funeral prayers, and he counseled the family to contact their funeral service to arrange for burial or to send the body "back to Morocco."

At Lyon, it is not the mosque's director who oversees these day-to-day tasks but the mosque's imam, who in 2006 was a Tunisian man, Najjar Mondher. Unique among imams serving in France, as far as either he or I could tell, he was sent by the Tunisian government to serve in the mosque. In fact, the Lyon mosque has contracts with both the Algerian and Tunisian governments to supply it with imams. When Najjar arrived in 2002 no one from Algeria worked there; between that time and my visit a delegated Algerian imam did work for a short time.

Najjar studied at Tunis's al-Zaytuna, the most prestigious Islamic university in Tunisia, where he specialized in *fiqh*, Islamic jurisprudence. He completed a master's-level degree in *usûl al-fiqh*, the roots of jurisprudence, before becoming the regional inspector of imams for his own home district of Monastir. He hopes he will be able to continue working in Lyon; he gets along well with the worshippers and with the mosque leadership, as well as with the Tunisian government. He has never been to Paris and did not know of the Paris Islamic institutes. His religious knowledge is grounded in the North African Mâlikî jurisprudential tradition, and his knowledge of French society is focused on the Lyon-region Muslims who come to pray or to seek his help or guidance.

Najjar oversees the mosque's complex religious-based financial transactions with the faithful. Local Muslims might present the mosque with gifts, but above all many choose to present their zakât, the tax on their wealth, to the mosque for proper distribution. The zakât is supposed to be distributed according to a limited set of legitimate recipients, including poor people, those newly converted to Islam, travelers, slaves (sometimes now interpreted as those suffering from worldwide oppression), debtors, the people collecting the zakât, and those struggling for God (*fisahillil-lah*), which could include a mosque trying to communicate knowledge or Muslims fighting in a war to help other Muslims. The Lyon mosque uses some of what it collects for its own expenses, explained Najjar, such as the costs for electricity. Indeed, a recent bill was posted on the bulletin board by the mosque entrance so that everyone could see the extent of the charges.

The mosque's assistance office is open every Saturday, and people in need may claim some of the collected zakât there for their needs. Najjar thought that schools also could present a legitimate claim to receive zakât, as they are working to spread knowledge (at least one institute in Paris has invited Muslims to donate their zakât to the school). "If someone needs to go to Paris for school, we might buy the train ticket for them. If someone is in the hospital and cannot pay the bill, we will pay something, maybe 150 euros. Each year thousands of people come to claim some of the zakât; that's why we had to be able to say, 'come Saturday when the office is open,' or we would spend all our time receiving them." A second kind of zakât, the zakât-fitrah, is a smaller sum paid by each Muslim, and the mosque distributes this to poor people and to students who are unable to afford their learning and living expenses. Most legitimate claimants each get 100–150 euros. The mosque also takes up collections each week: "Every Friday we have a single cause for which we collect money from those who come to worship, such as the Indian Ocean tsunami, or to help a new mosque that is being built somewhere else, or our own mosque expenses; the Mosque Association decides."

The activities that large mosques such as this one might undertake are virtually endless, limited only by their funds. Muslims ask for help with burial (either locally or in the "home country"), marriage and divorce, starting schools or prayer spaces, finding halâl food, and locating religious books. The Lyon mosque personnel give lessons in Arabic language and the bases of Islam for children and younger adults. You choose either Saturday or Sunday and come for three hours each week, and about 200–300 do so. In 2006, the mosque was about to add on a cultural center, which would include an institute to train imams and give refresher courses to current imams, for example in areas of *usûl al-fiqh*.[17] They hope to raise the money from the same foreign governments that aided in the original construction: "We will ask the consulates for help."

Najjar's main work is in leading prayers, attending to needs for burial or marriage, and, above all, receiving telephone calls or visits from Muslims needing advice, usually about marriage or divorce. Although his French is basic, it is adequate to talk through fundamental issues—the requirements for a marriage, why you should try not to divorce—and many of those who come speak Arabic. As we began our conversation he received a call from a woman who wanted an exorcism (*rukya*). He told her that the mosque did not do those but that he could give her the name of someone who might be willing to perform it at his house—nothing to do with the mosque, he emphasized. He then explained to me that he could tell right away that she had psychological troubles, because the devil works all the time trying to divert people from the right path, and particularly to come between husbands and wives (this was the nature of her troubles). Unfortunately, he explained, some people, *marabouts* (healers) from West Africa, try to make money from such cases, demanding five or six visits and telling people to kill a chicken, or to drink water that writing has been dipped into. An imam does not do that, but he can recite some of the Qur'anic verses that may help drive out the devil, such as verse 102 from al-Baqarah, or verse 255 from the same chapter (called *ayât al-kursî*, the "verse of the throne"), or the opening and closing chapters of the Qur'an. These verses also may be written down and the paper placed into a glass of water, which the patient then drinks. The Prophet, explains Najjar, left a hadith about chasing evil spirits with verses.[18]

When people come to see Najjar about marital troubles, he reads them hadith on how married life should be led, with affection for each other, that "each should be the clothing for the other," he said, quoting from the Qur'an. "I have to be social worker and psychologist in this job," he said. If a couple wants to divorce, he urges them to remain together. Other couples come to ask him to marry them at the mosque, but he refuses unless they have first married at city hall, as the law requires, and because without a civil marriage the wife cannot demand a divorce: the state will not consider the couple to have married, and there are no Islamic judges in France. For him, the only way forward is to create new Islamic institutions in France. "If we had an imams' council with some muftis," he explained, "then they could deliver a fatwa that would allow imams, such as me, to deliver divorces. We have no muftis now." [19] He saw the need for muftis as part of a broad need to understand the specific plight of Muslims in Europe. "We need to have jurisprudence for minorities," an idea he and most others associate with the scholar Yûsuf al-Qaradâwî, "because we are minorities in Europe."

Najjar wants to develop an Islam attuned to European life, and on this count he stands strongly opposed to the Salafis, people taking a literalist view of scripture without grounding in one of the main legal traditions. Many of the Salafis pray at his mosque:

> They don't think much of me but they pray and then go away. Every now and then one comes into the office to provoke me: they say that this or that is an illegitimate deviation, a bid'a; they say that we have to position our hands during prayer just as the Prophet did, and so forth, and that anything else is bid'a: and I say, in that case, the greatest bid'a is the collection of the Qur'an, because that was made after the Prophet's death! They have no answer to that. They say they have spoken with great teachers in Saudi Arabia: Ibn Baz, al-'Uthaymîn, Sheikh Arabi. In reply I say: "Have you heard of the works of this or that of the great jurists, or Ibn Ashur today," and they have never heard of these people. Sheikh Arabi, he wrote two or three books each of forty pages or so, saying everyone else is an unbeliever—"Qaradâwî is kafir, Ashur is kafir"—and this is not serious science.[20] We need the science of Arabic, Qur'an, hadith, usûl al-fiqh, the law's objectives, al-maqâsid ash-sharî'a. We need to know the reasons for which the Prophet said a particular hadith, the purpose of that hadith; that is why we study that hadith. They think that most acts are forbidden and but a small zone remained permitted, whereas with the sciences we understand that the permitted is very large. We have to understand the condition of society, the social reality, al-wâqi'.
>
> The Salafis say that we should all grow beards [he does not have one] and wear a long robe because the Prophet did so. If the Prophet were to live in Lyon today he would be wearing a sport coat! The elements of religion are

faith, ritual, and behavior, not appearance. They have no knowledge, so they rely on appearance rather than character. People here are not attracted to them but they approach the converts. We give the converts courses; I do not give a certificate of conversion until they have studied for three to four months. I tell them that you should read, but select carefully: if you are in a bookstore, call me. Often they do and I ask them who the author is and I say this book is alright but do not buy that one. [I asked if he suggested certain books and he said no, he just reacted to these calls. I asked him about the popular Islamic manual written by al-Jazaïri.] He is not as bad as the others, even though he lived in Arabia and so follows the Hanbalî legal tradition—what could he do; he lives there! I tell converts that his chapter on character is fine but to skip the jurisprudence part, because it is too complicated. We are Mâlikîs and little of that is translated.

Najjar shares many concerns with Karim back at the Paris Collective: that Muslims should rethink the bases of religion for European social conditions, that doing so requires looking at the objectives of the Qur'an, and that the Salafis, narrow readers of the sacred texts, are taking some Muslims down the wrong path. But Najjar comes to these conclusions from a very different starting point than Karim. Najjar is steeped in the Mâlikî tradition of jurisprudence and in the classical methods of thinking through fiqh, based on the science of the "roots of jurisprudence," usûl al-fiqh. His solution to the problem of adapting that school to non-Muslim societies is that of al-Qaradâwî, constructing a set of norms applicable only to Muslims in minority situations, a solution that does not require excessive tampering with the Mâlikî tradition. Karim is not trained in jurisprudence and reads in theology and jurisprudence with the goal of discovering Islamic bases for social positions that he already favors, about global warming and the headscarves and marriage. His aim is to make use of the construct of the "objectives of the Qur'an" to get more Muslims engaged as Muslims in projects of social change.

There are only a handful of cathedral mosques in France similar to the one in Lyon, and each one has its own story. The mosque in Évry, south of Paris, is closely associated with Morocco, and indeed was built thanks to funds from the Hassan II Foundation and the talents of Moroccan craftsmen. (Its carved concrete pillars are some of the finest in France.) The Paris Mosque, the first major mosque in France, continues to be directed from Algeria. Lyon, Évry, and Paris are the three mosques allowed by the government to certify sacrificers, and they realize considerable revenue from this privilege. The mosque at Mantes-la-Jolie received substantial funding from Libya in the 1980s and has been supported by the Saudi World Islamic League, but the principal imam was sent by the Moroccan government.[21]

MOSQUES AND SOCIAL DIVISIONS

Do mosques bring people together across ethnic or doctrinal lines, or do they reinforce such differences? When two French researchers studied the Comoro population in Marseille, and shared with an imam their observation that there seemed to be a "Comoro Islam," the imam laughed, then lectured them about the obvious unity of God and unity of Islam.[22] The tension between observing social differences among mosques or groups or practices, on the one hand, and acknowledging the idea and ideal of a single divine message on the other is characteristic of Islam everywhere, but the socially embedded ways in which it is manifest differ across countries. In Europe, and probably in most situations of displacement and immigration, mosques and other places of worship can become centers for enjoying familiar ways of speaking and socializing without becoming redoubts of an ethnically distinct form of Islamic practice.

The 50,000 people from Comoro who live in France provide a striking example of this dual character of mosques in France. Nearly all the Comoro immigrants and their children live in or near Marseille, where they are estimated to have formed some 300 local associations for sports, arts, and religion. They worship in the two dozen prayer halls, led by one of the approximately seventy imams identified in Marseille as Comorian. In the early 2000s, Imam Dhanoune stood out from the others, presiding over Friday worship at the Imam Chafi mosque in the Félix Piat projects.[23] The mosque and the prayer halls serve as centers for Comoro sociability, but many other Muslims, principally North Africans and people from Yemen and Egypt, also worship in the mosque, and some Sufi groups gather there for recitations (*dhikr*) sessions as well.[24] And the younger men and women who were born in Marseille find their Islam through reading French translations of Arabic writers—"The Permitted and the Forbidden" by Yûsuf al-Qaradâwî is one of the favorites. They are likely to have studied at the afternoon and weekend religious schools, which many of the Comoro adults consider to be a good way both to transmit religious devotion and to integrate the young into French society by equipping them with a solid moral base. This base is universalistic, not Comoro-centric. Some of these younger people become religious teachers, and they study in Saudi Arabia or the Sudan and return with an Islam without Comoro references. Here, then, is a situation in which a minority population among Muslims finds its unity through its own mosque, prayer halls, and associations but does not seek to construct an ethnically distinctive form of Islam or to keep others from participating in shared worship.

Let us remain for a moment in Marseille, where the population of Sufis from West Africa belonging to the Mouride order has a unique history.

Founded by Sheikh Amadou Bamba in the late nineteenth century in Senegal, the order is best known for its astute combination of rigorous prayer activities and cornering the market in peanut production and trade. From its center in Touba, Senegal, the Mourides have constructed religious-commercial networks throughout the world. Some Mourides lived in Marseille at the turn of the twentieth century, owning small hotels and cafes and in that respect resembling the Berber-speaking Algerians from the Kabyle region. But it was in the 1970s, after drought in Senegal and the worldwide economic crisis pushed many of Mourides into new transnational trade, that they began to come in larger numbers to Paris, Marseille, New York, and elsewhere. Marseille has maintained an important place in this network, both because of its port history and because it once was a stop on the route to Mecca for the pilgrimage.[25]

Today the Marseille Mourides are most likely to gather on those occasions when the sheikh of their order arrives from Senegal. After the Mourides had settled in far-flung places, the Touba sheikh transformed the pattern of visiting (*ziyâra*): whereas adepts once visited the sheikh to pay homage, now it is the sheikh who circulates around the globe to visit his followers.[26] As of the 1980s, and in more public fashion by the 2000s, the several thousand Senegalese Mourides in Marseille welcomed regular visits by the descendant of the order's founder. The members of the many Mouride worship circles, the *da'ira*s, where adepts regularly meet to recite religious poems and pray, come together to welcome the sheikh. He in turn brings signs of his charisma, his *baraka*, in images and cassettes. When, for example, Sheikh Sérigne Mourtada Mbacké visited Marseille in 2001, he urged his followers to build "Sérigne Touba houses," as he did at each stop on his circuit; taken together, these houses mark off the Mouride global space.[27]

If the Marseille Mourides mark off their own global religious space through their participation in what we might call "reverse pilgrimages" (*ziyâra*s), they do not choose a mosque for Friday prayer on the basis of ethnic solidarity or Sufi affiliation. Indeed, many of them live in the Félix Piat projects, and therefore pray at the nearby mosque—which is the main mosque for the Comoro people, and is presided over by their Imam Dhanoune!

Many other West Africans belong to other Sufi orders and participate in their respective global circuits of travel and study. The Tijaniyya order, founded in the eighteenth century by Sheikh Ahmad al-Tijani, is the largest in Senegal, and its followers include many Muslims in Senegal, Mauritania, and Mali, including Soninké and Pulaar speakers. One of the best-known leaders of the order is Tierno Mansour, who lives south of Dakar but makes regular visits to his followers in the Paris region and elsewhere in France. He makes his France base in an HLM apartment outside Paris. For many of his Pulaar-speaking followers in France he stands as a moral exemplar (and indeed as a saint, *wali*) in a land where upholding and transmitting Islamic values is seen as extremely difficult, and many of these Muslims credit his visits for returning them to the proper practice of Islam.[28]

Turks worship mainly with other Turks but for reasons that have more to do with the policies of their home country than is the case for West Africans. We saw in the previous chapter that Turks who came to France were much less likely to know French than were other Muslim immigrants; for that reason, they tended to settle together and, as one would expect, to build their own mosques. The majority of these mosques, around 100 by 2005, are controlled by the DITIB, the French branch of the Turkish state Bureau of Religious Affairs (the Diyanet). The bureau pays the imams' salaries, either directly or through an association, and even orders the prayer rugs from a single distributor in Turkey.[29] The DITIB has a parallel existence under a different name, the Coordinating Committee of Turkish Muslims in France, and as such sits on the Islamic Council as a thinly disguised direct representative of a foreign power.[30]

The major competing network of Turkish mosques is run by the Millî Görüs ("National Vision") movement, born of Necmettin Erbakan's succession of Islamic political parties in Turkey. When his National Order Party was banned in Turkey in 1971, party leaders took refuge in Germany and Switzerland, where they created the germ of the new movement. Some of the Islamic party leaders (including Erbakan's nephew) created the Millî Görüs in Germany during 1973–75, and opened a Paris branch in 1978. Turkish immigration to Germany and then to France increased drastically after the military intervention in 1980, and the Millî Görüs began to establish mosques throughout France, but especially in the eastern third of the country, where most Turks settled. The DITIB and Millî Görüs in France live in a tacit arrangement of live and let live, usually staying out of each other's territory. The relationship became easier when the Justice and Development (AK) Party, led by Recep Tayyip Erdogan and itself a spinoff from the Refah Party, won Turkish elections in 2002.

Because Millî Görüs remains focused on the issue of Islam for Turks, its leaders in France emphasize community solidarity over integration into French society: "integration of individuals might weaken ethnic and religious identity," said the imam of the Paris Millî Görüs mosque.[31] Millî Görüs organizes pilgrimages of thousands of Turks living in Europe each year to Mecca. The Millî Görüs has about seventy mosques in France, managed by a real estate corporation controlled from the movement's European seat in Cologne, Germany.[32] Of particular importance is the Eyüp Sultan mosque in Strasbourg, a population center for French Turks. In Paris, Millî Görüs controls the el-Faith mosque on rue du Faubourg-

Saint-Denis, where the sermon is given in Turkish. The movement's French offices are nearby. (Smaller numbers of mosques are affiliated with the Süleymanci and Naqsabandi Sufi orders, the Nurcu movement, and the Kaplan movement.)[33]

We have seen a number of distinct ways in which mosques are tied to foreign states. They may have received their initial funding from a single state. Large mosques in France have depended on foreign states, associations, or private donors for at least part of their funding. Even the Paris Mosque, created in the 1920s as an element of French foreign policy, also receives major support from foreign sources. Recently constructed mosques were largely subsidized by Morocco (for example, in Évry) or Turkey. But others have received moneys from multiple sources—the Lyon Mosque here is a good example: diversifying its "development portfolio" prevents it from becoming associated entirely with one country.

In some but not all cases the foreign donors also retain some control over the policies or leadership of the mosque, a second dimension of foreign state–mosque imbrication. Algeria sends imams and appoints the director of the Paris Mosque; the Turkish government does the same (plus the carpets!) for the majority of Turkish mosques. Here again, Lyon's politics have involved efforts to avoid this dependence, in receiving imams sent by the governments of both Algeria and Tunisia.

Finally, some mosques are frequented mainly by people from one country of origin and their children. Fewer and fewer mosques are worshipped in only by one North African population: more commonly, the presence of substantial numbers of Moroccans and Algerians leads to a dispute over the selection of an imam—as in the case of the Clichy mosque, which then turned to the Tunisian Dhaou Meskine, or in that of the mosque at Bagneux, south of Paris, which appointed a Comoro imam to lead worship of the mainly Moroccan and Algerian faithful. Either because of language—Urdu is used at the one Pakistani mosque I found in the Paris region, Turkish at others—or because of a sense of ethnic or national solidarity, some other mosques have a clientele predominantly drawn from one or another country.

For some groups this ethnic specificity may remain longer than simple generational accounts of migration would suggest, insofar as Muslims continue to participate in global networks of trade and communication. Turkish and West African communities in France continue to be replenished with fresh arrivals from the home countries and even from specific regions within home countries. Many in these communities see this reaffirmation of home ties as a positive feature of transnational orientation in that it reaffirms moral values and cultural traditions. In the case of Turkey it also is part of a transnational struggle for the future of Islam back home, as the competing groups see their diasporic communities as likely to return home. Mosques then remain part of transnational communities, not because Muslims do not wish to be French but because their life projects involve movement and communication across national borders.[34]

By looking at a range of mosques we are able to understand how Muslims have organized vis-à-vis a number of features of the French landscape in which they now find themselves: ethnic diversity, state management of religious bodies, and demands by some of the faithful for education, financial assistance, and help in fulfilling religious obligations. Many mosques develop educational and social branches; they function with steering committees and in fund-raising they target those who frequent their services. Mosques thus take on some degree of the "congregational" character noted by many observers of American religion, suggesting that to some degree it is the social need for certain services and not specific features of worship traditions that shapes religious institutions.[35]

Within the social contours of these mosques, schools, and networks such as the French Muslims' Collective, teachers and religious leaders have had to develop new ways to advise Muslims in France about how to live as French Muslims. We have already seen that the socio-Islamic landscape tends to push some of these leaders toward modes of reasoning that facilitate new solutions and broad alliances. We now turn to focus on the content of "Islam": how do some of these imams and teachers bring past traditions of knowledge and norms to instruct people living in French society?

CHAPTER FOUR

Shaping Knowledge to France

As TEACHERS have developed Islamic institutes and schools in France, they have had to negotiate with French officials and meet the expectations of Muslim students. In some respects the first challenge has been the clearer of the two. The working relationships between elected or appointed officials and Muslim leaders are always unstable, sometimes tense, but occasionally productive, and in any case are situated in the long-term logics of electoral politics and of the state's sponsorship and control of religious institutions.

The contours of the Islamic educational field have been less clear because they are still emerging. Teachers have to translate a language of religious norms, practices, and ethics, developed and learned in societies suffused by Muslim institutions and practices, for a new territory characterized by the absence of such institutions and by strong professions of secularity. In France, many Muslims try to improve their knowledge of Islam, but not all are certain how to go about doing it. In bookstores and mosques, at lectures or on the Internet, they encounter a vast array of positions, often strident, sometimes subtle, and often difficult to situate and adapt to their conditions in contemporary Europe. Visiting preachers might urge a separation of men and women in everyday life, but those same men and women go to work every day in a gender-mixed France. Books or lectures might set out detailed rules of Islamic finance, but to buy a house in France means visiting a European bank that charges interest.

How, then, to teach Islamic norms to women and men who plan to make their lives in France? Teachers, scholars, imams, and anyone who cares to post opinions on the Web have offered a confusing variety of answers, but I think we can group them into three broad ways of framing the question of Islamic norms: as a set of absolute rules, as one among several legal traditions, or as a set of principles based on Scripture. Each of these frameworks has its firm place in Islamic history and its own attractions as a base for shaping a Muslim life in France today.

RULES, SCHOOLS, PRINCIPLES

The conceptually easiest approach to imparting a sense of Islamic norms, of God's way for Muslims (the *sharî'a*), is to construct a rule-book of

Islam, stipulating what a Muslim must do and must not do, and what actions or objects lie on a continuum between these end-points. Indeed, compiling and referring to such a list, sometimes referred to as "the *harâm* and the *halâl*" (the forbidden and the permitted), is part of practical Islamic life throughout the world. Muslims throughout the world learn rules of this sort: they must pray in certain ways at certain times, they must avoid certain foods, and they should slaughter an animal on the Feast of Sacrifice. Muslims may learn such rules as they grow up, or they can seek out advice or find rule-books in their own language. Potential converts are told to learn these rules as the first step toward living as a Muslim, and some Muslim groups, such as the Tablighi Jama'at, focus almost entirely on such rules as the basis for living a Muslim life in a non-Muslim society. This approach can be very attractive to a Muslim who, feeling adrift, looks for sources of certainty: do this and avoid that, and you're a good Muslim.[1]

But many problems of contemporary life—in Syria or Indonesia, as well as in France or Canada—are not so easily resolved. Should one eat meat killed by a Christian or Jew? May one take out bank loans at interest to buy a house? Is it acceptable to give money to the poor in the place of sacrificing an animal? On these and many other questions about practical life, Muslim scholars differ. Moreover, even core ritual practices have developed along divergent paths in different world regions, and Muslims who have come together in lands of new immigration may find themselves not all praying in the same manner. So the rule-book approach is not always sufficient even on its own terms, that is, as a safe, noncontroversial, "best practices" guide for getting through life.

A second approach promises to do better in this regard by urging Muslims to follow one of several established legal traditions or schools. Most of the world's Muslims do generally follow teachings of one or another such tradition, a *madhhab*, which sets out conventions for most of the disputed details of ritual and religious life, drawing on the accumulated body of rulings made by respected jurists (sing. *faqîh*) engaged in the pursuit of legal knowledge or jurisprudence (*fiqh*). North African teachers (and historically those living in Andalusia) generally follow the Mâlikî tradition, named after the scholar Mâlik ibn Anas (d. 795). Those living in or coming from the former lands of the Ottoman Empire and in India will likely follow the Hanafî tradition, after Abû Hanîfa (d. 767). Ahmad ibn Hanbal (d. 855) gave rise to the Hanbalî tradition, which predominates in Saudi Arabia and Qatar. Muhammad ash-Shâfi'î (d. 820) gave his name to the Shâfi'î tradition, followed in Southeast Asia and to some extent in Egypt and Central Asia.

The picture is more complicated than this: there are other schools, particularly several major Shi'ite ones, and some Muslims select from among the teachings of more than one school. The main idea behind the Sunni Muslim traditions, though, is that, on the one hand, all four traditions are legitimate (one is not a better Muslim by following one or the other), and on the other hand, agreement within each one is desirable as a practical matter of establishing conventions and agreement in the face of understandable uncertainty about the precise instructions from the Divine on many matters of everyday life. One does not have to argue whether Muhammad (the penultimate arbiter on all religious matters) held his hands in this or that manner while praying; one follows the convention of one's school and says that, in the end, "only God knows."

This second approach differs from the first primarily in the way it frames the question. It also involves learning rules of correct behavior, but it short-circuits potential bickering about ritual details and introduces a sense of rule pluralism into teaching itself: we do it this way; other ways also are legitimate. Conversely, it allows teaching minute details without having to constantly say how every school approaches every issue or justify why those details are followed rather than some other set. But it involves learning ways of living a Muslim life that were developed in traditionally Muslim lands. Some teachers and scholars find that new approaches are required to address the new issues facing European Muslims. They ask whether or not Muslims might create new sets of legal norms, either by drawing from more than one of these traditions or by developing new approaches.

Across the new lands of major Muslim settlement in Western Europe and North America one finds an assortment of efforts at normative bricolage, involving notions such as a "jurisprudence for minorities," the "objectives of the Qur'an," or the shared importance of contracts in Islamic and European societies. Those who advocate these new approaches base them on ethical postulates or on general objectives found in the Qur'an, or on their readings of the reports (hadîth) of the Prophet's statements and actions. In the last chapter we heard both Karim at the Paris Collective and Najjar at the Lyon Mosque invoke the idea of shari'a's objectives, al-maqâsid ash-sharî'a, as providing the groundwork for offering Islamic justifications for social projects and for adapting practices to European social conditions.

This third general approach to teaching Islam in France is less a school of thought than a shared sense that Muslims must seek new principles in scripture, and that these principles ought to be related to one another in a systematic way. Teachers in France adopting this approach often refer to the work of modern scholars, including Muhammad ʿAbduh (1849–1905), Hasan al-Banna (1906–49), and Muhammad al-Tahir Ibn Ashur (1879–1973), as well as the fourteenth-century scholar Abû Ishâq al-Shâtibî. They also may draw on the works of the contemporary Egyptian scholar Yûsuf al-Qaradâwî, who broadcasts from Qatar on the al-Jazira television station. But in reformulating the thinking of these scholars they are taking new paths.

Although teachers may combine these approaches, how they frame "learning how to live as a Muslim" maps roughly onto the sociology of Muslims in France. The rule-book approach has its closest affinity with individuals and groups seeking to live uncompromisingly Islamic lives in what they see as a relatively hostile environment, such as the Tablighi Jama'at (or "Tabligh") mentioned above, or those groups, often labeled Salafi, that proclaim a desire to reproduce the life conditions and life ways of those who learned directly from the Prophet.[2] Teachers who advocate following one of the legal schools—usually the Mâlikî school—generally were educated in a Tunisian or Moroccan university and have sought to create institutions of Islamic higher learning in France. Those advocating developing new sets of principles are more eclectic in their training as they are in their teaching, but include some with historic ties to the Muslim Brotherhood and individuals who have studied in more than one country, or in subjects other than Islamic jurisprudence or theology.

Individual Muslims who live in France and who seek greater religious knowledge thus have options. Many try out more than one possibility, perhaps starting in a mosque, then enrolling in one school and perhaps transferring to another later on. Some prefer to read books and attend lectures, and may approach an imam or try the Internet for answers to their specific questions. Now and then, the demands of some of these seekers intersect with the institutional supply, and a school succeeds.

Hichem El Arafa's CERSI

One such success story, at least as of the close of the first decade of the 2000s, is Hichem El Arafa's CERSI (Centre d'Études et de Recherches sur l'Islam, Center of Studies and Research on Islam), located in Saint-Denis, north of Paris. Several scholars and activists, including Hichem and a young convert to Islam, Didier Bourg, created the school in 1995, and found housing in the Saudi-sponsored World Islamic League building in Paris.[3] In 1999, Hichem moved it into the back rooms of the Tawhid bookstore in Saint-Denis (the location of the Islamic Collective described in the previous chapter). In 2003, after several failed efforts to relocate back to Paris, Hichem was able to move the center to a building close to the University of Paris's Saint-Denis campus and on the tramway that links several of the northern Paris suburbs. The new quarters provide two large classrooms; a library with books on immigration, French law, and Islam, in both French and Arabic languages; a lunchroom; and several offices.

Figure 4.1 Hichem El Arafa, 2001

I examine Hichem's approach in some detail here because it shows us how a leading teacher has fashioned his approach over time as a set of responses to alternative ways of framing Islam for France. When I first met Hichem in 2000, he was in his thirties, with a short goatee and mustache, and usually wore a sports coat and mock turtleneck sweater. He has a thoughtful, soft-spoken manner, pausing to reflect before answering. Running the center is his main employment, but he also is often called to give Friday sermons or nighttime talks and to field questions from young couples worried about their marriage or from people unsure whether their workplace was halâl. During the month of Ramadan he is in nearly constant circulation around the Paris region.

Hichem lives with his wife and four children in Aulnay-sous-Bois, in the northern Paris suburbs. In 2001 his oldest daughter was thirteen; he initially had enrolled her in a private elementary school in Paris because she could learn Arabic there. (Arabic was taught in some schools as a legacy of the idea that the state should teach children the languages of the countries to which, one assumed, they would "return.") At the time, he did indeed think that he would return to Tunisia with the family and that his daughter and the others would attend an Arabic-language school, so he wanted to make sure she knew the language. In the end, the family remained in France. Hichem had received a university degree in Paris and was planning to continue on for a doctorate in Islamic studies, but he decided that to support his family he should find work. "The opportunity to teach at the institute turned up and promised steady employment, so I decided to stay." He then decided that they would all speak Arabic at home to give the children a strong base in the language, but over time it has become mixed with French.

Hichem has been moving all his life—"I feel like a nomad," he told me in 2001. Born in a small Tunisian town, he moved to nearby Bizerte for high school. Although he traveled home on weekends, the move "really changed my relationship to my parents, because I was not with them all the time, and far from sight, far from the heart, as they say." He studied philosophy and religion at university in Tunis before traveling to the Imâm Muhammad ibn Saʿûd University in Riyadh, Saudi Arabia, where he spent four years studying Islamic sciences. He came directly to France from Riyadh in the early 1980s and began teaching in 1993 at a precursor to the institute. Unlike some who were forced to flee Tunisia because they advocated an Islam-based political reform, Hichem is able to return to his birthplace, and travels with the family most summers, sometimes to Tunisia or Morocco.

CERSI clearly follows the third general approach to Islam mentioned above, that of teaching on the basis of a set of Islamic principles. Its Web site states that its purpose is to develop an "adapted approach" to teaching and research, but Hichem finds that this process of adapting is a series of experiments. When he first began teaching in 1993, "I did what most of us do," he told me in 2001. "I took the books on a specific topic and compared what they said and made a synthesis on, say, how to understand revelation, or I took one book that seemed to offer a good approach and taught from it, adding elements from others. I taught for the first two years like that, but I found that it was not right for the students, that they had a different background from students in a Muslim country, so I modified the course to give them a global vision, and to analyze problems, asking how and why."

I asked him to talk more about the differences between students in a Muslim country and those coming to his institute:

> In North Africa, students live with mosques and radio all around them, and would have gone to the mosques at least a few times and heard people talk about things, and heard words on the radio, so that they have perhaps 1,000 concepts and words about Islam, many of which the young people here do not have. For example, I had been talking about *sahâbi*, which I translated as the Prophet's companions, and a student here asked me what that meant. He took "companion" to mean "a good Muslim," which I can understand, but it was far from the word's meaning. So I had to return to the basics, make things more accessible for them.

Indeed, translation poses constant challenges for all the teachers.

> Another difference lies in the reasons for which people take the course. In North Africa students take courses to prepare for roles as teachers, or imams, or religious officials, whereas here they already have work, and they take the course more for their general knowledge of Islam. It also means that they do not have that much time to spend on courses, so giving them a perspective, tools, keys, is more important than giving them a vast quantity of facts.

I asked him to expand on why people chose to take the courses:

> They come because they have concerns, usually about practical matters such as ritual. They rarely pose questions about theory; they feel surrounded by different opinions and want to feel sure of themselves. Sometimes they say that their parents do not know very much about Islam and that there is a hole in their lives.
>
> The younger generation, those born here, do not know their own language and culture and could never go back to their country of origin. I could do so: even though I left Tunisia twenty years ago, I could reinsert myself somehow, but not them. They are always going to be here. They have been excluded from French society, growing up in the projects; those who come to the Institute are looking for some sort of order; they find attractive the structure of the daily prayers, and so forth. They start to consider themselves responsible.

Hichem himself refers to "their own" language and culture as that of the northern or western African countries from which, in most cases, it was his students' *parents* who had emigrated. He, like them, finds himself caught between two sets of social and cultural references, even in his ways of speaking. Identifying oneself as Muslim rather than trying to choose between Africa and France is one solution to this problem: it provides the "order" that many otherwise fail to find.

Students signing up for courses at CERSI choose either a three-year sequence of Islamic studies conducted in French or a one-year introductory course on the Arab language, or both.[4] Most students take the former, in which they study Islamic history and civilization, the "sources and sciences" of Islam (including Qur'an, hadith, and jurisprudence), and "faith and spirituality."[5] The entire set of courses is given three times each week—Saturday, Sunday, and over Monday and Tuesday evenings. Most students opt for one of the weekend times. Hichem also calls on activists and academics in the Paris area to give "general courses" on Islam. During the period I attended courses, a Muslim from south of Paris talked about elections and naturalization, a leading female Muslim scholar talked about the history of women in Islam, Didier Bourg discussed his research on marriage issues among young Muslims in France, and I discussed Muslims in the United States.

Hichem has had difficulty locating and retaining teachers. They must be competent in Arabic and French, know a subject matter, and be comfortable with the school's general orientation. But there is no single teacher profile: "I keep experimenting with ways of teaching; the classroom is a laboratory," said Hichem. "The people who do teach are of so many tendencies—UOIF, Tabligh, and so forth—but also [have] different ideas about whether religion is public or private, the role of faith in their lives, and so forth." Although the teachers have quite varying styles, they all base their teaching on Islamic texts, either classic works or their own compilations of Qur'an and hadith.

As Hichem indicated, those who attend CERSI (or other similar institutes in France) usually do so to fill out their religious knowledge and improve their religious practice, not to seek work as a religious specialist.

In their own accounts, students generally emphasized the importance of correct religious practice. The comments of one young man born in France of North African parents were typical. When I asked him why he chose to study at CERSI, he answered, "I had only studied Islam at the mosque before, and little groups there just talked about Islam in terms of what was forbidden [harâm] and what was permitted [halâl], and then I heard some people give lectures, particularly Hassan Iquissien and Tariq Ramadan, and they had a much more open spirit. Here I really learn about Islam, as an open, tolerant religion. I want to be able to teach my children [he is still unmarried]: 'the first lesson is this, then this. . . .'" A man from Mali explained that "[i]f I just studied by myself, I would be likely to go in the wrong direction, that of obscurantism. Here I can study from people who know about Islam, and this knowledge helps my practice." His main worry was that he would pray or fast or tithe in the wrong manner, not that he would misunderstand Islamic history or fine details of theology.

As other scholars of Islam in France have noted, many young Muslims make the effort to understand "true" Islamic norms, without distortions and free of "traditional" elements, by which they usually mean the Islam practiced or taught by their parents. Some women who enroll at CERSI do so despite their parents' wishes to the contrary. "They ask, for example, that we not send enrollment forms to their homes," Hichem explained. "Their parents oppose their general turn toward religiosity."

Most of the CERSI students have not taken formal classes on Islam before, although most had been to mosque lessons, and I met several who had studied in the small circles of the Tablighi Jama'at. Nearly all had grown up in households where some rules of Islam were observed, usually fasting and at least occasional prayer. Most had learned about CERSI through word of mouth, or from visiting its booth at the annual Islamic gathering at Le Bourget. In the early 2000s, 200–300 students were enrolled in classes each year. Although some drop out during their first or second year, after a decade of existence CERSI has taught thousands of youngish Muslims in the Paris region. Most students live around Paris, particularly in the département of Seine-Saint-Denis. Around 100 students take the course by correspondence each year; most of these live in other parts of France, but some correspond from French-speaking parts of Canada, and a few even live in Saudi Arabia.

Some students find CERSI to provide the kind of learning not available elsewhere. One man in his twenties often came to CERSI to help out even after he graduated. In 2001 he was still in his second year of study. His parents had been born in Algeria but they were not at all observant; indeed, he had learned to pray at the institute! He lives in the same city as Hichem and had heard Hichem give the sermon at the local mosque. He thought he would check out his school, and ended up enrolling. At his mosque, "there is little to interest the young people, everything is done in Arabic, even though the young do not know it. If young men come at all it is because there are sports and some other activities. Now they have started to have someone come in once a week and give a *dars*, religious talk, in French, although that is not very deep either."

As the institute expanded to become CERSI, the profile of the students shifted somewhat. In February 2004, Hichem noted that students were more advanced in their own studies of Islam than before, but that more of them were beginners in practical religious matters than before as well: "The change means that we have to adapt the curriculum to them." Hichem had hired a new teacher who also works as imam south of Paris to teach a course on the basics of Islam, including ablutions, prayer, and other obligations—just the sort of knowledge a child might learn at home or in a mosque. "I had to answer these sorts of questions in the mosque, and now I can teach the same subjects here," said the new teacher. In other words, the center had taken over the functions of a mosque or a family in teaching complete neophytes how to practice their Islam.

Hichem sees students as self-selecting into his school. When I asked him in 2004 what was true in general of the students, he replied, "I know what they do not share: a literalist reading of texts. If they thought in that manner they would have left in the first year. Probably some of those who do leave early on disagree with what we do; others leave because they have too much to do between their work and their studies. And there are some who come to see if we have mixed classes, men and women together, and when they learn we do they do not return. That is why the Salafis do not like this school." In class as well as in our discussions, Hichem contrasts his approach to that of the Salafis, those with literalist approaches who take from scripture only a list of what is forbidden and what is permitted—"*harâm-halâl*," as he put it.[6]

Hichem said he knew the Salafi approach well from his years of study in Riyadh, Saudi Arabia:

I could smell the closed-off approach the minute I stepped off the plane. In some sense I had been vaccinated against it, because in Tunis in the late 1970s, I had debated people taking all sorts of positions, including union organizers and Communists. I was thought of as of the "Islamic left wing," so I was used to dealing with many different opinions without just accepting them. The Saudis have a general attitude toward theology, which is to not look too deeply into questions. So the people who study there and return to France, they themselves are not that educated, maybe one year after high school, with some Arabic. Or perhaps they speak Arabic, but although they can cite Qur'an and hadith they have not been trained to be jurists. So they give simple answers to questions, say do this and do not do that. They give people rules to which they have to adhere, and reject all alternative ideas.

Once I was giving a talk in a prayer hall and I gave as an example how a hadith urges people to brush their teeth before they pray. "Well," I continued, "the Prophet used a small stick, but that is because that was what was available at the time. Today he would use a toothbrush and toothpaste." This got around to many of the groups the young belong to, and then it came back to me; one young man approached me on a subsequent occasion and told me he had heard that I had said that, and that at that moment, in his heart, he had tried, judged, and executed me. [JB: Did you ask him what he used to brush his teeth?] You know, if you go into the bookstores that you find around Belleville or other neighborhoods, along with the books are little gadgets for sale, including these little sticks for brushing called *mishwak*, wrapped in plastic, which come from Saudi Arabia, also small flasks of perfume, made without alcohol, because that is what the Prophet used.

Toward the end of October 2001 we were discussing the institute. The attacks on the World Trade Towers, and the claims that Muslims were responsible, hung over our conversation:

Many young people do not study here because they think we are too soft [*laxiste*]; they are unhappy with the fact that girls and boys sit together, and that some girls do not wear headscarves. Sometimes someone calls first to ask whether the seating is mixed, and we know that when we say "yes" they will not come. They consider al-Qaradâwî to be too soft and instead they follow others, local imams who just give them answers out of their own heads. They do not like it that we study al-Ghazzâlî, his books on the faith of Muslims and the morals of Muslims; they want to be taught what is forbidden and what is permitted, and that's it. These Salafis are the extremists, the next step to people doing violent things, but I do not understand how one could go from holding Salafi views to committing such a violent act.

(Few Muslims in France with whom I spoke just after the attacks were willing to agree that Muslims were responsible, and even by 2008 many thought that the real story was still to be told.)

Many students know the sort of response Hichem will give to some questions and so do not pose them. In the months after the attacks on the World Trade Towers in 2001, for example, ordinary Muslims did not ask about jihad. "Several reporters did so, but not Muslims," he told me in 2003, "because if someone asks that question it is because they want to go on jihad and they want a yes answer, and they figure, well, an institute probably will not say that, so they ask the imam at their local mosque, and he may say yes. These local imams give answers on their own, yes or no; they do not ask others or consult Web sites to see what others have said."

As Hichem knows all too well, CERSI sits in a larger environment that includes other institutes, mosque classes, Internet sites, and Saudi fatwa phone banks. Students at CERSI often have arrived there by way of earlier experiences with these other institutions. They all seem to be on journeys. A bit of purposeful hanging out in the corridors reveals a lot about the pathways leading some of these young Muslims to Hichem's school. Some began their quests with simpler approaches, either the Tablighi Jama'at or various Salafi groups. In 2001 I talked with two men, who had tried both approaches. "Some of the Salafis give courses in mosques where they study the fatwas of the Saudi scholars. We also went to some of these, and found them fine for studying the Prophet's life but much too narrow for fiqh, so we gave them up." They then tried the Tabligh, "but we realized that there were lots of debates and differences, and figured that we needed to study more."

Khalid is a convert to Islam in his mid-twenties who had seen the Salafis, and reacted against them:

> The groups who call themselves "Salafi" wear their long gowns and beards and follow people in Saudi Arabia. They are more interested in pointing out the forbidden than in exploring the permitted. [JB: Why?] Ignorance, mainly; they know very little. I was in Saudi Arabia for the pilgrimage and met people who had similar opinions about Islamic matters, but they were very open to other points of view.

He said they followed al-Albâni (see below), that he was "the Sheikh" for many of these groups:

> He writes in a way that is very clear and very narrow. They listen to his Arabic-language cassettes. They say that everyone must have "their own sheikh" and that ours is al-Qaradâwî. They do not like al-Qaradâwî; they say he is too open to Europe in his views of hadith. But we don't listen only to him; we listen to other scholars too, such as [former Saudi Grand Mufti Abdelaziz Abdullah]

Ibn Baz, and Muhammad al-Ghazally. These people have looked over what it is like in Europe and only then do they pronounce fatwas.

Those others follow people who have never been here but produce fatwas, which the Salafis follow, for example against Muslims associating with non-Muslims. Well, that is fine elsewhere; in Mecca you can separate people, so much the better! But in Europe, you have to buy bread from somewhere; you have to go to the store. I know some people who have decided that they cannot live in Europe, they must live in a Muslim country; one friend, born in Algeria but living here for many years and married to a French convert, left two months ago to live in Dubai; he is a trader and that is what they will do there, they are trying to see if it will work.

Two years later Khalid reported that this friend had returned to France, as had most others: "they had become used to life here."

Paris-area Muslims have followed several different pathways. One young Tunisian man studies with Hichem and studied at a Tablighi school, "where we sit on the floor, at low desks, and learn to recite Qur'an, all Qur'an and very little else." Of course, my encounters were only with people who had rejected Salafi views, but students spoke of friends who had moved from the Tabligh into the Salafi movement, "because they have a very strict and limited view of things." Others defended the Salafis. I sat with two men in the back of the Tawhid bookstore. One said "they are not all the same, some are good people. If you join them they tell you right from the beginning, 'people will approach you and say this or that [referring to jihadist preachings]; do not believe them,' and this insulates them. And they do not practice politics; they are like the Tabligh in that respect." His friend disagreed: "If you say they do not do politics, that misses the point that they keep to themselves, do not exactly contribute to an integrated society." Here is one of the main fault lines: between pursuing an Islamic path within France and becoming part of it.

What does Hichem offer as an alternative to Salafism and the Tablighis? He reaches back into the traditions of Islamic epistemology to emphasize the complexities of knowledge, and also builds on a set of general Qur'anic objectives or principles to extend that knowledge to new domains. His teaching tends to highlight the former, based on the science of the hadith, the "reports" of what the Prophet did, said, and refrained from doing or saying. He can focus on the science of hadith to underscore the complex nature of Islamic knowledge and to argue that scholars must weigh alternatives and make judgments. He also teaches that the reliable hadiths converge with common sense, even now, in France, and they cohere into a logical system. Muslims thus have no need to abandon the traditions of learning for a simplified approach to their religion in the form of a simple rule-book. But neither does it make sense to Hichem to teach from the standpoint of one or another of the legal schools, as these were developed in societies far different from today's France.[7]

Hichem himself teaches classes on the Qur'an, hadith, and jurisprudence, and I followed his lessons on these topics over several months. In all his classes he often drew diagrams on the whiteboard to schematize the internal logic of one normative domain. He also frequently cited hadith to support his points, referring to all four founders of the main Sunni legal traditions. He told stories to illustrate a point, and sometimes these stories merged with the stories contained in hadith of the form: "One day so-and-so came to the Prophet Muhammad and said. . . ." Hichem's "meta-message" was that Islamic knowledge is based on the science of studying the Prophet's sayings and that this science yields complex results, not easily reduced to a set of rules. Students often are unhappy with this message; many would like to find those rules.

THE SCIENCE OF HADITH

Classrooms at CERSI resemble modern classrooms anywhere. Students sit at desks in rows; the teacher uses a whiteboard to diagram or to write phrases and terms. Most classes had twenty or more students, more or less equally men and women. Most but not all women wore headscarves. Generally, men and women sat in different areas of the room, but sometimes they sat next to each other. Classes combined lecture and rather free-form questions and answers.

In May 2001, Hichem was teaching how to know what degree of reliability to assign to a particular hadith. This question is central for this branch of knowledge, which sifts through the many such reports to determine their relative reliability, and only then makes efforts to adduce general or particular rules. To talk about reliability, Hichem used a term from the law courts, the "admissibility" of reports. He explained that the first question to ask of any claim about a hadith is how reliable are those who transmitted it. "For example, if someone says to you that your father has asked you to send him 10,000 francs, and that he will take the money to him for you, you ask yourself if you know this person and what you know about him before entrusting him with the money. Above all you ask about the honorable character of his conduct."

> The scholars of Islam looked to see if liars were found in the chains of transmission, because if you did not pay sufficient attention to other norms in your society you also might lie about a hadith. So they created some conditions for admitting a hadith. First, you may not have committed a major sin, one for which there is a penalty. [A student asks, "How did they know?"] Perhaps

because punishments were applied in public, and then people wrote biographi-
cal dictionaries with details of the lives of many people, including those who
transmitted hadith. You also may not have persisted in committing small sins.
What counted as a small sin changed with the times, so perhaps then if you
ate a sandwich in the street that was something that people did not normally
do, and so you would not be believed if you testified in court, or not wearing
a long garment. Neither act proves that the person would lie about a hadith,
but they mean that the person was not terribly bothered by the opinions others
had of him, and so was more likely to lie about something; better to avoid him
entirely. It is the fact that the person acted without following the norms of the
day that makes him likely to lie.

If there were contradictory statements, these scholars would lean toward
doubting the transmitter. Perhaps they pushed the fear of lying to the extreme;
several hadith warn of the gravity of lying, that it secures a place for you in
hell. One hadith even says that complicity in a lie disqualifies someone because
it shows a failure to exercise a critical spirit. Bukhari writes that he saw a man
catching a horse by holding out a sack as if it had food in it, and then tossing
it aside once the horse had approached and he had grabbed hold; the sack was
empty. He reasoned that if the man could do that then he could easily lie.

The transmitters also had to have sound intellectual quality, *dhabt*, a word
that now means "military officer" [the connecting idea is "discipline"], and
requires strength of memory, that there be no major errors in what the transmitter said.

One week later, Hichem picked up the discussion from this point. How
did people decide whether someone's memory was sufficient? One way
was to question the same person at different times. For example, hadith
no. 2673 in the compilation by Muslim mentions a companion of the
Prophet. The hadith says that the signs of the last days are when God
takes from you one by one each of those who is learned, so people will ask
questions of those who do not know, and they will be led astray. Hichem
comments, "We are not too far from that state now in France. Someone
who has one year of experience and grows his beard sufficiently long becomes the 'neighborhood sheikh,' transmitting what he hears from Saudi
Arabia. Sometimes now he will even telephone there to answer a question." (Some in the room chuckle at this comment.) Hichem continues:
"So, Â'isha"—a wife of the Prophet—"had her nephew ask the men who
said they had heard the Prophet say the hadith if they would recite it to
him. A year later when she heard the nephew was coming by where they
lived she asked him to ask them again, and not a word had changed."

Hichem then explained a second method of verifying memory, by com-
paring the hadith of different transmitters. The more people who heard
a hadith at each stage of transmission the more reliable is the hadith. He

used an analogy: "For example, we do not doubt that Napoleon invaded Egypt, because so many people know this. If someone claims that he did, we don't then proceed to ask, 'Do you drink [alcohol]? How good is your memory?'" (The class laughed at this.) He explained that reports that do not have many independent lines of transmission are judged according to the character of the transmitters. He gave the Arabic and French terms for these categories quickly and orally; students learned the general idea of the subcategory but not the terms. Students often asked for clarification. (In general, the women in the class had better French and were quicker to catch on than the men, and also tended more often to challenge the teacher with their questions.)

At this point Hichem made one of his frequent disparaging references to Salafi ways of knowing the shari'a:

> Other scholars accept different hadiths. Al-Albâni, for example, prohibited jewelry; he was the only one to do so. Surely you have heard of him; he is a "star of the *banlieue*." Young people will take what someone has said ["and change it," commented a student]; no, not deform it, but they make that one person the one and only reference, without looking for others, and then they say "this is the only way." There is for example a controversy over whether you have the hands hanging down during prayer or crossed in front. One sheikh said you must fold your hands in front of you while another said that doing that is a *bid'a*, straying from the path. But the essence of prayer [*salât*] is not in those details; you could have both hands cut off and still perform the salât.

Hichem's target here was indeed one of the best-known writers on matters of Islamic norms available to French Muslims. Muhammad Nâsir al-Dîn al-Albâni (1914–99), who was born in Albania and lived much of the last part of his life under house arrest in Jordan, stirred up a great deal of indignation among established legal scholars by his strident condemnation of followers of the legal schools, and also for his absolutist pronouncements on a variety of matters: forbidding fasting on Saturdays, condemning women who wore gold jewelry, stating that income from commerce was exempt from the 2.5 percent zakât tax, and many more. But many others, particularly Ibn Baz, grand mufti of Saudi Arabia in the 1990s, extolled al-Albâni's knowledge of the hadiths. He is thus a formidable competitor to those who would argue for a more pluralistic form of Islamic knowledge—and he is very popular in the bookstores and the mosque discussion groups.

Hichem did not argue with the details of al-Albâni's pronouncement but with the degree of certainty associated with it—an attitude that leads some who follow al-Albâni to condemn any who disagree as outside of Islam. Hichem intends his detailed analysis of hadith to undercut the way in which these "black-and-white" thinkers issue pronouncements by contrasting it with the deeper knowledge contained in the work of the students of hadith and the founders of the legal schools, such as Imam Mâlik. He also pointed out the difference between the major issue, the essence of prayer, for example, and the relatively superficial issues often debated, such as how one holds one's hands. Outside of class Hichem told me that he increasingly was asked questions by young Muslims about these ritual details, such as whether the hands should be crossed or at the sides when rising up to one's feet, or whether it is the knees or the hands that should touch the ground first when prostrating. "These issues do not matter; it is the spirit in which you pray that counts. They raise them because different imams are telling them different things, and they are confused and afraid to make mistakes."

But even among those who followed Hichem's classes were many who wished for something a bit more absolute from their teacher. In the classroom one woman asked Hichem, "How then do we decide which thinker has credibility? We do not know where we stand after all this!" Hichem answered that the problem lies with the effort to explain everything from one element and to discredit all others; it is better to be more nuanced. But neither she nor some of the other students were satisfied by this response.

Hichem made things worse by continuing with a story:

> There was a companion of the Prophet who was assigned by the Prophet to guard the storehouse, and one night he found a man trying to steal the food. He caught him, but the man promised he would do it no more, so he released him. The very next night he caught the man again, and the man said, look, let me go and I will give you something to ward off the devil. He taught the guard the *âyat al-kursî*.[0] The guard reported all this to Muhammad, who replied, "Do you know with whom you were dealing? That was Satan, and of course he lied to you when he said he would not come back a second time and steal, but he told the truth about the *âyat al-kursî*." So this goes to show that you can learn even from Satan.

Several students exchanged dubious looks among themselves, and the woman who had posed the earlier question objected: "Are we supposed to laugh at this?" Hichem: "Well, not 'Satan,' but we can learn from anyone." Hichem's point was that the charismatic character of several "stars" such as al-Albâni had led people to accept their claims without critical examination, and to reject claims made by others. What we should do, Hichem argued, was to examine what everyone says, but also take learning from whatever source we find. Muslim scholars around the world will cite the famous hadith, "learn even all the way to China" in support of this rationalist, anticharismatic approach to authority that naturally fits with the way in which Hichem presents the science of hadith.

Hichem's stance is particularly important in that at times he has used textbooks that themselves present unilateral statements of what Muslims should and should not do. For several years he taught from *The Way of the Muslim* (*Minhaj al-Muslîm*) by Abubaker Jaber al-Jazaïri ("the Algerian"), available in two French-language editions (one in three volumes and another in pocket format) and a perennial best-seller among Muslims in France. Al-Jazaïri left colonial Algeria for Saudi Arabia, where he became close to the mufti, Ibn Baz, and lectured frequently in Europe in the 1980s and 1990s. The *Minhaj* is popular because it covers all the basics, from faith to prayer to social relations, and gives unambiguous directives to Muslims, backed up with citations from the Qur'an and the hadith. In Hichem's words, "al-Jazaïri is more enlightened than some other books, but only relatively so, only compared to what many people get in the mosques."

The difficulties presented by the *Minhaj* for someone trying to adapt Islam to France are clearest in the volume on social relations, where the author declares that Muslims are forbidden (except under conditions of extreme necessity) to transact even with most banks in Islamic countries, because those banks practice usury. He devotes a long section to jihad, presented as the armed confrontation with unbelievers (*mécréants*), and not as primarily a struggle with oneself. He also sets out in detail the conditions under which a man may repudiate his wife but does not mention the major avenues by which, in most Muslim-majority societies, wives can petition judges for a divorce. The book sets out rules that do not correspond to those of any existing society, and it admits none of the innovations or compromises worked out by Muslim scholars from Asia to Africa.

Hichem switched to using a volume by Yûsuf al-Qaradâwî when it became available in French in the mid-1990s. Although its title, *The Permitted and the Forbidden in Islam*, suggests the rule-book view of Islamic norms, al-Qaradâwî's approach was much more acceptable to Hichem, for two reasons. First, the book itself takes a theoretical approach, allowing a teacher to develop specific arguments as he might wish. Second, the author's rather flexible stands on a number of issues regarding Muslims in Europe has made him a symbol of an open-ended and open-minded approach to Islamic norms—just as the Saudi scholar Ibn Baz, justly or not, has become a symbol of a strict, uncompromising approach. In 2006 Hichem reaffirmed his preference for al-Qaradâwî, emphasizing that he remained within the tradition of Islamic legal reasoning and sought ways to adapt it to Europe, in contrast both to those who remained inflexible, such as Ibn Baz, and those who reasoned from outside the tradition, such as the popular Muslim author on Islam Malik Chebel. Indeed, the Qatar television station al-Jazira, which features al-Qaradâwî, was playing in the restaurant as we were eating lunch. "Qaradâwî has advised banks and is on most of the fiqh councils, so he has had to learn about concrete problems of banking and arrive at solutions."

Al-Qaradâwî begins his treatise with the general observation that in Islam, everything is permitted unless God has forbidden it, and quotes Ibn Taymiyya, usually thought of as a source for a strict version of Islam, as saying that "We forbid only that which God has prohibited, because prescription and proscription belong to God's Law."[9] The book makes no mention of jihad. Al-Qaradâwî reiterates the prohibition on interest, argues that the religious traditions of Jews and Christians also forbid it, and provides a socioeconomic justification for the prohibition, arguing that interest increases economic disparities. He argues in a tone of social explanation of the divine word, rather than condemnation of those who transgress it. He argues that divorce is forbidden by Islam unless it is justified by a great need. In other writings (although not in this book, perhaps to avoid controversy), al-Qaradâwî explains that his approach is based on the objectives of Islamic law (al-maqâsid ash-sharî'a), such as preservation of the family and of religion.[10]

Although Hichem admires al-Qaradâwî—above we heard one of his assistants stating that "everyone has a sheikh, and Qaradâwî is our sheikh"—he tries to ground his interpretations directly on hadith; he learns from al-Qaradâwî but justifies in terms of the Prophet. He therefore argues that, with proper interpretation, all the reliable hadith remain true today. In class he said that "the collectors of hadith were careful not to put their own subjectivities into their weighing of hadith, such that centuries later we can still use what they did. For example, the hadith that there is no such thing as contagion is very reliable, but we know that epidemics spread through contagion. So do we then say that the hadith is not good, that we cannot use it?" He paused to say he was very glad to see that Rashid, a man from Algeria who had medical training, was in the class, and could help him answer the question. A woman put up her hand and suggested that perhaps the hadith did not refer to medical contagion. Hichem replied that it did, and continued: "I read a doctor's article, a Muslim doctor, of course, that said that only a small number of the instances of transmission of a virus result in illness." Rashid then added: "Right, there can be 'healthy carriers' of a virus, such as the AIDS virus." Hichem: "So what the hadith says is that contagion is not automatic. There was a nurse in Johannesburg who died of the Ebola virus from caring for someone who had it. All those who had come into contact with her, 350 people, were tested, and none of them had it, nor did anyone in her family."

For Hichem, the science of hadith rests on epistemological criteria that make good sense today. In our everyday lives, we are more likely to believe statements made by reliable people than by unreliable ones, and we are more likely to believe statements that many people have made than those made by only one person. The content of the hadith also makes good sense. Time and time again, Hichem would say that the Prophet's statements differ not at all from what we derive from our common sense and our reason. If the content of a hadith does not immediately appear to be consistent with our knowledge of the world, as in the case of the hadith about contagion, then it is up to us to find a way to make it consistent, to reinterpret it.

THE OBJECTIVES OF SCRIPTURE

Although Hichem argues that the hadith are applicable today, not all questions that arise now, in France, can be answered on the basis of hadith scholarship, but require reasoning outward from the relatively accepted norms of Islam to new situations. Hichem encounters such questions frequently. He is relatively available for questions from Muslims in and around Paris: he keeps regular hours at the institute, he often gives sermons or talks in mosques, and he is available by telephone—although only at work, and he refuses to carry a cell phone, fearful of the volume of calls he would receive. He has written answers to commonly posed questions for magazines or as leaflets. Younger Muslims frequently come to him about practical matters.

It is in his reasoning about these issues that he engages issues of adapting to France in a more immediate way than he does in the classroom. Although some of these questions concern basic elements of Islam—how to pray, when to cease fasting—and are easily answered, others lead Hichem to reflect critically on alternative ways of understanding Islam in the modern French context. I spoke with him several times in early 2001 about the questions Muslims brought to him. Often they ask about how to marry or divorce, he said. Sometimes the question is more a request for personal advice. "They ask, 'Should I marry someone whom my parents disapprove of?' They want a counselor as much as a religious person. Sometimes I can bring Islam to bear on the question."

In general, if Hichem does not find a satisfactory answer to a question in the Qur'an and the hadith, he turns to the opinions of al-Qaradâwî and others, and then to contemporary fiqh councils. "There also is a doctors' site about fiqh across the Muslim world whose findings are very useful because they have fiqh specialists and doctors together; it is multidisciplinary."

I asked Hichem how he developed his current approach to finding answers. "I began to think through things in my twenties—at that time I was a cultural Muslim, I had taken my baccalauréat in humanities and I was especially marked by philosophy, which was quite intense, with five hours a week, and it was secular thought, analysis, so I posed questions to myself about Islam, and read in Islam, rediscovered elements of Islam and decided that its components did hold together." On another occasion, he reflected that "it must be the case that our pasts, where we studied, shape how we teach, but I cannot say exactly how that is true for me. . . . It is true that I studied in Riyadh, but I did not completely accept what I was taught there." He hopes to complete a more systematic work on fiqh, "to show what the reasoning was behind the new *ijtihâd*," by which he meant the writings mainly in Egypt by such scholars as Muhammad al-Ghazally and al-Qaradâwî.[11]

Hichem also has drawn on Pakistan's Abdullah al-Maudûdi in teaching.[12] Indeed, he distributed to his students in the class on fiqh a photocopied, eleven-page document called "Introduction to the Study of Fiqh," which is a translation of the final chapter of the influential book by Maudûdi, *Towards Understanding Islam*, written in the late 1920s in Hyderabad. Maudûdi developed the idea of Islam as an ideology, comparable to Western ideology and opposed to it. He emphasized the importance of understanding the system of Islam as a set of institutions and practices, distinguishable from those of Western societies. But thinking about Islam as a system leads Hichem to seek points of overlap between Islam and other systems, by looking for ways in which diverse institutions could satisfy the purposes or objectives of the Qur'an, *al-maqâsid al-Qur'ân*. We will see the term *maqâsid* cited again and again in this study. It offers a term that resonates with the history of Islamic scholarship and at the same time offers a mechanism for justifying innovative practices, for mediating between a practical exigency and a system of Islamic norms.

The contemporary scholars who invoke the idea of shari'a's objectives usually identify a prestigious lineage that stems from the Prophet to the caliph 'Umar, then to the scholars Abû Hanîfa, Ghazzâlî, and Shâtibî, and, in the twentieth century, to Ibn Ashur and Yûsuf Al-Qardâwî. In the twelfth century, Ghazzâlî had identified the interests of Muslims, their *masalîh* (sing. *maslaha*), as "the preservation of the *maqsûd* [objective] of the law [*shar'*], which consists of five things: preservation of religion [*dîn*], of life [*nafs*], of reason [*'aql*], of descendants [*nasl*], and of property [*mâl*]."

Of continuing importance to modern debates is the work of the fourteenth-century scholar al-Shâtibî, who distinguished between the timeless principles, *maqâsid*, found in the Qur'an and the historically changing products of jurisprudence.[13] Shâtibî elaborated the idea to say that the shari'a was created to protect these five universals (*kulliyyât*). These "necessities" (*darûriyyât*) are supported by desiderata of lower rank: the "needs" (*hâjiyyât*) and the "improvements" (*tahsîniyyât*). Performing salât, for instance, is necessary to protect religion, but human needs require allowances for travel, sickness, and so on, and local customs regarding cleanliness and dress should be seen as "improvements" that contribute to this maqsûd.

Successive authors have broadened the range of these objectives. In the mid-twentieth century, the Tunisian scholar Muhammad al-Tahir Ibn Ashur and the Moroccan political activist and scholar Muhammad ʿAllâl al-Fâsî expanded on the objectives identified by Shâtibî, and al-Qaradâwî offered more general definitions of the maqâsid as that which defines "public interest" (*maslaha ʿâmma*) and includes "the institution of justice and shared responsibility in [what ought to be] a model community, and everything [else] that makes life easier for [the people], removes oppression, perfects their character and guides them to what is best in manners and customs, in [social] arrangements and in interactions."[14]

In the practical use he makes of this form of reasoning, Hichem prefers to look to overall meanings or principles, rather than follow the reasoning contained in the fiqh manuals of the Mâlikî or other legal traditions. He is as willing to derive those principles from practitioners in a non-religious domain as he is to look to Islamic scholars. In one conversation he mentioned his recent reflections on two issues that local Muslims bring to him: abortions and bank loans. "Contemporary scholars tend to oppose any interruption of pregnancy, and I follow them," he explained. "You might think that the scholars would have been strict on this issue and the doctors more flexible, but in fact the four law schools were more flexible, in that the majority tended to tolerate abortion at some point in the process of pregnancy, usually for the first forty days, but some also for the first four months. After that point everyone condemned it. But then the Muslim medical doctors took as their starting point the fact that the embryo is living, and so they urged all abortions to be prohibited. The scholars have ended up going along with the doctors. This change, towards a stricter position, started in the 1970s."

He pointed out a similar progression in thinking about bank loans:

> Until recently, scholars hesitated to condemn interest. They would analyze the operation of charging interest into several stages, and could find a way to declare each one halâl, and so therefore declare the entire process halâl. But more recently, starting in the 1960s, Muslim economists urged us to see the process as part of an entire economic system, with certain motives and objectives, and to declare it harâm. Since the 1970s, all fatwas tend to condemn it.

In both examples, Hichem points to what would surprise some, that classical jurists showed more flexibility than did modern medical doctors and economists. Jurists perhaps thought too much, taking apart things into units and justifying them. Hichem favors the modern positions because they look at the overall meaning of the act under judgment: an abortion is ending a life; a loan is part of a system that extracts interest without participating in risk. He accepts these ideas as "the current consensus" rather than as the only possible approach.

If this part of his overall reasoning process sometimes leads him to be more likely to condemn a practice than would someone remaining within a specific madhhab, the next part builds in a great degree of practical flexibility. When he applies his general conclusions to the case of a particular person, he looks to the probable outcome of a decision before providing advice:

> What I do is try to start with the current consensus, but Islam gives us a certain room to maneuver, so that, for example if a woman comes to me and says she is pregnant, I consider her particular case. Perhaps she has two young children already and is poor, and another child would really strain their budget, then I might tell her that she has some choice in the matter, that there are several options, and that what counts is that she has made this effort to think through the problem. For even in the case of a jurist, there is a hadith that says that if he is correct in his fatwa he gets two benefits, but if he is wrong he still gets one, so not only is he not punished, he benefits from having tried. But I also consider the type of person I am facing. If she seems like someone for whom giving her choice will just confuse her all the more, then I might urge her to make a particular decision; but if I think she can reflect on it and decide, then I will urge her to do that. There is not one law, but one way (*pas une loi, mais une voie*).

In these instances, Hichem's recourse to principles is tempered by a look toward the consequences of one or another decision. Although in this case he did not use the notion of sharī'a's objectives, his reasoning is similarly pragmatic.

Hichem's particular strategy of interpretation and application—grounding in the ever-relevant hadith, a search for the current principled consensus, application on a case-by-case basis—defines one of several possible normative and pedagogical niches. CERSI focuses on the religious domain: it is about Islam, not the world of social issues facing Muslims in France. It offers a general curriculum, not specialized training for imams or preachers. It models a world of gender mixing, free discussion, and also the observance of prayer times and fasting. It offers one future for Islam in France, but not the only one imaginable. To situate it in a broader field, in the next chapter we consider the ways students and other teachers evaluate the alternatives.

CHAPTER FIVE

Differentiating Schools

WHEN WE LISTENED to Najjar at the Lyon Mosque or Hichem at CERSI
talk about their pedagogical projects, they explained what they were
doing in contradistinction to teachings they labeled as Salafi and considered to be simplistic. I now want to continue this ethnography of distinc-
tion-making but to turn our perspective around. Rather than looking
outward from within a particular institute, let us consider directors of
all such institutes as pedagogical entrepreneurs, looking for niches to
occupy. We can then understand the way in which each presents his approach as an effort to claim distinction (and a market niche) by way of
a particular understanding of Islamic knowledge.

DIMENSIONS OF PEDAGOGICAL DIFFERENCE

We can provisionally distinguish three dimensions along which these institutes differ. The first, *professionalization*, concerns how far the institute seeks to prepare Muslims for work as Islamic professionals—imams,
chaplains, or teachers—or focus on imparting a general knowledge of
Islam. Hichem's CERSI makes no claims to offer professional training;
others offer only that. *Language* is the second dimension: teaching at
CERSI is entirely in French, with optional courses on the Arabic language, while others require mastery of Arabic before a student may
begin to take classes on Islam. These first two dimensions are related
but distinct, in that a school might train imams but mainly through
the medium of French, and conversely, a school might teach the Arabic
language and even teach some courses in Arabic, but as ways to enjoy
the full range of Arabic arts and television as well as to read religious
texts. Finally, institutes highlight different combinations of *sources* for
learning about the Islamic tradition. Some start from one of the four
Sunni legal traditions; others avoid these traditions and work directly,
and interpretively, from the Qur'an and hadith. Of course, anyone starting from a legal tradition will cite scripture, so this dimension really
regards the degree to which the teachers refer to one or more of the legal
traditions.

Hichem's View

Let us begin by returning to Hichem, who always thinks about what he does with respect to the competition. As we saw in the last chapter, he designed his school to oppose what he sees as the simplistic approach of Salafis. He also wishes to reach beyond the four main legal traditions of Sunni Islam, the four Sunni *madhhabs*. North African judges and jurists followed one of these traditions, the Mâlikî, and most of the scholars directing institutes and schools in France today learned Mâlikî jurisprudence, even if they then went on to study other legal traditions. Some of these teachers prefer to start with Mâlikî teaching and then add opinions from the other schools, but Hichem prefers to bypass these traditions, though not the masters themselves.

In May 2003, over lunch, Hichem asked me about another institute in Paris, and I explained that the director of that school, Ahmed Abidi, would present students with the opinions from all four legal schools on a subject. Hichem immediately replied that he did not see that people were interested in the traditions, and that he preferred to choose specific problems that concerned people. He also distinguished CERSI from a school sponsored by the UOIF that seeks to train men to serve as imams (mentioned by Fouad Immarine in chapter three). The school's name reflects the UOIF's desire to position itself as a major force within European Islam; it is called the European Institute of Human Sciences (in French, Institut Européen des Sciences Humaines, IESH). The IESH has its oldest branch in a rural area in Burgundy, Château-Chinon. Students who come to this institute live on the grounds and commit to four years of preprofessional study. Near CERSI in Saint-Denis is the newer Paris branch of the institute, which does offer to train people to become imams but also has more general courses, and offers courses in the evenings and weekends, as do most other institutes, allowing students to live at home and hold down jobs.

As we were talking at CERSI in February 2004, a student came by to greet us; he had tried the imam training program in Château-Chinon, but because he could not work while there he had to drop out; it was too expensive. But CERSI also has made a trade-off, as Hichem explained: "Because we teach in French, we get a great many students, and this has the advantage of teaching them in their everyday language, but it also means that we have to keep the program not too advanced." Hichem has tried to offer higher-level courses and research training, but these are not major dimensions of the school.

In 2001, a young African man in his first year at Hichem's institute approached him to ask how he could study Arabic more intensively. Hichem tried to find out what he wanted exactly, and told him about the Château-

Chinon program, which required seventeen hours a week and (in 2001) about 15,000 francs a year. The man asked about programs overseas, and Hichem replied that Saudi Arabia and Syria had such programs, but not geared toward French-speaking students. The man had just completed a program in computer science, and Hichem counseled him to not leave France, lest he lose his competitive edge in the job market. The man said he wanted to read Islamic works in Arabic, and asked if it was not better to do so. Hichem replied that after a year of studying Arabic you can read the Qur'an, but that even after two years you cannot easily read, say, a book of fiqh, because words have special meanings, and you would need to consult other works. You would do better to study Islamic sciences in French or, even better, in English, he said. Hichem had gone to one of the major Paris libraries with holdings on Islam and found much more in English than in French. After a long discussion, the man left. Hichem said that many of the younger people are on a spiritual search; he can tell that when they do not really know what their goal is in studying Arabic, or they say they want to study everything in Arabic. Those who are more realistic say, for example, that they want to read the Qur'an.

These encounters display, from Hichem's perspective, the specific situation of CERSI with respect to the alternatives. By staying with the French medium, it signals a centering of learning in France, and plays down the tie between learning Arabic and learning Islam. Hichem even considered letting students choose English rather than Arabic as their additional language. CERSI remains generalist, and caters to people who are already holding down full-time jobs or engaged in full-time studies at university. Finally, as we saw at length in the last chapter, it starts with questions of scriptural interpretation and with real-world problems, and seeks a meeting point. It refers hardly at all to the scholarly traditions represented by the four legal schools

Now let us consider how some of the other institutes position themselves in this three-dimensional space defined by degree of professionalization, choice of language, and choice of sources. I start by filling out our picture with some brief examples and then turn to a long discussion of one other institute, one that tries to remain within the Mâlikî legal tradition.

The Great Mosque of Paris

The Paris Mosque—Grande Mosquée de Paris, in its full, glorious title— is not only the oldest mosque in Paris, it also trades on its reputation as the most moderate Islamic institution in France in order to retain close ties to the state, to welcome a secular public to its famous tea room, and to allow a wide range of Muslim figures to hold meetings on its premises. As we saw in chapter two, it was the favored partner in a series of state-initiated efforts to domesticate Islam, from attempts in the mid-1990s to form a national Islamic body around the mosque, to the formation of the Islamic Council in 2002–3, to sporadic projects to create state-supported institutes to train imams. An old but prominently displayed plaque explains to the visitor that the mosque is part of an Institute that is "private with a public and international aim."

Abdelkrim Bekri taught in Oran, Algeria, before the mosque's director, Dalil Boubakeur, recruited him to lead their Training Institute, housed in the mosque's elaborate, tiled building. A thin, animated, friendly man with rudimentary French, he explained to me in June 2005 that he sought to overcome the linguistic limitations of French Muslims who seek to become imams. "Even if they know Arabic, they know it in a French-ified way, so we require that they learn Qur'anic Arabic before they begin." (They offer courses in Arabic students may take before starting the other sequence.) The mosque offers two tracks. In one, people working as chaplains in hospitals and prisons train men and women to become chaplains. The track takes two years, and the students visit hospitals and prisons to see what problems come up. "Women are especially needed; this year we graduated six women and three men."

Abdelkerim also trains imams over a four-year course of study. He bases the curriculum on that used in Oran, "because most of Islamic learning is the same. We teach the Mâlikî tradition, but we learn something of the others." Students also learn the foundations of jurisprudence and the maqâsid as-sharî'a, continue to study classical Arabic, and take courses from French professors on the history of France and Western thought. In 2005 their first cohort finished their third year of the program; they had about seventy students enrolled in total. Courses are held on the weekends and during the late weekday afternoons. All the students live in the Paris region and continue to study or work. In 2005 they paid 80 euros a year for their course. Few find work afterward: "There are no paying jobs. Some work for free; others are paid a small amount by associations."

The Paris Mosque Institute teaches the objectives of scripture, the maqâsid, as a part of fiqh, using works by Shâtibî and Ibn Ashur, and they subscribe to the idea of a fiqh for minorities. They also have a telephone number for questions about religion, and "every five minutes someone telephones with a question; we have two and sometimes three people answering the phone." They draw on the fatwas produced by the European Council for Fatwa and Research associated with al-Qaradâwî, but most questions are simple, about how to carry out the prayer, for example. I asked for other types of questions frequently posed. "They ask, 'I work in a bistro and serve wine; should I leave?' and they ask about bank interest and whether a Muslim woman may marry a non-Muslim man. That last issue is under debate, because some say that as long as he respects her right to keep her religion, why not?"

Abdelkerim would like to see their institute create branches to better serve other parts of France, and to train people who could then train imams, "which would require us to create institutions at the same level as universities, similar to an École Normale." Among the other institutes in the Paris region he considered the IESH in Saint Denis, run by Ahmad Jaballah, as closest to his. "The basic materials are the same, but he emphasizes Arabic less." He is less favorably disposed to the older IESH branch in Burgundy. "I find the atmosphere there very narrow, closed off from society—of course, it is off in the woods! That a student would memorize sermons by Sheikh Kishk [the well-known Egyptian preacher] from cassettes, when he does not yet know [classical] Arabic: I find that shocking!"

Teaching the "Middle Way"

The IESH does indeed try to sustain two tracks of Islamic education. The branch in Burgundy focuses on training imams and chaplains, and when the directors opened a branch in Paris in January 2001, they thought they would offer similar training. But the directors quickly realized there was more demand for more general theological studies than for imam training, and by 2003 they had created a two-year plan for general Islamic studies that resembles Hichem's at CERSI and that attracted twenty students in its first year. But they retained the four-year program to train imams that resembles the Paris Mosque program (and that attracts a smaller number of students, five to ten per year).

The institute's director is Ahmad Jaballah, a friendly, somewhat reserved man with short dark hair and a close-clipped beard. He completed his master's degree in Tunisia in Islamic sciences and finished a doctoral course in sociology and Islamic studies in Paris. One of the founders of the UOIF, he sits on the European Council for Fatwa and Research and routinely presents fatwas on behalf of the UOIF at their annual gatherings at Le Bourget. His wife directs the Muslim Women's League.

The Paris IESH is housed on two floors in a nondescript building near the Saint-Denis RER train station near the Seine. Even by 2006, no signs directed you to the building; you turned in past a long metal gateway, noticed a sheet of paper taped to the front to indicate you had arrived, and buzzed to be let in, then walked up to the first floor. I sat in on Ahmed Jaballah's class on Islamic legislation one evening in 2001. Ten students (seven men and three women) attended. Jaballah taught the course from photocopied handouts, which presented fiqh as "the elaboration by interpretation and reason of the shari'a," and shari'a as the "divine law". It describes the Hanafî school as allowing more room for interpretation than the other schools. The text emphasizes that truth is multiple and that God intended this multiplicity, and mentions that the "Salafi school refuses to study in the framework of the four legal traditions, because they say that the traditions place themselves between God and humans; this claim results in superficial texts." Among the works students use to learn fiqh is a text from the Shafî'î tradition (and an overview of fiqh by Saïd Ramadan, the father of Tariq Ramadan). All works are in French.

After describing these sources of knowledge, the photocopied text refers to the "collective ijtihâd," which takes the form of legal counsels, including the World Islamic League's Islamic Law Assemblies at Mecca and Jeddah, national councils, and the European Council for Fatwa and Research. To the class, Jaballah explained that all questions that arise from social life, for example about medical techniques, require ijtihâd. He asked the class what the sources for reasoning were, and they all said together: Qur'an, Sunna, *ijma'* (consensus), and *qiyas* (analogy). Then there are additional sources, such as *'urf* (customary norms) and *maslaha 'âmma*, the general interest of Muslims. "But it comes down to two kinds of reasoning: texts plus ijtihâd, since qiyas and ijma are kinds of ijtihâd."

In his text, Jaballah also mentions the six "principles" (the *maqâsid*) that lie behind interdictions, those being the objectives of safeguarding religion, life, reason, procreation, honor, and property (the five principles proposed by Shâtibî plus honor, added by al-Qaradâwî). He then explains that we can deduce specific rules from these principles: for example, from the principle of safeguarding procreation we can derive the prohibitions against fornication (because it destroys families) and "abusive abortion." A footnote explains that the Hanafî tradition says that abortion can be tolerated up to the end of the third month of pregnancy. Jaballah is able to produce a more tolerant stance on abortion than that explained by Hichem (discussed in chapter four) by interpreting an objective (safeguarding procreation) rather than by deducing an opinion from a principle (that life is sacred).

In front of the class, Jaballah diagrammed this relatively permissive approach by explaining that Islam is "valid for all places and times," but it is also adaptable to all contexts. There are universal elements and those that we change. Most acts are neither prescribed nor prohibited, such that they are in the large domain of "the permissible," which is a "legal vacuum." He drew a circle on the blackboard, with a shaded portion representing those acts for which there are texts and the much larger remainder representing that vast area of "the permissible," for which no relevant texts exist. He asked the students the difference between law and fatwa, and they responded correctly, as he saw it, that the former is general and the latter a response to a specific case.

He then explained that it is not that God forgot to discuss these activities for which there are not texts but that he left things open for us because of his mercy. You cannot go beyond what is in the texts, should not try to overly expand the area covered by rules.

> It is not the objective of Islam to multiply the number of prohibitions. The Prophet once said to his companions, "Do not ask me too many questions." They asked him why not, and he responded, "Because then I will have to reply," and because his word was revealed; which means that if he spoke he would create another limit to the realm of free choice. So, for example, if you are invited to someone's house and you know it is a Muslim, do you ask if the meat is halâl? No, because it is enough to know that he is a Muslim; do not ask too many details. The Qur'an says: "If you ask something you will get a new obligation; accept the grace of God." But there also always people who keep on asking.

Jaballah's pedagogy reflects the UOIF's broader view (consistent with that promoted by al-Qaradâwî) that scholars should pursue a "middle way" or "the just middle" between arguing entirely from objectives and principles, on the one hand, and arguing entirely from positions derived from one or the other of the four Sunni legal traditions on the other. Jaballah reflected this position when he answered a question I posed on another occasion, concerning the scope of reasoning from objectives. In late 2003 the importance of wearing a headscarf was at the center of public debates about Islam, and I asked him if the objective (*maqsûd*) of a woman's wearing a head covering were not protecting her dignity and honor, and if that objective could not be better served in other ways in France, given the degree of resentment it had generated. In his response he emphasized the methodological priority that scholars must give to clear scriptural texts, such as those telling Muslims when and how to pray, and to the analysis of a text's reason or cause, its *'illa*. The reason or cause of a text has to do with why it was revealed or uttered at a particular moment and is much more tightly connected to the text itself than is the objective it might further:

> Yes, we do advocate relying on the maqâsid of verses, but the texts concerning headscarves are not tied to contexts. Take the example of prayer. The objective of requiring prayer is to bring the praying person closer to God, but you could not say that praying twice a day is enough to accomplish that objective, because there is a clear prescription in the texts [about the frequency of prayer] that we must follow. God has said that this rule is required to guarantee the objective. It is as with a red light. There is a rule that says that we should always

stop for a red light. Now, it may be night, and no one coming, and you might say that the principle of the rule is to prevent accidents and none could happen, so it is alright to drive through it, and that might be true, but if you did it other times it might produce an accident: the rule is required to guarantee safety.

Things change if the prescription is tied to a context. [JB: As with slavery?] Yes, exactly. Laws are based on causes, 'illa, and if the cause disappears or changes, then the law changes, too. For example, at first God forbade Muslims to visit graveyards because this practice was associated with polytheism and they might have returned to those ways. But then he ruled otherwise, because that danger was gone and the practice had an alternative potential objective, namely, to remind you of the hereafter. So, a practice can have more than one objective associated with it.

The prescription for wearing the scarf is different, because it is a general rule that is not tied to a specific context. It has to do with modesty and with the general relationships between men and women.

In this account Jaballah restricts the scope of reasoning from objectives. He gave the examples of prayer and stopping at a red light, which would not seem to have much in common with the rule on scarf wearing, in order to emphasize their common element: they are all rules that indicate specific forms of action: you pray at certain times, you stop when the light is red, and you cover your hair because these specific practices are required. We are not free to propose that other courses of action could equally well accomplish the objectives of these rules. Nor is scarf wearing limited to a specific time and place; rather, it is a prescribed way to achieve modesty that is valid for all times and places. One must pay attention to the objective (guarding modesty) but also to the prescribed form.

Teaching the Four Traditions

A very recent entry into the field of higher Islamic education gives the legacy of the four Sunni legal traditions a higher profile, but this teacher, too, draws on the logic of maqâsid reasoning. The Tunisian scholar Ahmed Abidi studied Islamic law at the University of Damascus, Syria, before coming to France in the early 1990s. His French is only passable, but perhaps to compensate he adds strong expressions of emotion about particular points of interpretation. In 2003, after having taught with Hichem and elsewhere, he opened his institute in an office building in the southern Paris suburb of Boissy St.-Leger. Short of funds, he offered to renovate and paint the offices in exchange for one month's rent. In April 2003 he proudly showed me around the new quarters.

Early in our conversation, Abidi differentiated his project from those of other scholars. He saw Hichem's CERSI as teaching general Islamic culture, whereas his "is more serious, and students get lower marks, maybe 12 or 15, whereas at Hichem's you probably saw all 18s and 20s [of 20]!" He knew that in fiqh classes Hichem had used the books by al-Jazaïri and al-Qaradâwî, "but neither is a legal scholar [faqîh]." He requires his teachers to write out their own lessons for their students. "Often I have to correct their French, so I am here until late at night." He is not married: "I am married to the office right now." To the UOIF institute at Château-Chinon in Burgundy he contrasted the better quality of the French language instruction he offers. Indeed, although Arabic is taught, all substantive classes in the track of Islamic sciences are in French; in the other tracks, on Qur'an and the Arabic language, instructors use both languages as media of instruction.

Although he studied in Damascus with the well-known scholars Sa'îd Ramadân al-Bûtî and Wahba al-Zuhaily, he took issue with al-Bûtî's tendency to condemn all who disagreed with him, preferring himself to let truth emerge out of disagreement. He teaches on the basis of maqâsid, and indeed wrote a short treatise on the subject, but he also integrates the legal traditions. "I give students what each of the four legal schools says, and the equipment they need to make up their own minds, and then I let them do that." He showed me an example chosen at random from the volume he had written, concerning how to use water for ablutions before prayers, and indeed he gives the teachings of each of the four traditions without selecting among them. He covers the ablutions and prayer in the first year of teaching fiqh, marriage and divorce in the second, and eventually commercial and criminal law.

We can best follow his teaching style by inspecting one specific analysis he conducted in his classroom. I attended his second-year class on fiqh on June 4, 2006. He dictated the lesson for one and a half hours that afternoon to the four men and four women in attendance. He would not provide them with references to the Qur'an: "You are in the second year and you should be able to find them."

That afternoon Abidi discussed matters regarding filiation: how a man could establish or deny paternity, and why adoption was forbidden, because it was tantamount to denying filiation. He explained that if a man denies paternity, then that denial stands unless someone can prove the contrary. In this matter, one woman's testimony suffices to counter the denial, because women are assumed to know about such things, unlike public matters, in which it would not be sufficient. A man's testimony also could suffice if he had reason to know about a birth, for example a doctor, "like a gynecologist today."[1] He cited his former Syrian teacher al-Zuhaily to the effect that if it is generally women who know a certain subject, then one woman's testimony suffices.

Abidi took this opportunity to argue that differences in witnesses' religion counted for little in court. He referred to the Hanafî legal position that in the case that two men disagreed on the facts of the matter, even if one were a Muslim and one a Christian, whoever had the better proof would prevail. In addition, he said, if a Christian claims someone as his child and a Muslim claims him as his slave, then the Christian will win, if the level of proof is the same, because Islam favors the eradication of slavery: "Humans were created to be free, and judges decide based on that principle." Here he appealed to one of the maqâsid as the basis for selecting among possible rules of interpretation, after drawing on the Hanafî position to argue that one's religion does not affect one's reliability.

Regardless of claims to lineage that someone might make, adoption was forbidden, because "every human being has two real parents," according to the Qur'an. The family is the most important element in society, and preventing adoption protects it from being dissolved. Adoption takes a child from his parents, for example poor people, and gives him to "illusory parents," and the new parents are trying to meet their own needs rather than showing compassion. Some parents, once they have had their own children, abandon the adopted child. Islam orders that we help natural children and orphans if they are needy; one may leave up to one-third of his heritage to an illegitimate child.

A female student who came from the Comoro islands said, "*Chez nous,* an illegitimate child is neglected." Abidi retorted sharply:

> I have never heard of an illegitimate child being maltreated in a Muslim society. For example, Egypt has residences for them. If we allowed adoption we would be encouraging adultery, because people would assume that someone would adopt a child if they had one. Adoption has close ties to adultery, because to recognize the effects of adultery is the same thing as recognizing adultery. Doing so would be to break the norms that hold society together, especially the norms of harâm and halâl, and the family in Islam is based on well-known principles that must not change.

Abidi felt strongly that adoption was a social evil, raising his voice in his enthusiasm during this portion of the dictée. We gathered in the hall briefly afterward, and he commented that "they buy children and then abandon them." He never explained who "they" were, but it was this crass self-interest, the absence of respect for the natural relationships of lineage that Islam protects, that upset him, not the mere matter of legality. His focus on objectives, the maqâsid, made the matter still more a source of passion. At that point one of the students came by to offer us some chocolate cake.

OBJECTIVES AND IMAM MÂLIK

Dhaou Meskine occupies center-stage in the next chapter; one of his many projects has been to create the Advanced Institute in Islamic Sciences (Institut Supérieur des Sciences Islamiques, ISSI). His institute is similar to Hichem El Arafa's CERSI in that it offers classes in French, teaches Arabic, and introduces students to knowledge about Qur'an and hadith. Dhaou and Hichem share an emphasis on the science of hadith, and although Dhaou uses different diagrams and examples, they do not disagree on fundamentals of understanding scripture.

But the schools do differ in three main respects. First, ISSI aims at a higher level of training than does CERSI. Although Dhaou did not construct it to train imams (there is not the training in professional duties such as chaplaincy that an "imam school" would include), the institute does offer advanced courses in Qur'an and hadith, and some students have taken up the role of imam in a mosque after completing courses. That is not the case with Hichem's school. Second, the ISSI includes courses taught in the Arabic language and attracts some students whose Arabic is far better than their French. (When I lectured there in 2006, the director translated my talk from French into modern standard Arabic). Arabic is required of all students. By contrast, Hichem's school operates entirely in French and mainly attracts students born in France; Arabic classes are optional.

Third, Dhaou's institute tries to combine two ideas about how to teach Islamic norms in France today. The first is the idea also advocated by Hichem, that one ought to emphasize principles or objectives of Islam, the *maqâsid*. As we have seen, this term is grasped by many across France as a way to reconcile Islamic jurisprudence with modern French society. But a second idea also runs through the institute's teaching, namely, that one ought to begin with one of the legal schools, because each of the schools represents an effort to construct a consistent and total set of answers to religious questions. Because the Mâlikî tradition was used in North Africa, where most French Muslims have their origins, teachers who adopt this approach choose that school (rather than combining views from different traditions, as does Ahmed Abidi). In the end, most teachers favor some combination of the general, "principles first" perspective and that from within the Mâlikî legal school.

As with most such schools, the ISSI offers courses on the weekends and on some evenings, and as with many, it has moved from place to place. Initially housed by the World Islamic League in Paris, by 2001 it was offering evening classes at the Islamic secondary school (La Réussite) in Aubervilliers and weekend classes in Paris's fashionable sixteenth arrondisement. In 2005 they found new quarters in the city of Saint-Ouen, just west of Saint-Denis, but in 2008 they moved back to La Réussite. The institute has attracted 100–150 students at any one time to its various courses.

In 2002 the teachers were dictating their lessons to students, in the traditional French manner, but Dhaou planned to ask them to write out their materials and distribute them to the students. "This will force the teachers to work more in preparing their courses and allow us to go twice as fast, because students can come with questions already prepared." He was unable to find suitable books written in the Mâlikî tradition: "They are out of phase with society; one of these books discusses what to do when the nursing mother cannot nurse—well, now she will use a bottle, so the problem never comes up!"

What do students hope to get from courses in fiqh? "They want to learn how to pray and to fast and to know the relevant hadith. Often they have heard a lot of conflicting ideas and they are confused. They are never sure of whichever choice they make among the different ideas. One man was about to go on the pilgrimage. He came to me and said that he had read seven different books on how to carry it out, and they each listed different obligations and prohibitions, and he was totally confused. So I drew up a chronology—these other books just list things to do and not to do—and that satisfied him."

Foregrounding God's Objectives

One day in February 2004 I took the subway to the rue de la Pompe stop in a quiet part of the sixteenth arrondissement. I was headed for the current weekend seat of the institute—on the fifth story of the Iraqi School, an Arab-language college and lycée for Iraqis distinctive in that it is the sole Arabic-medium school to have its baccalaureate degree accepted by France. It had fallen into a dilapidated state since the Gulf War in 1990. Papers posted in the windows advertised after-school tutoring and courses in Arabic or French.

Abdelkarim Sabri teaches fiqh and Qur'an at the school. He studies law in his native Morocco and completed a master's thesis in Paris on the idea of public order in Islamic law. He continues to work in Morocco to advance legal reform. He said that the Moroccan family law code followed the Mâlikî legal tradition but that it has to be flexible to work. "I follow the Mâlikî school, but even Ibn Mâlik was not Mâlikî. He changed his mind and developed a great deal of flexibility in law. When I teach, I take from other schools when they offer something." When not teaching at the institute he is an apprentice in a Paris law firm.

He teaches fiqh in French to about thirty students, divided into several levels, but only five women showed up that day—it was exam time at the universities, and most ISSI students are also pursuing degrees in subjects such as business, languages (particularly English and Arabic), and computer science. One of the women wore a burqa, covering all but her eyes; two wore black headscarves, and the others had colored scarves. We sat in a classroom furnished with two-person desks and lit by two large windows, from which we benefited on this slightly chilly but sunny day.

Abdelkarim was discussing details of religious practice, and indeed that is all the students learn in the first two years—how to pray, fast, perform the pilgrimage, and so forth. Abdelkarim longed to be able to teach more advanced topics. The students, clearly trained by years of taking dictation, in the old-fashioned French pedagogical way, took down his words, especially when he spoke slowly. (Dhaou's hope to get past the dictée stage of teaching had clearly failed.) All five students were of college age and had been born in North Africa—one in Morocco, two in Algeria, and two in Tunisia. They had no books with them, and only one had brought the outline for the course. Abdelkarim had before him the text *La Voie du Musulman* by al-Jazaïri (the text once used by Hichem), but he referred only to his own notes, written on typewriter paper.

They were studying the rules for taking ablutions. They are of two sorts: the "major ablutions," required after sex or menstruation, and the more ordinary ablutions, performed before every prayer. Abdelkarim encouraged the young women to go beyond the rules and reason from principles. One woman stated what she thought to be a principle, that once you have performed major ablutions, for example by taking a bath, you did not then need to go through the usual steps of purifying yourself—washing the hands, feet, mouth, and so forth. Abdelkarim said that on this point she was wrong, that you should still perform the ordinary ritual ablutions "to be certain," but praised her for looking for a general principle rather than just learning a series of rules.

In the course of working through one facet after another of the ablutions and then the steps in prayer, Abdelkarim stressed a number of general points: that the worshipper must say that he or she is about to worship for the worship to be valid (because the Prophet emphasized having the right intention), that it is important to know which of the legal schools take what positions (we did not learn why this was important), and that women cannot be excluded from any social role. When referring to a hadith that had been reported by Â'isha, the Prophet's wife, he stopped to observe that "she reported the second greatest number of hadiths and so we cannot exclude women from any position in society. A brother argued with me on this point and I said that a woman could be a judge," and here he quoted from Abu Hanîfa, the founder of the Hanafî school, in support of this general point.

Abdelkarim consistently argued that we must make reference to the objectives of the Qur'an in order to understand the scriptural text. As an example, he approved of the way in which Tariq Ramadan had translated the word *zakât* as "a purifying social tariff" (*impôt social purificateur*) rather than as "alms" or "tithe" (the usual translations), thereby emphasizing its objective, which is to purify individuals and society of sins.

His discussion of how one performs the major ablutions illustrated his general approach. The four Sunni schools and major Shi'ite legal scholars agree that water must pass over the entire body, from the hair to the feet. "Oh, I forgot something: what is it?" he asked the class, to which one of the girls responded, correctly, "the intention," reinforcing his point that the general principle applied for every ritual act. "Intention is what distinguishes the major ablution from just bathing," he clarified. But the four schools differ about what we have to do when we arrive at the head. Must you put water into the nose and mouth? For the Hanafi and Hanbalî, it is an obligation, but for the Mâlikî and Shafi'î scholars it is only Sunna, or recommended. He then posed practical questions to show how one can apply the principles to everyday life, usually answering the questions himself. "If I wake up at 8 and I have a class at 9 and have no time for a shower and I am in a condition such that I need to make the major ablutions, what can I do? I can put my head under the faucet and then make water flow down my body."

The following Saturday I returned for more courses. In the first-year course were five additional students, including a man and woman who sat together, making ten in all. Abdelkarim continued the discussion, now turning to details of prayer. This time he dictated to the class from the manual by al-Jaïziri. "What are the objectives of the prayer?" he asked. "There are both material and spiritual objectives." The students ventured answers: drawing close to God, achieving tranquility, fulfilling an obligation to God. "What do you do when someone else does not pray?" he then asked. One girl answered that he would not be a Muslim believer, but Abdelkarim shot back that this was a "backward response"; the nonworshipper must not be excluded but rather be told that he had left something out of his life. He wrote the names of the five prayer times in Arabic on the board, and the students copied them, and then he recited a hadith in French, in slow dictée style, from the text lying open in front of him: "God has obliged us to perform the five prayers, and for those who do not, God can punish them or not, as He wishes." He then glossed the text: "You see? It is entirely up to God what to do." They finished the hour by discussing the nonobligatory prayers, and what it is that makes a room into a mosque.

When Abdelkarim was unable to derive principles from rules he became profoundly bored, as in the following class, on the steps one must go through in the hajj. Abdelkarim was so bored he simply read out the steps from a book.[2] He was out of sorts in this class because the steps of the pilgrimage do not at all lend themselves to an analysis in terms of objectives: they track step by step the actions of the Prophet when he returned, victorious, to Mecca, and simply must be learned. "The scholars do not have a great amount of room to maneuver here, because the texts are so clear," he told me later. He kept searching for principles, nonetheless. When he read the rules for expiation of major sins committed while on the hajj, he noted that even after you sacrifice a sheep or a camel, the pilgrimage is annulled for you if you have committed one of those sins, but nonetheless you have to remain part of it and finish out the steps. He then turned to the class and said, "I have always wondered at the logic of this, but I suppose that the objective is that were you to quit the pilgrimage you would create disorder." (Avoiding disorder is a major objective of politics in Islam.) He continued on in a bored tone, and when he mentioned that when circumambulating the Ka'ba you should take the first three turns at a faster pace, one of the students asked why. He brightened up at the opportunity to leave the reciting of steps behind: "Good question. I have read that in the time of the Companions people were threatened by others, so they took the first turns quickly to show they were strong, that they could resist oppression."

Abdelkarim's distaste at teaching Islam as if from a rule-book was linked to, perhaps motivated, his broader perception of the pedagogical alternatives. He saw himself in a broader field of teaching styles. After class he told me that "teaching the rituals frankly bores me because it is just 'you should do this or do that.' I much prefer studying transactions, commercial law. These involve the use of reason; this is what is most important. Too many young people just hear an imam say 'you should do this or that,' and they do, without thinking. Frankly, I am for the law against the headscarves, because it places learning above everything else."

I visited the institute on subsequent occasions. As I mentioned above, by 2005 it had moved to new quarters in Saint-Ouen, easily accessible by Paris subway line 13. One Sunday in June 2006 I found my way from the Saint-Ouen City Hall subway stop across a pleasant square, along the municipal cemetery, and to the building now housing the institute. There was only a small piece of paper with the institute's name next to the intercom on the outside of the building. When I pressed the button, glass sliding doors opened, giving access to the elevator, and I had to know that the institute was located on the third story. On leaving the elevator I had to feel around for a light switch and find my way to the door. Inside were several classrooms, with good light. I could look out over older brick buildings and see cranes in the distance: the suburb was expanding. A driving musical beat was coming from downstairs.

As of 2003 a Tunisian scholar, Abdurraouf Boulâbi, had taken over the direction of the institute, at Dhaou's request. Boulâbi writes scholarly articles about Islamic law in which he emphasizes objectives or principles. I congratulated him on his recent book, which he had written, he explained, to trace commonalities between Western theories of power and Islamic normative theory. He found these in ideas of legitimacy. "Then I looked for the maqâsid, the most general principles underlying shari'a. I found them in Shâtibî, and the writers in Andalusia, as well as such later writers as Ibn Ashur in Tunisia and Muhammad 'Abduh in Egypt and Malek Chebanni. It is thinkers in the Mediterranean who write about the principles underlying law, because they had a dialogue with the West and had to look for common elements across the Mediterranean. You do not find these writings in the East." He attributes problems in Islam today to younger people who are attracted by the more extreme writings of "the East," meaning Saudi Arabia and the Gulf states, but also Syria.[3] "Men who had been delinquents like that sort of writing because it is the mirror image of what they used to be like. Some come here and talk to us. They always ask whether the classes are mixed and whether the professor is a woman. Some then leave, but others stay, and we talk with them, and then they follow the courses."

What Nullifies Prayer—for a Mâlikî

Abdelkarim continued to teach in the new setting, but Dhaou was able to find another teacher who followed a consistently Mâlikî line. Dhaou was suspicious of those whom claimed to take a broader view. "The UOIF says that they teach 'all the schools,' talking the way the Saudis do, but what this means in the end is Wahhabism." He sees staying in a single legal tradition as a bulwark against extremism.

The new fiqh teacher was Corentin Pabiot, a Frenchman in his forties who converted to Islam when he was twenty and then went to Syria to study. He recommended the works of René Guenon to me; he had been introduced to them by an American scholar, Zaid Shakir, in Syria. "Guénon denounces the great mistake that was the rationalism of the sixteenth century and the creation of the current world, which has gone in the wrong direction." Two of his classes on fiqh illustrate how to combine an effort to remain within the Mâlikî tradition with a higher level of consideration of all four traditions. He teaches one series of classes focused on practical issues of everyday devotions, and a second series on rules concerning social life. In the classes I attended, the first focused on the behaviors that would annul a prayer and the second on an issue surrounding divorce.

This first-year class had twenty-two students, young men and women in equal proportions, who eagerly wrestled with the practical difficulties posed to those who wished to ensure their prayers were always received by God. Corentin led off by asking what sorts of physical movements would make one's prayers null and void in God's eyes, and then proceeded to explain that it depended on the number of steps involved: if you take a step to keep someone from blocking your space of prayer you may continue praying, but if you took two or three steps, that would nullify the prayer. A young woman asked, "What if my small children come and hang all over me while I pray?" "You are free to move them off you and gesture to where they should sit, without nullifying the prayer, as long as they are not impure, for example, with soiled diapers." "But what if they cry while we are in the mosque?" "Ah, it is really a bad idea to bring small children to the mosque. People say, 'in the time of the Prophet they did that,' but just because it happened in time of the Prophet does not make it Sunna to bring crying infants to the mosque!"

He explained that for Mâlikîs, you can turn from side to side as you pray, but not for the three other traditions, which say that you must remain oriented in the direction of prayer. You may move sideways, backward, or forward to respond to a problem but all the while remaining facing it. If you turn your back on the direction of prayer, then all four schools say the prayer is nullified. "Now, inside the sacred space of Mecca these rules do not apply; the Prophet prayed with women in front of him, for example. Imagine 2,000,000 people; you have to suspend these rules." He then added what seemed like a non sequitur but was intended to forestall objections that his last remark showed him to be too lenient on gender separation. "Now, if you wanted to have a curtain placed in this classroom, to separate the boys from the girls, I would not object, that would be fine.

"Now, if someone greets you while you pray you may respond, indeed you are obliged to respond, because this is the opinion of Imam Mâlik, and we are all Mâlikîs here. Here is what you do: I am standing, praying, like this." A woman asks, "Is it alright to have the hands crossed in front of you like that?" "Yes; having the hands down at the sides is recommended, but the hands in front is alright. Then someone greets me, says 'Assalâmu 'alaykum,' and I hold up my right hand, like this, but do not say anything."

Corentin reviewed a number of other particular issues about prayer, some in response to student questions, and for each he contrasted the position of Imam Mâlik to those of the other traditions. Then he paused to address the differences among the traditions in a more general way.

"Imam Shafiʿî tried to synthesize, to take the eclectic norms and use superior principles to unify them. Imam Mâlik stayed closer to specific hadith, and tried to reconcile differing hadith by way of exceptions, and without any overall principles." He said that he was going to Morocco that summer to look into some of the specific questions posed in class within the Mâlikî school and that "if I get two or three differing opinions, then I will look for the best one."

Throughout the class the students posed many questions deriving from their own past errors in prayer. One man once forgot whether or not he had said the opening recitation, the al-Fatiha, while praying; another mistakenly said the closing greeting before the imam did (an error), and so forth. They were clearly interested in the subject and passionately so; as a body, they asked Corentin to continue on after the end of the hour because they wanted him to finish the lesson on what nullifies prayer—even after he had said these details would not be on the exam.

Although Corentin reminded the students that "we are all Mâlikîs here" and that Mâlik tended to synthesize less than did ash-Shafiʿî, nonetheless Corentin emphasized the internal logic of the rules. He also spoke in French at all times and avoided using Arabic terms (for example, saying *prière* rather than *salât* to refer to the prayer) unless he recited a text of Qur'an or hadith, in which case he would recite at length and at great speed from memory. At the end of class he asked them if they would like an invocation, or closing prayer; they said yes, and he recited a very long one, fast and clear, hands upraised.

When May a Judge Pronounce a Divorce?

In his advanced class eleven students were present: nine younger women, one older woman (all the women wore headscarves), and one young man. Corentin picked up from the last session of this class, discussing what happens if a husband fails to give his wife enough money to live. Because the issues were not ones of everyday ritual practice and thus probably would not be put into practice by the students, Corentin had greater leeway to present alternative opinions without always arguing for the Mâlikî over the others.

"The Hanafîs often engage in more complex reasoning, as you know, and say that failure to support the wife is not grounds to annul the marriage because there are other solutions: the wife can support herself and then force the husband to pay her back later. The judge will imprison him." He recited chapter 65 of the Qur'an here, clearly and quickly. He always recited the Qur'an from memory and then consulted the French translation by Jacques Berque, lying open before him. "You see that in Islam, obligation is followed by facilitation."[4]

> The other schools say that the judge may dissolve the marriage when the husband fails to support the wife. The legal basis in the Qur'an—because we always have to have a legal basis in the Qur'an or the Sunna—is [he reads the French] "either you keep your wife and give to her what you should, or you free her." There is not an opposition between these two positions; the difference is how to resolve a concrete problem. The Hanafîs look for solutions other than divorce because God looks negatively on divorce; the others give the wife that right. Now, Syrian courts use Hanafî law, so they follow the first option—they also sometimes draw on other schools. So the Syrian judge will see if the husband owns property and will sell it off to pay back the wife.
>
> Now, if one of them decides that life is impossible together, what do they do? Mâlik says the judge should try to reconcile them, use arbiters. [He explains the procedures.] There are other ways to dissolve a marriage that date from before Islam, for example when the husband says, "I swear that you are to me as my mother's back," which places the wife into a state of suspension, neither married nor divorced. Islam had to regulate this practice based on equity and by way of contract. Qur'an 65:2 provides the legal mechanism for this regulation, when it stipulates that the husband could not have sex with her unless he expiated the oath by freeing a slave, because Islam wanted to abolish slavery, contrary to what people say, that Islam tried to preserve slavery; that is absurd. He also must fast for two consecutive months or, if he cannot because he is too old or ill, then he may feed sixty poor people.

He explained that the oath he had described now is forbidden by Islam but that it does have legal effects in Islam, and that Islam tried to regulate it. He likened this apparent contradiction to the rule that selling something during the Friday prayer is illegal but still is a sale. Islam recognizes these older practices as valid oaths, he explained. (At the end of class he joked that they had not brought presents for him, and they said "after the exam." "Do you mean I have to come back after the exam?")

Both Abdelkarim and Corentin try to find principles underneath rules. They differ in their emphases, Corentin trying to construct a purely Mâlikî version of Islamic norms, in keeping with that pole of the school's mission, and Abdelkarim giving greater emphasis to maqâsid, but together they demarcate the intellectual space that Dhaou Meskine and Boulâbi wish to create.

How do students respond to this particular approach? Many of them take the institute's courses because they simply want to learn about their religion and they find the teacher appealing. Ibrahim, for example, came to France from the Cameroons in the mid-1980s to study, did postgraduate work in engineering, and in 2003, when we talked, was working as a computer technician. He followed Dhaou's courses because he wanted to get Islam right—"The Prophet said that you study and go straight ahead and then you are in the right"—and chose to study with Dhaou because the daughter of a friend attended the secondary school La Réussite.

After class at the institute in June 2006, I talked with a dozen students, all in their twenties and thirties and all near the end of the first year of their three-year program of studies. At present they were following only eight hours of class per week and hoped that the institute would increase the course load so that they could petition the state to recognize their classes as earning them the equivalent of a regular French first university degree, the *license*. I asked them why they were in the class, and they said it was to improve their own religious practice, because they were taught their Islam by their parents and sometimes those teachings were not correct. Because the instruction all followed the Mâlikî tradition, I asked if they all followed those teachings. "That is what our teacher says," replied one, "but in fact, we come from all over, and the teacher is Shafi'î, so sometimes we learn that too. The theory is that we learn Mâlikî and then we can choose, but how can we choose if that is all we know?" Two girls in the group had taken courses at Abidi's institute, where "we learned the four traditions, and take from each." One man added, "I do not think I follow any tradition because I do not know any one of them yet."

Although the students emphasized that learning Islam was important for their own lives, I wondered whether all the subtleties, such as the "on my mother's back" oath, had anything to do with life in France. I posed this question to Samia Touati, who for many years organized some of the debates at the Adda'wa mosque in Paris's nineteenth arrondisement, and who tends to view these normative matters in terms of everyday Islamic life. She said they did matter: "In fact these practices *do* come up in everyday life here in France—the oath you mentioned, and different forms of divorce—so you need to know them if you want to be prepared for things people say. In addition, the fiqh of marriage, divorce, and so forth is such a large part of Islamic knowledge that if someone wants to study Islam they want to understand it, too. There is intellectual curiosity but also a sense that they should know the structure of fiqh, have the resources to respond to questions."

The students also clearly appreciate the time they spend in an Islamic space of learning and open discussion. Although those with whom I spoke in 2006 were born in France, they did not feel accepted as French. One girl said that the main problem was that she could not work with her headscarf on; she had to take it off when she arrived at work each day. A young man complained, "It was a shock for me when I started work, because I always had lived in the Seine-Saint-Denis, and was used to all sorts of people around me, and then when I started work [at a finance company] there were two blacks and one North African out of 2,000 employees!" The girl who had first spoken to me added: "I am French, born here, but I am considered a foreigner and people say *chez vous*, meaning Algeria, but when I go *there* they see me as a foreigner also."

The value of an "Islamic ambience" is evident in other spaces in the field of Islamic education, where the ostensible reason for attending school is not religion at all—and yet where the schools provide an Islamic social space for those who attend.

PRACTICAL TRAINING IN AN ISLAMIC AMBIANCE

Some Islamic public actors have set out to teach other domains of knowledge and skill, not limiting their schools to Islamic matters. In the next chapter we will see the first attempt to build an Islamic day school within the French national system, but other efforts are oriented toward teaching practical skills. These efforts take account of Muslims' demands that there be spaces where young people, and sometimes their parents, can feel "at home" among other Muslims, without the suspicions that a young man's beard or a woman's headscarf arouse elsewhere. Muslim schools, institutes, training centers, and even summer camps seek to square the circle of social integration and religious integrity, to make pursuing education in a Muslim ambiance be the most effective way for Muslims to achieve success in mainstream French terms.

France has seen a rapidly rising demand for technical training institutes (*centres de formation*) in high-demand fields such as computer skills and English. Those run by Muslims have mixed and matched several kinds of knowledge in an effort to attract clients through a strategy of horizontal integration, offering language classes, technical knowledge, and Islamic sciences under one roof.

The Future

Near the main market street in the Paris suburb of La Corneuve sits the Institut de Formation l'Avenir (Training Institute: The Future). The institute also houses a private primary school run by Muslim families. Habib Mokni, a quiet, thoughtful man, directs the institute. He came to France in 1981 as a political refugee from Tunisia. He had worked as a journalist and editor in Tunisia, and he brought those skills with him, editing two intellectual reviews and in 1985 starting a school to teach Arabic and the Qur'an to children and adults, on weekends or afternoons. But he insists that "it is not an Islamic or Arabic institute, we are registered with the Labor Ministry to teach modern languages and computer science." French and English are offered, but 80 percent of the approximately 500 students were taking Arabic, and about 100 were taking computer lessons. "People take Arabic mainly to have access to the Qur'an, it is for Islam. The teaching is about one-half language and one-half science: the Qur'an, the Prophet's sayings, the pillars of religion, ethics. But it is not an institute to train people in religion; for that we send them to Jaballah, Hichem, or Dhaou Meskine. Those people have a notion more or less following the Muslim Brotherhood, like Qaradâwî, of adapting to the society, but in a limited way. We need more capabilities in all fields."

Habib Mokni stresses training Muslims in useful skills, but he does not neglect the religious dimensions of education. Indeed, his school's major effort was to produce their own books for teaching Arabic, four volumes to cover two years. The covers for the first two volumes have a mosque in the upper-right, in the background, resembling the Taj Mahal, with a carpet coming out of it and cascading downward to the Eiffel Tower in the bottom left. On the carpet are Arabic letters, disconnected. Riding the carpet is the large figure of a boy, who also appears in the book riding a skateboard and wearing a backpack. Inside are lessons with illustrations showing some people falling into drug use or crime, others succeeding, and still others teaching the food groups and urging pupils to exercise regularly.

Institute of Useful Knowledge

Growing out of Mokni's school is an institute directed by Chokri Hammrouni, a young, energetic man and a former football player in his native Tunisia. He started his Institut de Savoirs Utiles (Institute of Useful Knowledge) to teach languages and computer skills to adults and adolescents. After several years of borrowing space, he opened his doors in early 2005 in the southern Paris suburb of Alfortville. Outfitted with new computers and DVD players (used for Arabic classes), the institute emphasizes skills—"non-Muslims take the Arabic; even the secret police are welcome!" says Chokri.

Not surprisingly, the Arabic classes incorporate an Islamic dimension. I attended a class intended to teach adolescents about "everyday expressions" in Arabic, such as Bismillah, "in the name of God," Subhanallah, "praises to God," and phrases used to express submission to God's will when there is a disaster: "When an Israeli rocket falls on a Palestinian house, people say this phrase, and it is from a Qur'anic verse, and there is a recompense for reciting it at those moments."

On a different weekend, the teacher explained a series of verses from the Qur'an. One text concerned punishment, and the teacher added that "torture is forbidden in Islam; Saddam Hussein practiced that. Muslims do not torture and must fight against torture." A student asked, "What if someone protects Islam by killing someone?" The teacher answered, "If someone is colonized by people who have weapons and who are going to kill him, then he may defend himself by killing them first. But the attacks in New York and London: is this Islam? No, it is terrorism, madness."

A different verse concerned God's judgment, and the teacher added, "God will facilitate judgment; he will not hold many sessions, not like the trial of Saddam Hussein." He then continued on, leaving the Arabic aside for the moment to draw out certain conclusions from the children:

TEACHER	STUDENTS
Do you follow his trial?	
	Yes! I saw it on al-Jazira!
	He is a tyrant, betrayed his own people, killed Shi'a and children!
Who judges him?	
	Americans.
But I saw the trial, is it not Iraqis?	
	But the Americans have the authority.
Is Iraq independent?	
	No.
What is it?	
	Colonized!
By whom?	
	America.
So what about the trial?	
	He is a tyrant.
Who has the right to judge him?	
	Iraqis
As a colonized or independent people?	
	[No answer]
Brahim?	
	They are obliged to judge him.
Who has the right?	
	Americans.
How so?	
	Iraqis [same pupil].
The Iraqi people? Who, realistically?	
	Iraqis.

So now is the trial just or unjust?

>Unjust!
>
>Unjust!

Why?

[Teacher just keeps going, does not answer.]

So, we must free Iraq, and then judge; we will return to this.

A Muslim who sees injustice and remains silent is unjust.

>But what can we do?

You can write a letter, to the Pentagon or to George Bush, and say it is unjust.

>He will read it?
>
>I know some one who wrote a letter
>
>and got into trouble.

I don't mean that you should threaten, just invite George Bush to change his policies.

The "useful knowledge" thus returns to religious education and its political implications. Students and their parents find at this institute a well-equipped training institute that does not teach religion but offers an Islam-friendly pedagogy. The next chapter considers the effort to advance one step further into secular education, by creating a school in the French national model but retaining something of the Islamic ambiance.

Of all the areas in which Muslim teachers and scholars are active in France, that of Islamic education might be considered to best resemble a "field," in the sense indicated by Pierre Bourdieu. There are forms of cultural capital, including the religious expertise claimed by teachers and the skills and knowledge promised to graduates, and there are clients selecting among these possible schools.[5] But if it is useful to underscore the specific forms of economic and religious legitimacy that teachers and leaders bring to their institutions, to speak of these forms using the language of capital employed by Bourdieu suggests that students quantify the degree of knowledge or of Islamic correctness they see in each of several institutes or in the directors of those institutes. This view does not quite capture what we have seen in the discussions of students and teachers in the sections above. Each has his or her own set of ideas about the best way to learn more about Islam, but these involve differential weightings of various aspects of education: whether or not employment is the goal, whether knowledge of the legal traditions is important, and so forth.

Moreover, Bourdieu's own analyses of religion emphasize forms of power created by the strong division of the religious from the secular, or the world of the clergy and the world of laypeople. These emphases derive from his own experience of the "vision and division" exercised by French Catholicism, and may, as with his other field ideas, be most appropriate to the worlds of France, imagined (at least by some) as closed off and structured internally. But it is precisely this view of quantifiable symbolic capital, a well-bounded field, and a strong division of religious and secular that many Muslims would question. If, then, I use the term "field" in this chapter, I use it in a weaker sense: as a set of repertoires and pedagogical possibilities, all having to do with "education," but with reference to various ideas about Islam and to various strategies for advancement within French society.

In the chapters that follow, we will see with greater precision how French Islamic institutions lie across the boundaries of distinct realms of justification. In the next chapter we trace ways in which an Islamic school is subject to evaluation as a way of transmitting Islamic values and as a school corresponding to secular criteria for educational quality. Subsequent chapters examine how stances taken with respect to Islamic norms are evaluated differently by actors located within France and outside France, across boundaries that mark both political and normative breaks.

CHAPTER SIX

Can an Islamic School Be Republican?

Now WE MOVE even closer toward the French educational mainstream and ask, Is the phrase "Islamic Republican school" an oxymoron? But one also could ask, Are *all* confessional schools not at odds with France's Republican mission?

French Republican thinking makes the public school the primary instrument for making everyone into citizens. From this perspective, all children should attend public schools. Successive governments have tried to create a truly universal public school system, from Jules Ferry's project in the 1880s to create secular schools for all French children, to the efforts early in the twentieth century to remove clergy from teaching, through the current debates about the best ways to include all children in the school system. But in the early twentieth century the Republic was unable to ignore the opposition posed by the Catholic Church to efforts to remove religion from the field of education. In the compromises reached in the 1920s, but stabilized only in the 1950s, the Church won the right to create private religious schools, and the state agreed to supply teachers at its expense if the schools taught the national curriculum and admitted students regardless of their religious beliefs. Jewish, Protestant, and in theory all other religious bodies also were granted this right. Today about one-fifth of secondary school pupils are in Catholic schools at any one time, and as many as one-half of all French parents use a religious school at some time for at least one of their children.[1]

Only a few Muslim private day schools (as I shall refer to them) exist. The first on French metropolitan territory was École La Réussite, Success School, located in the northern Paris suburb of Aubervilliers and developed by the Tunisian educator Dhaou Meskine, whom we have met as the imam at Clichy-sous-Bois and as the force behind an Islamic institute.

I spend this chapter on Dhaou Meskine in part because the portfolio of his activities says something about the desire to have a broad umbrella of Muslim-ambiance institutions. At one and the same time he directs the school, the institute, a summer camp, and a network of imams. His challenge is to maintain good Islamic credentials as a figure independent from the state and yet also take advantage of the opportunities the state provides. From one side, the question becomes, Will the French state tolerate this sort of independent figure? From the other side, it is, How broad a group of Muslims will find someone working with the state to be a credible Islamic public intellectual?

DHAOU MESKINE'S SUCCESS SCHOOL

Aubervilliers, like neighboring Saint-Denis, is part of the inner ring of Paris suburbs that once lodged workers and elected Communists, and to some extent continue to do so. Today the ethnic mix of the workers has expanded from French, Belgian, Italian, and Portuguese to include Algerian, Senegalese, Indian, Chinese, and many others. Aubervilliers resembles Saint-Denis without a basilica to attract tourists and with a much smaller market area. But it is not grim, not isolated, and not "communalist," the favorite slap-down of central Paris intellectuals for the suburbs they never see. It is as ethnically mixed a place as you could find in France.

You reach these suburbs from Paris by passing through one of the old "gateways" (*portes*) that encircle the capital and from which roads radiate outward. To reach the Success School I usually take the bus that runs from the Gateway to Aubervilliers (Porte d'Aubervilliers) to the Aubervilliers city hall a few kilometers away. The bus winds along a road lined with import-export clothing businesses named Fadil, Lucky, Rosetta, and Wan Fa, and a couscous café whose store-window sticker shows that the Paris Beth Din certified its food as kosher. My busmates are schoolgirls with or without headscarves, older Algerian men, women from Senegal in bright print dresses, and Chinese families.

From the final bus stop—the Aubervilliers city center, with city hall, the main church, the marketplace, general bookstores, and several restaurants serving good and reasonably priced prix fix lunches—I walk down a side street past mechanics' shops and workers' cafes to a small, dead-end side street, the Impasse Charles-Cousin. On my first visit, in 2001, I was told to look for the school at that point, but I could see nothing but a parking lot and a garage. I was standing waiting for something to happen when a boy of about six walked up, turned a corner, and disappeared through a small, unmarked metal door. I followed. As of 2009 there is still no sign indicating where the school is—"we have enough applicants anyway," explained Dhaou—and even after dozens of visits, if I do not pay attention I am likely to walk right by the side street, forgetting where to turn in.

Once inside you see that the place has the dimensions of the warehouse it once was, with high ceilings—enough that most of the building was made into two stories—and a wide footprint. The outer door gives onto a large hall used for prayers, recreation, assemblies, and lunch. One Wednesday in February 2004 I arrived in late morning, when parents were showing up to get their children—Wednesday is a short day for all schools in France, as the afternoons originally were reserved for Catholic catechism. Everyone was smiling, the mothers in flowery headscarves and the children engaged in play. In a room on the upper story, a film crew from the Canal Plus cable station was filming an interview with Abdur-rahman Dahman, a self-styled "secular Muslim" who was trying to find his way in national politics. Photographs from the summer vacation lined the walls, next to photographs from the mayor's recent visit to the school. On other visits I encountered the entire school in Friday prayer, or staging a play on the Prophet Muhammad's birthday; at night I attended courses in the study of hadith. Religion, electoral politics, and the lure of summer leisure all mix here in an Islamic way.

The Success School is a multidimensional space, all Muslim ambiance but offering a regular day school curriculum, night classes for adults in Arabic, after-school and weekend tutoring and courses for children, and weekend vacations and summer family camp. Dhaou Meskine holds all this together. A large man with a full beard, usually dressed in a dark sport coat with an open-necked shirt, Dhaou is at the center of a network of institutions and activities that include, in addition to the school, his imam duties in Clichy-sous-Bois, the institute we read of in chapter five, his position as the secretary-general of the national Council of Imams, and his role managing two properties in Normandy, which he is building into permanent sites for weekend and summer activities but, as we shall see, which landed him briefly in jail in 2006.

A Teacher's Trajectory

For most of his adult life Dhaou has combined the roles of educator and imam. In the 1970s, in his native Tunisia, he started a private secondary school that, like Success School, taught the national curriculum in a Muslim ambiance. He also worked as a state-appointed imam at a mosque in the eastern part of Tunis. He had graduated from the famous al-Zaytuna University, specializing in the foundations of religion, *usûl ad-dîn*, and the science of hadith, but by the late 1970s, President Bourguiba had begun to act against those imams and teachers whom he considered Islamist and a threat to his rule, and in 1981 Dhaou left for France. He was offered the possibility of returning three years later but chose instead to accept a scholarship to study at Imâm Muhammad ibn Sa'ûd University in Riyadh. He spent five years writing, but not completing, a dissertation on the Tunisian sciences of hadith of the twelfth to fourteenth centuries, work that left him impressed by the struggle of the Mâlikî scholars of jurisprudence against the forces that wished to forbid fiqh and allow only reliance on the hadith. These impressions shape his teaching in France.

Even while he was enrolled in Riyadh, however, Dhaou spent much of his time in France, and, as we saw earlier, took up the post of imam at the mosque in Clichy-sous-Bois. By 1987, near the end of his scholarship period, he had started to look for a way to earn a living directing a school in France. "I had directed a private school in Tunis called the al-Ghazzâlî school, so it made sense for me to start some kind of a school here," he told me in 2003. In 1992 he was living in a housing project in Clichy, near his current mosque, and saw there were lots of children who needed after-school tutoring, and thought of finding a way to train them in trades and placing them as apprentices with butchers or bakers. He then began a decade-long struggle to establish a school. Dhaou found the current site, which was an abandoned factory, "but because I would not play ball with the Communist Party [then in power in Aubervilliers], the mayor kept putting obstacles in our way; for eight years he kept bringing me to court on grounds that the building was not going to be used for the right purposes, or that it failed to meet safety standards." Dhaou won some of those court decisions, and in 2001 the mayor relented and visited the school in late 2001; photographs of that visit lined the walls when I first set foot inside it. In the meantime, Dhaou had decided to open a middle school rather than a technical training school, got the mayor's permission, and opened the doors of the school for regular classes—one week after the events of September 11, 2001.

All during this period Dhaou had been teaching: at first he worked with Hichem El Arafa, but soon he threw most of his energy into tutoring secondary school students. "We did not set out to start an Islamic school but to help Muslim children succeed at their school," in particular in contrast with the middle school across the street, the Collège Rosa Luxembourg, which has a low success rate on the middle school-leaving examination (the *brevet*), as do most of the public schools in Seine-Saint-Denis.[2] Levels of performance were so low that a minister of education, Claude Allègre, once suggested there be a separate and easier high school–leaving examination (the baccalauréat) just for Seine-Saint-Denis pupils.

By 1992 Dhaou's teachers were tutoring children after school in core subjects (math, French, history) and offering classes in Arabic to children and adults on weekends and Wednesdays. He added regular day classes for the kindergarten levels with authorization from school inspectors, and in 1999 he added adult courses on Islam to the Sunday program.[3] By May 2001, when we first met, about 600 children were enrolled in one or another of these classes, with 350 more on a waiting list. One quarter of them came from the northern arrondissements of Paris, another quarter from Aubervilliers, and the rest from other ring cities around Paris. As of 2007, on Wednesday afternoons and Saturday and Sunday mornings groups of young children were coming to the school for courses on the Arabic language and on the basics of Islam. Dhaou explained that they began the courses on Islamic ethics after the events of September 11, 2001, "to protect them from radical movements."

When his first regular secondary school class opened in September 2001, Dhaou had received approval from the Ministry of Education to begin offering classes that were equivalent to those given in the public school, adding one class every year, beginning with the *sixième*, the first year of middle school (*collège*). The initial cohort had eleven pupils, selected from among the twenty-seven who had applied for slots. For the next six years the school has added a new class of *sixième* students and the previous year's classes have advanced up one level, such that by 2006–7 about 115 pupils were distributed across six classes, or just under twenty per class. Since 2003, about 150 students have applied each year. Financing Islamic private schools without subsidies is difficult because most Muslims in France do not have large disposable incomes. For 2008–9, Dhaou charged 1,500 euros per pupil, far less than the real cost and less than fees charged by other private schools not subsidized by the state. Indeed, each time Dhaou adds a class to the school it adds a burden of around 60,000 euros, even after all tuition has been paid. For the first year the teachers worked without pay, but since then the school has depended on contributions and loans from local businesses and individuals.

Over the years I have seen Dhaou's level of enthusiasm and emotions change as a barometer of how he saw the fate of his school enterprise. In 2001, he was excited and fresh from obtaining permission to open the school, and when we spoke in early 2002 he fêted me with couscous to mark the beginning of the school. He was looking forward to exchanging teachers and laboratories with other schools in the city; anything was possible. By late 2003, when it became apparent that a law forbidding headscarves in schools would pass, Dhaou was deluged with calls from people who were interested in starting Islamic schools so that girls could attend in headscarves. This attention plunged him into despair. He had never hoped to start a wave of separate schools, he explained, but to raise the level of education for Muslims. Building new private schools would affirm the victory of those who sought to ban Muslim girls in headscarves from the public domain. "I want the private schools to be there for those who wish to use them, but not for people to be forced into them. People are coming to see me about setting up schools, and it is taking a lot of my time, so I held a meeting with people to tell them about all the money it takes, and then we will have another in a few months. I am trying to slow down the rush toward creating them," he said. In fact, he found that for the 2004–5 school year, when the law against scarves in schools went into effect, very few people mentioned scarves as a reason to choose his school.

He gradually recovered his old enthusiasm, and in September 2004 he told me proudly that the school had been entirely repainted and that the parents had provided all the supplies and labor and even bought new chairs. "We spent not one cent," he said several times. The following spring the first class had come to the point where the pupils sat for the brevet, the examination that regulates passage from the middle school to the high school. "100% success at the brevet for the Success School," read the headlines in a story on the results.[4] The next highest figure in Seine-Saint-Denis was 74 percent, at a school in Pantin, east of Paris.[5]

Financial worries continued to plague the school. In 2004 Dhaou had decided that he could not afford to add another new class, but the news led some parents to worry that the school might be in trouble financially and to begin fund-raising, which generated enough in loans or gifts to cover the new class. (That was the year they repainted the school.) When I saw him in June 2005 he said he was worried sick over what to do with the current final year middle-school class: whether to send them into the public schools or to create a high school. He decided for the second solution, but this meant finding new space and teachers. "When they move from *collège* to *lycée*, the pupils need to feel that they are changing schools, taking a big step in their lives, and we could not keep them in the same building and with the same teachers." They had leased space in a building next door, enough for one class but expandable. In the end, he was able to borrow additional money (interest-free) for the new rent. In 2006–7 the school weathered another funding crisis—it became harder each year to go back to the same contributors—and had been able to offer the next year of high school. By then, children who came for regular classes, tutoring, or Arabic and Islam classes added up to 900 pupils in any one week. But by the start of school in 2008, the school's debt had mounted to 360,000 euros, and he had lost a number of his pupils. He was forced to cancel the highest two levels of instruction, and once again parents set about on a new fund-raising campaign.

School as Symbol

Although one might assume that the Success School would meet with general acclaim as a successful Islamic effort to fit into the French model, such is not the case. The idea of a Muslim private school has great symbolic significance in France, and many French are conflicted about such a school. On the one hand, to have such a school, or a number of them, would further signal the integration of Muslims into the state system, where Catholic and Jewish schools have long existed. Somewhat more cynically, many in government see such schools as providing a safety valve for Muslim "communalist" sentiments: let those who insist on Islamic scarves and food go to a private school and not bother the public school teachers. On the other hand, such schools would provide enclaves for Muslims to remain visibly different and would give Muslim pupils less contact with non-Muslims than they otherwise would have. Given that many French see "integrating Muslims" as an unfinished task, they carry different attitudes toward Muslim schools than toward Catholic or Jewish schools.

One senior member of the Paris government told me in 2006 that "French people find it very hard to have Islamic private schools. The private schools were made for Catholics, and there always have been Jews; the kippa [yarmulke] does not shock people, but Muslims are another story." He mentioned a Web site that is urging Muslims to dress their daughters in burqas and has a picture of a woman all covered up with the netting across her eyes. "The law of 2004 forbids headscarves in all schools, public or private under contract with the state, but it will not be enforced." His last comment was particularly striking because it does not correspond to the text of the 2004 law, which prohibited religious signs only in public schools. It does indicate what he considers to have been the general will expressed in the law, namely, that headscarves should be kept out of all schools.

Even one city official who had worked energetically with Muslims to build a mosque in another Parisian suburb criticized Dhaou Meskine for creating a school that had a strongly Islamic ambiance. In 2006 conversations with me he said that "in the Catholic schools, they have Catholics and Jews and Muslims and others, so they cannot teach Catholicism, even though there is the catechism and students may learn it. But at 'our friend's' school it is only Muslims." He used the occasion to broaden his criticism, saying that "if we had never publicly recognized religions and given Muslims mosques and so forth, and let each person keep his religion at home, then we would not have today women appearing in hospitals asking to have a woman doctor and separate hours at pools for women." This sense of a "slippery slope" regarding Muslims' presence in public life is frequently touched on in mainstream television programs.

Not surprisingly, headscarves surface as an issue for the Success School. The school does not require that girls wear scarves, and whenever I have visited the school I have seen about two-thirds of girls in scarves, whether seated in class or playing games, with more of the older ones and fewer of the younger ones wearing them. Girls and boys sit together in class. Whereas some French officials (including the municipal official quoted above) take the presence of headscarves to indicate the school's "communalist" quality, some parents of prospective students ask Dhaou about headscarves and mixed seating, and some decide not to use the school because of its relatively liberal policies. At least one potential source of outside funding from a Gulf state dried up when the visitors to the school saw that the classes had mixed seating. "To get such funding you have to have someone from the Muslim Brotherhood or the Salafis support you, and they condemn us for allowing boys and girls to study together and for not requiring scarves," explained Dhaou. Some Gulf organizations did fund another school in the Paris region that separates boys and girls in class. "The school directors made a short film showing that everyone wore a scarf, and that they had some spare scarves for any pupils who showed up without one, and on the basis of that film they got financial aid."

Dhaou has found politicians on the political Right to be more open to his activities than those on the Left, both because he finds common cause with Catholic school personnel and because he views greater freedom in France as coming from a more free-enterprise view of education and re-ligion, where each is free to practice and to create new institutions. "I see positive and negative sides. On the positive, the competition and choice are good. On the negative is the likelihood that the poor will be further marginalized. So we will need to have ways of ensuring that bright poor children have a chance, through government aid for their school of choice or through different levels of teaching within the public schools," he told me in 2004.

Dhaou and his associates also are trying to gain municipal support for building a mosque in Aubervilliers. The mayor agreed to rent them land at a subsidized rate. "He can say it is for the cultural association, which will have cultural and sports activities, rather than for a mosque—you know the secular jargon [*patois laic*]!" The Mayor also provides a space for Ramadan prayer free of charge, to the Muslims' Association of Aubervilliers.

These efforts, have led some of those associated with the school to enter more directly into local politics. One of Dhaou's colleagues at the school, Fayçal Menia, spearheaded an effort to have an independent slate of representatives elected to represent local Muslims in the national Islamic Council, and in 2008 he led the Aubervilliers slate for the center-right governing party, the UMP.[6] The very existence of Islamic institutions—schools, mosques, centers of any kind—requires at least tacit approval from local officials, and at any time can become elements in local electoral political battles.

How to Teach a Secular Curriculum in a Muslim School

By 2005, the middle school had its four classes in place, and the directors decided they needed a full-time principal—a requirement to receive state subsidies. They found Mme Fazilleau, a small, bustling woman who likes to address me in English (but declines to shake hands), and who had taught English for many years in a public school. For a number of years after her conversion to Islam she had worn a small headscarf while teaching, but by 2004 "the other teachers became very worried that because of the new law I would get them in trouble. So I resigned." The school also has a director and several assistants, who keep the pupils on time and in line (literally) to move from class to recreation or lunch and back again.

As long as they follow the national curricular guidelines, teachers may devise their own teaching plans. These teachers cover the same subjects as in a public school, except that one hour of religious education and four hours of Arabic language are taught during optional periods on Wednesday and Saturday, following the plan adopted in Catholic private schools. (Spanish and English are taught during the regular hours.)

Mme Fazilleau explained that of the fifteen or more teachers working at any one time (all but one or two are women), most also teach in public schools and have their school head's permission to work at Success School. A few have decided to teach in scarves and hence can only work in the private sector. Teachers receive a salary, but a modest one compared to those available in public schools.

I have met a number of the teachers while visiting the school or by accident on other occasions. Muslim educational life in the Paris region is like that: despite the size of the metropolitan region, lives intersect. Decent halâl restaurants, of course, attract conscientious Muslims, and once at lunch with Dhaou we found ourselves seated near the school's recently hired French language teacher, a woman who also writes a regular column for one of the major French Islam-oriented Web sites. When she is not teaching at Success she teaches French at a public high school in Paris (without her headscarf). She remarked that the Success students were two years ahead of the public-school students.

French is taught the same way in both sectors, but I was particularly interested in domains where there might be an Islamic twist given to standard courses of study, such as civics, biology, and religion itself. In the spring of 2006, with the instructors' permission, I attended some of these classes; the following are three instances of teachers trying to maintain an Islam-informed distance from the materials they are teaching without compromising their duty to fully instruct the pupils in those materials.

Civics and Gay Couples

The instructor for civics class for the *seconde* (the next to last year of regular course work, and in 2005–6 the school's original cohort of pupils) is a young woman wearing Islamic dress, who tutors public school students in her home when she is not teaching at this school. She has students carry out team research projects on topics described in a brochure sent out by the Ministry of Education. Among topics for 2005–6 were unrest in the poor outer cities, discrimination, and civil unions (PACS).

This class of eleven pupils (six boys and five girls) meets in a well-lit, second-story room in a building newly rented by the school, one block away from the main building. The students, in teams of two, write and present reports on assigned topics, one team each session. On one day in May two boys reported on civil unions. They circulated a photograph from a newspaper story of two gay men, one from Madagascar and the other born in France. The two men had entered into a civil union and hoped that the foreign-born man would thereby qualify for a long-term visa. Never during the class did I hear expressions of judgment or disapproval by students or the teacher about the couple's sexuality. There were spontaneous expressions from pupils, but on other, more practical issues. When the teacher explained that in order to inherit you had to pay a fee to the state, one boy blurted out "*O putain!*" (Whore!) The pupils mentioned current efforts to recognize gay marriages, but made no comment.

The teacher explained in a matter-of-fact way that there was no promise of fidelity in a civil union and that "in society today, people prefer to make a civil union first and then marry." In their questions, students were mainly interested in figuring out the legal logic of the relationship. The teacher explained inheritance laws for marriage and civil unions, and at this point introduced a contrast with "Eastern societies," where boys inherit larger shares than girls do, and explained this contrast in terms of legal responsibility. "If the women have debts the men must help them from their own share of the inheritance, but if men have debts the women do not have to help them out. In Western societies, however, boys and girls have the same shares, but also they share equally in the debts. They can decide to take over assets and debts from their parents, or to have neither—most people take the assets and debts." A pupil asked if the eldest child did not receive a large share in France; the teacher replied that the children could go to the notary and give more to the eldest. One pupil then asked, "Even in our societies [*chez nous*]?" and she responded, "Yes, even in Eastern, Arabic-Muslim societies."

By explaining the logic of the French system of marriage and inheritance, the teacher made it possible for students to understand the society in which they live without embracing it as their own. The norm that "people conduct civil unions first and marry later" would seem foreign to Muslim children (and to their parents)—although the dual system presents an interesting parallel to the distinction between religious marriages and state-sanctioned marriages made by many Muslims in Europe (see chapter eight). Most Muslims in Europe would not approve of gay unions. The teacher encouraged a subjective distance from French social norms by affirming the one pupil's contrast between the society they were studying (and where he himself was born) with "*chez nous*," the Muslim-majority societies that may provide a frame of personal historical reference even for Muslims in France who have never lived in them.

Religion versus Culture

A similar distancing, but on a different register, shaped teaching in the course in religious education for pupils in the *cinquième* (equivalent to U.S. seventh or eighth grade). Mme Keffi teaches that subject for all the grades and otherwise works with human rights organizations. She is a short, energetic, friendly woman who had no trouble getting the students to talk. We were in a bright room with stained-glass windows all along one side.

She alternates sessions on ethics with sessions on how to worship correctly. On one day's class in 2006 she gave out photocopied sheets from a book on Islamic ethics, with hadith (in Arabic and French), followed by principles concerning behavior toward others. She began by completing the discussion from the previous session on how to treat one's parents before moving on to the lesson for the day, on neighbors.

She kept up a dialogue with the pupils: "How should you be with your parents?" (Responses: Honest, respectful, show affection, obey them.) "Why obey? What have they done for you?" (Educated us, brought us up.) "And before that?" (Kept us in the womb.) "Yes, and for how long? Nine months, and the birth was painful for the mother—and for the fathers? We don't speak enough of them.

"And when the wife works, what does she do with her wages?" (The husband controls them; she can give them to him if she wishes.) "In Islam she has the right to keep her salary if she wishes, but in the family we share everything, money, affection, but her wages, her inheritance, she can keep them if she wishes." At this point one boy remarked, "The husband forces her to share it," leading Mme Keffi to ask, "Is that religion or tradition?" and the same boy shouted out the reply, "Tradition!" Mme Keffi continued: "You have to distinguish between religion and tradition. Many people do not know their rights; they are ignorant. Is ignorance an excuse before God or before the law?" Several replied at once: "No! We should look for knowledge!" Mme Keffi: "Who knows the first verse of the Qur'an, which speaks of this? Pupil: "Iqra' bismirrabilqal." Mme Keffi: "Which means?" Same pupil: "Read!" Mme Keffi: "In the name of?" Same pupil: "God!"

Mme Keffi extracts the right answers from the children by making it quite clear what is expected. When in the context of a discussion about Islam a pupil said that the husband has rights over his wife's wages and she then asked whether that claim was out of religion or tradition, clearly the question implied that the pupil had mistakenly interpreted Islam; the right answer then had to be what he quickly gave, "tradition." Relying blindly on tradition is implicitly associated with ignorance; religion requires study.

In the lesson for that day Mme Keffi showed pupils how to draw general lessons from hadith or Islamic stories. On the photocopied sheet was a hadith on the question of the status of a neighbor. She read the hadith in Arabic and had pupils one by one read the French translation and commentaries. One line of commentary asserted that the neighbor has the same rights of inheritance as a relative. "What does this mean?" she asked the class. "Even in families there is discord," replied one student. A girl said she heard a story of the Prophet Muhammad, who had a Jewish neighbor and looked in on him when he was sick.

"Yes, even if someone retains their religion"—she did not say "Jew"—"he has the right to retain his religion and has to be respected. If our beliefs are sound and well-founded, then they won't be threatened," she explained, giving a rationale for interfaith tolerance. She then asked the class what their obligations are to neighbors: "Visit when he is ill or in trouble, loan him money, let him do laundry at your house," they replied, and she nodded at each. "I know a man in Nice who lived in the center of town," she continued, "and when he died lots of people came: all his neighbors, although none of them were Muslims, and the mayor, and it was because they had all given him their keys to take of their pets when they were away. Why? It is because Islam teaches us to watch over our neighbors' concerns." Here she recited a hadith (in Arabic) from memory and explained its meaning, that you get merit if you do something to be good and not to show off, and then she repeated the hadith. She finished the class with other parables concerning duties toward neighbors; the last underscored our neighbor's right of first refusal to buy our property.

The Islam that pupils learn in Mme Keffi's class consists of a set of obligations, including ritual obligations to God, and a set of ethical principles. Her lesson plan does not focus on the particularistic history of Islam, or its specific institutions; it underscores a universalistic Islam, one that is particularly well-suited to life in a religiously pluralistic society.

Evolution and Islam?

My third example comes from the course on biology and geology, combined in French curricula as *sciences de la vie et de la terre*. I was interested to see how principles of evolution could be taught in an Islamic school. In June 2006 I attended the class held for students in *seconde* (the same eleven pupils I observed in civics class). Their teacher is Mme Ben Ouadday, a very friendly woman in her forties who wore a beige headscarf and a white lab coat. The pupils met in a classroom containing three banks of desks, with a faucet and sink in the middle of each. An overhead projector sat in front of the whiteboard and cabinets at the front of the room.

Mme Ouadday handed out work sheets at intervals, either to be filled in or as guides to their discussions. She kept the class moving at a brisk pace for two hours. She upbraided pupils who did not raise their hands to answer questions, but treated them in a friendly manner. The six boys and five girls did their group projects as four self-selected working groups. Boys had chosen to work with other boys and girls with girls, and the swifter ones with others of similar capacities. One group of three girls said nothing unless prompted; two girls talked more, and one of the two groups of boys did much of the talking. Three of the boys had taken the examination for entry into the public sector for their last year of high school, because it was as yet unclear whether would be such a class added for them at Success. As class began, these boys reported to Mme Ouadday that they were quite happy, because two-thirds of the content of the examination was material they had covered with her.

Today they studied the organization of the internal organs of the body, moving from the results of a dissection of a mouse they had performed the previous week to the human body, taking note of the similarities and differences across groups of animals. Most of the class was in the form of questions and answers, as in Mme Keffi's religious education class, punctuated by moments when students wrote answers on worksheets or their teacher drew diagrams on the whiteboard. Mme Ouadday directed the pupils in how to answer questions: "Hold your head up and speak clearly, and use complete sentences: subject, verb, object."

As they examined similarities across animal species they spoke about limbs and tails. Their teacher explained that "the tail disappeared on humans in the course of evolution." When they discussed the unity of all living things, she explained what that meant, then paused.

> Now let me open a small parenthesis. The curriculum is designed to convince you of the theory of evolution but it is just a theory, it is not absolute truth, I cannot say that in twenty years a scientist will not say, no, that is not any longer true—that is how science progresses. For example, with the cell, we used to say that it was like a room, and then we became able to see the parts, and then there were biochemical studies. Science is knowledge that is constructed bit by bit; it does not fall from the sky. So, now we teach about the unity of all living things, but perhaps in twenty years we will speak in a different way.

The lesson continued, and a few moments later she was explaining that "animals have limbs—some do not have them anymore because in the course of evolution they lost them. Take the snake: it lost its limbs as it developed a new way of moving through its environment."

I talked with her after class. She came from Tunisia, and had received a doctorate in cellular biology in France. "I should be teaching at a university, but because of my headscarf I cannot." She teaches only three classes at La Réussite and otherwise takes care of her children. I asked her if pupils ever objected that she taught evolution. "I am sure that some of them do not believe it at all. At the beginning of the year I tell the parents, 'Here is what I am going to teach them because it is in the national program and if you want to brainwash them afterward or deform the teaching it is up to you!' I do believe in all the stages that humans went through, *Homo erectus* and so forth, that we evolved, and also in the unity of creation, which was by God, but I do not think we have a common ancestor with other species; I do not know what happened in between." She said she teaches the national curriculum "as if there were always an inspector here in class."

As with the civics class, pupils learn the official scientific position about evolution, and their teacher embraces much of that curriculum—the mechanisms of change through adaptation to changing environments, the evolution of hominid species—but she is careful to present the thesis of the unity of all living things as a provisional claim. Pupils must learn it to succeed—and she must teach it for the school to be accredited and subsidized—but it is not God's truth.

The three subject matters lead these three teachers in different directions, but they present their subjects in ways that emphasize an ethical distance between the believer's source of certainty (scripture) and the particular norms or teachings that characterize French society. For the teachers of biology and civics, this ethical stance means that the teacher presents the curriculum as an external set of claims to be learned for very specific purposes. The national curriculum says that all living things are united and we must learn that, but who knows if they will say the same thing in twenty years' time? Civil unions are part of French society and reflect how that society has developed, and we must obey all French laws, but pupils and the teacher know that this is not the same as "Arabic Muslim" societies or, as one pupil put it (despite his birth in France), *chez nous*. The teachers' main concern is to impart knowledge that France requires—about biology, or civics, or for that matter English and history—without giving up an independent religious stance. For the religious education teacher the relationship of the subject to France flips around, and now the concern is that pupils treat the object of study as having an objective value, one that is quite distinct from the particularities of tradition or culture—and one that dictates norms of neighborliness across religious lines.

An Islamic Ambiance

Inside the school but outside the classroom, La Réussite maintains its Muslim ambiance through religious practice and celebrations of feast days. At regular prayer times, Dhaou or other teachers lead teachers and students in prayer in the large common area. The school puts on special events to mark the feast days in the Islamic year.

In April 2006 I attended the celebration of the Prophet Muhammad's birthday. It was vacation time, and the pupils participating in the event were not the regular middle school students but some of the students who came on Wednesday afternoons for Arabic lessons. They had been invited to spend the day at school at the celebration and to join Dhaou in an outing to the countryside the following Wednesday. There were about eighty pupils, six to ten years old, full of fun and noise; the adults kept telling them to pipe down. The walls were covered with exhibits of calligraphy, mostly by professionals but also one area of the pupils' own work. Several young boys began by reciting from the Qur'an; one five-year-old wandered off until the announcer gently picked him up and put him on stage. Students saw part of the film *The Message*, though the staff had difficulty with the player, so we kept seeing the introductory bit, with its dramatic music and dancing flame (a nonrepresentational stand-in for Muhammad), over and over again. After the first ten minutes of the film the staff switched to a series of slides containing lessons for the pupils about the importance of seeking out knowledge: a hadith reminded them that seeking knowledge was a way into heaven; the explanation said that when they were at school, they were following God's will.

After the film one man told some didactic stories about the Prophet, from time to time stopping to ask questions of the students to see how much they knew of the Prophet's life. His stories all concerned the Prophet's patience. In one, a neighbor hated the Prophet ("he was an infidel [*mecréant*]!" offered one small boy) and would dump his garbage in front of the Prophet's door, whereupon the Prophet would emerge, clean it up, and never say anything. One day there was no garbage and the Prophet wondered what had happened, went to see the neighbor, and learned he was ill. The Prophet visited him, and the man said, "What is this, I show my hatred for him and he visits me?" Here was the same lesson as that delivered in the religious education class: one has ethical obligations toward a neighbor that do not depend on a common faith.

Muslim Family Camp

Dhaou Meskine sees his role as part counselor, part scholar, and part administrator. He has taken special pleasure in arranging ways for Muslim children and their families to leave their surroundings in crowded areas of Paris and have time in the countryside. Some of these excursions are as school field trips, usually to "green spaces" (*espaces vertes*) in Normandy.

One of these was in June 2006, when he led a group of students to Normandy to set up a telescope, where "for the first time I saw the moons of Jupiter!" and the school's physics teacher showed students how to launch small rockets. Dhaou also takes students to the theme park called Futuroscope in Poitiers. (JB: "I suppose they really like that." DM: "No, that's for me, I love it: huge screen, 3D."). But he saw family outings as the major way to help Muslims feel at home in France while keeping their Muslim identity, as he explained to me in 2003:

> Because I work as a local imam, I am trying to help children integrate into French society without breaking their sense of who they are, their origins. It is important for their psychological development to be proud of who they are, and only then can they act appropriately toward others in society. In the past, some men who came to work here would send their wives and children back to their home country so that they would not lose their Arabic language and culture. The men would return for a month or so in the summer, bringing gifts; and all was well. But when they would retire and return to stay, they would no longer feel at home, and they would travel back to France regularly because they had become in many ways culturally French. It is worse than sad. My small village in Tunisia, every family has someone in France.
>
> So we try to keep the families here. We send the families with children on vacation, to touch the sea water for the first time, so that they can grow up as do other kids. The families can relax: you have a family where the mother and father both work all the time, the least thing will cause them to get angry at each other, but if they can relax then things can get cleared up. For example, there was one family with five children; they were in great difficulty, and they divorced, the kids with the mother. So I told her that she and the children could go to the summer camp, and I also told the father this, and over the course of the camp period they grew back together and remarried. All they needed was to relax.

In 2003, Dhaou created three legally registered associations, each with its own executive board, in order to keep distinct the fiduciary responsibility for each set of activities. Réussite Enseignement (Teaching Success) directs the school and after-school tutoring; Réussite Culture organizes art exhibitions, Arabic language and literature courses, and various other clubs, and Réussite Loisirs (Recreation Success) takes care of excursions and the summer camps.

This change was motivated by Dhaou's decision to purchase property in Normandy. He had located two parcels in the Pays de Caux, between Rouen and Dieppe, and began to negotiate to buy them. He met a mixed reaction. National media were featuring scare-stories about Islamists in 2002 and 2003. Although Dhaou and his wife had been bringing families there for short-term stays, most people were not yet used to the beards and scarves. "It's hard to be accepted there," he told me in 2003. "The priest is from a village twenty kilometers away and *he* is regarded as a stranger; you can imagine what they think of *us*." Mme. Meskine said, "No one would talk to me; they would give me looks in the street. It was even worse when word got out that we were buying property; I heard one woman in the market say, "and on top of that, they are now *chez nous*!"

In 2003, Dhaou showed me the dossier he was assembling on his efforts to buy the land. Two villages were involved, Saint-Laurent-en-Caux, and Saâne-Saint-Juste. The mayor of the former was reported as having said in a public town meeting that the Muslims "would have to cross over my body" to buy the land. At some point (you never know for sure, because Dhaou loves to make good stories out of these events) Dhaou claims to have retorted: "As Muslims we never step over someone's body, the one exception being during the war, when Muslims came to save all you in Normandy." In Saâne-Saint-Juste the notary had tried to prevent the sale by claiming that the owner did not really own it, but it turned out that the owner had notarized his purchase of the land the previous year—at this notary's own office! Dhaou threatened to sue, and then let it drop.

Others, including some local journalists, made an effort to give the new arrivals the benefit of the doubt. Dhaou showed me a story in the local Normandy newspaper about them, which was rather favorable except for the statement that Dhaou was "one of the great architects of the French Islamic Council," which irritated him. They tried to fit in: "We always take care to buy things from the local villages and hire people from the villages to do some of the work, buy bread and newspapers there, buy our gas there—it's not as if we are creating a supermarket there!" By 2005, Mme Meskine reported that "lately it has gotten a bit better; the baker will speak with me; people are getting used to having us here."

The summer camps continued to be held in local vacation villas. In August 2005, I traveled with my wife and children to Val de Saâne to spend the night at the *Village Vacances* where Dhaou Meskine had located his ten-day family camp, housing 120 people, parents and their children. He guided me in by cell phone, from Rouen northward toward the sea. The site consists of a large hall and separate multifamily houses (*gîtes*). The layout was not ideal, because unrelated people shared lodgings. Mme Meskine: "Like this, we cannot relax; we have to keep our headscarves on all the time, because we never are just with our own families. When we have our own property it will be better, because each family will have its own room." Mme Meskine explained their logistics: "We get our meat from an abattoir nearby, buying directly from them and storing it in our freezers; we have large ones here. We only buy lamb and veal; no one likes the taste of beef; the kids say it is hard to cut up. We get frozen fish and chickens, too." They ended up buying from the large stores because the prices were lower.

During the day there are classes and outings, one or two each day to the sea, to a farm, or to an historical monument. Dhaou uses the occasion to introduce the adults to aspects of France they do not know. One of his favorite sites is the museum to Victor Hugo, "the greatest French writer," and he has taken the group to Reims to talk about the reconciliation between the Germans and France carried out there by de Gaulle and Adenauer. He asked me if I knew who had made the red tapestry on the floor of the Reims cathedral: "A Muslim from India, and you have the Chagall windows, so made by a Jew, all in a cathedral!"

At one point they had hired someone to generate adult activities at the camp, but they had to economize, and now Dhaou gives lectures in the mornings for the adults. The Success School's assistant director, Youssef Riahi, comes along to supervise all the other activities. He organizes children's games, liberally using the whistle he keeps around his neck, and makes sure that the lights and water are working. Over breakfast, some adults told me that their children loved the camp but that they themselves sometimes were a bit bored.

We arrived for the camp's final evening, featuring an outdoor barbecue followed by group songs and skits in the hall. A young man who had served as assistant imam at the large mosque at Mantes-la-Jolie sang Qasidah with the aid of a synthesizer and acted as master of ceremonies. A group of adolescent girls put on a skit about prayer. In the skit, three of them debate which city is most likely to be chosen for the Olympics for 2012. (Paris had just lost out to London, a defeat highly publicized, to the great chagrin of Paris's mayor.) One of the girls bets a pizza on Paris, and they hear on the radio that the winner will be announced in a few minutes. At that moment the girls note that it is time to pray, and they begin, aligned on a prayer rug. While they are praying, the radio announces that London has won the competition, and one of the girls stops her prayer and says, "Enough prayer, let's have the pizza!" The skit ends with all the girls singing, "Prayer is more important than pizza in the eyes of God."

The next day, Dhaou took us on a tour of his two properties. The 4.5-hectare site at Saint-Laurent-en-Caux is a small farm once used to raise livestock. The house had been fixed up by a painter, who used the attic as a studio, and the barn stood untouched, with a wide array of farm implements. Dhaou is fascinated by the machines and tools, and described for us the complicated multistep system once followed on the farm to thresh and winnow the wheat. He plans to turn the barn into a museum of farm implements. This week he had taken the camp group to a farm where the cattle are milked via computer, the computer knowing how much each should be milked. The children love touching the farm implements, planting trees, seeing the cows, he explained, because these are concrete things, and the rural areas are new to most of them.

The second, eleven-hectare parcel lies within the village of Saâne-Saint-Juste. It consists of a meadow sloping down into the Saâne river, with a small house built near the road. As we approached the river we saw two black swans swimming, and a flock of small geese flying over head. We tromped through the tall grass down toward the river. Dhaou lets a neighbor turn his cows loose on the meadow: they eat their fill and at the same time keep the grass from getting out of hand. As we made our way over the boggy ground, Dhaou was fielding Arabic-language calls on his cell phone. (He continued to receive calls as we toured; later, when we had arrived at the sea, someone called him with a question about zakât; he explained that if someone is not married then he does not have to pay zakât, because he is still a dependent of the family.)

The village of Saâne-Saint-Juste is politically well to the right—64 percent voted for Le Pen in the 2002 presidential elections—and the mayor remains opposed to Dhaou's presence. (Dhaou no longer has trouble with the other village's administration.) One of the most vocal critics is an American with a house bordering their land, "who is trying to show that he is more French than the French" by urging others to oppose the Muslims. They purchased the land from a local man who owns a number of land parcels in the area and whose parents came to Normandy from Belgium: "people still call him 'the Belgian,'" explained Dhaou.

To look after these properties Dhaou found a local man, Jacques, who he said was "the only Normand willing to work with Arabs." Jacques had been an activist in the Socialist Party in the 1970s and 1980s—"it helps that he is Socialist," said Mme Meskine. For his part, Jacques told us that he respected how "the Arabs" view things. "They think first in the long term, about life in general, and then after that, like the rest of us, they think of themselves," he said.

The family camp is akin to the training school we saw in the previous chapter: an attempt to build an institution with a secular set of activities and universalistic goals (training, recreation, introduction to rural France) that yet preserves an Islamic ambiance. This is religion outside the narrow French official definition: religion suffusing everyday life. If the religion in question is Catholic, it is part of the French heritage. Will France accept it if it is a religion that had been thought of until recently as alien?

ARREST

Even as relations with local people were improving, a plan to arrest Dhaou was being concocted in Paris. On June 19, 2006, Dhaou and his son Malik were arrested in Paris along with seventeen others, all of them members of one of the boards of the three Success associations. Dozens (Dhaou says hundreds) of judicial police and secret police (the Renseignements Généraux) were involved in different aspects of the investigation and the interrogation.

The judicial police made a number of accusations, reported in the Paris newspapers.[7] They said Dhaou had financed terrorism, because in 2001 he had sent a wire transfer to an account in Germany held by someone under suspicion. (It turned out to be the money paid for their white van; he bought it from a local Tunisian, who directed him to transfer the money to his friend.) The police raided his home and the offices, and found a videocassette of a play put on by girls at the Success School. The play dramatized a death that occurred in a Palestinian family after an Israeli air attack. The police claimed it was made to encourage hatred, but as it had never been distributed, this and most other charges were dropped. As of 2009, only one set of accusations (and no indictments) remained standing: that the three Success legal associations had transferred funds among themselves without filing tax reports.

The most salacious charge levied against Dhaou was that the Recreation association had permitted al-Qaeda training to occur on the Normandy properties. The woman who lives right across from the Saâne property had called the town's mayor on February 2, 2006, saying she had seen terrorists shooting on the land. The mayor then notified the police, and the investigations began. Later that summer, two local men came forth and told the newspapers they had asked Jacques for permission to hunt game birds on the land in preparation for the general hunting season. They wore their camouflage. Jacques forgot to inform Dhaou, so when he later was questioned he had no idea how to explain the "al-Qaeda sighting."

Dhaou, his son, and the others were held and questioned for five days. Dhaou was released on bail of 80,000 euros. His lawyer, a man who usually defends Jewish causes, gathered letters of support from the Orthodox rabbi, the heads of Catholic and Protestant associations, and, notably, the prefect of Bobigny. The deputy representing Dhaou's district in Aubervilliers, Eric Raoult, issued a public statement of support. In January 2007, Dhaou was called before the investigating judge, who returned to the charges of terrorism, asking about ties between people associated with La Réussite and Islamic movements elsewhere in the world. As it happens, the names were of people who worked with the mayor of Aubervilliers—the mayor had even granted them space for prayer.

The various Success activities—at the school and in Normandy—continued throughout the investigations. The efforts to gain state funding for the school were stalled, however. Only two weeks before the arrest in July, the Academy (school district) had delivered a report favorable to the granting of a contract to the school. After the arrests, with all the required inspections and requests completed, the case seemed to have disappeared into the bowels of the state, from which, as of early 2009, it had not emerged. Moreover, in 2005, the banks used by the associations had been instructed to place a partial freeze on the association accounts, allowing them to withdraw money already deposited but not to deposit or transfer.

It is never easy to discern what lies behind these raids and investigations—France is little different in this respect from the United States or Britain. Perhaps the secret police were annoyed that Dhaou had insufficiently cooperated with them in the past and wished to pin a charge on him. Perhaps someone in the Interior Ministry (the location of the judicial police) was unhappy that he was not forthcoming with information about foreign Islamic movements. Indeed, when the police raided the Success School they were accompanied by two men from Tunisian government offices. There is also the role Dhaou played in Clichy during the riots: praised by some, resented by others. Some saw Dhaou as interfering with the project of assembling all major Islamic groups under the umbrella of the French Islamic Council, the CFCM. Dhaou's criticism of the council is in part in his role as secretary-general of an association of independent imams, the Council of Imams (Conseil des Imams). He considers the state-backed council to claim prerogatives over matters on which the Council of Imams also works, such as the difficulties faced by imams in obtaining long-term residency permits or the expulsion of imams. Creating the CFCM has not made it easier for imams to obtain their residency papers, and even the imams working with the Paris Mosque have difficulties.

Dhaou perhaps has had greater difficulties than they have. After seventeen years residing in France, he received his first permit (*titre de sejour*) on September 11, 2001. "One year later, on September 11, 2002, an agent of the secret police [the Renseignements Généraux, RG] asked me how I felt about that day, and when I replied that it was the most glorious day of my life he went crazy, until I explained why, that it was the first anniversary of receiving my identity papers!" How does someone live without these proofs of legal residency? "The police would say, 'We know you are here, and when you pass by a checkpoint we will look in the computer and it will say that we know you.'" The RG frequently makes calls to Dhaou, as they do to other prominent Muslims, and he tries to keep them at bay by barely complying with their requests. Frequently, in his office, he would field such a call and say that he had no special information about such-and-such an event.

But one must also take into account the potential electoral gains that someone who wished to move from the Interior Ministry to higher office might reap from making high-profile moves against Muslim leaders. Indeed, Dhaou had been brought in for questioning during three previous periods of pre-election fever. And during this particular runup to the residential elections, in which former Interior Minister Nicolas Sarkozy was victorious in May 2007, other actions were taken in the name of security that later were dropped. During 2005–6, seventy-two persons, mostly Muslims, who worked at the Paris airport terminal (Roissy-Charles de Gaulle) were told to turn in their security badges. The prefect of Seine-Saint-Denis, where the airport is located, claimed that the actions were intended to stop "fundamentalist movements with potentially terrorist aims" and that they had targeted selected individuals who had frequented "radical mosques" or had undertaken "religious travel" and had been unable to prove they were not likely to endanger airport security. One of those who lost his job twice had been awarded medals, once for discovering a weapon and again for his work during Sarkozy's visit to the airport! The police stated that they wished to ensure that these persons would not "eventually be used by radical movements"; they did not even make the weak claim that the detainees were involved with such movements. Some of the employees brought suit against the prefecture.[8] By May, immediately after the presidential elections, the prefect had dropped the charges and restored the badges to those detained, before the courts could pronounce on the employees' complaints of harassment.

The arrests and charges make credible those who criticize the French state as not playing by its own rules. The French institutional game offers state support for those who create religious schools, but these rules were created to appease Catholics, and were extended to Protestants and Jews. It may be more difficult to play the game when one is visibly different and setting out to take seriously the notion that Islam ought to have the same privileges as Judaism and Christianity.

Thus far we have explored ways in which Islamic public actors have created Islamic institutions that make use of (and yet challenge) the French cultural and political environment, and ways in which teachers have shaped Islamic reasoning to those conditions. I have examined how reasoning is situated in these schools, institutes, and mosques, but not yet analyzed the debates about the forms of Islamic reasoning themselves. I now turn to this complementary question: Given the institutions, how have Islamic public actors approached the question of Islam's fit with France?

PART THREE

Debates

CHAPTER SEVEN

Should There Be an Islam for Europe?

LET US STEP BACK for a moment and consider where we have taken our inquiry. We began with the forces that have shaped the present landscape of Islam in France: Muslims' trajectories of arrival and settlement, a growing identification with Islam, and the state responses that applied the long tradition of French state control-through-support of religious institutions. This perspective allowed us to understand the development of Islamic institutions—mosques, schools, and institutes—as responses to the possibilities afforded in France and to the demand growing among younger French Muslim men and women.

Then we turned to a more detailed study of a set of "mainstream" Muslims institution-building projects that have been developed according to the French rules of the game—although contradictions within the French "game," particularly around education, continue to bedevil some of these projects. Some mayors still oppose mosques; some religious schools still find their ways blocked within the bureaucracy. These projects show Islamic public actors seeking practical solutions to a double challenge: how to survive in the French public landscape and how to teach about Islam (or in an Islamic ambience) in a way that attracts a new generation of French Muslims. We paid little attention to discussions outside these schools or institutes but focused on the ways in which the scholars directing them combined various available Islamic approaches to social life. We found that running across the range of their answers to everyday questions, as well as their ways of teaching Islam, lies the idea of the objectives (maqâsid) of the shari'a as underlying the specific rules contained in scripture. This idea can be used to justify efforts to go beyond these rules, to explore new avenues for Islamic lives.

But most of these scholars and teachers also seek to bring together the discourse of objectives with older scholarly traditions linked to one or more legal traditions. Some take a slightly different approach, seeking to discern general principles in scripture or causes of a particular revelation, rather than the objectives of scripture. They each choose a particular way of weighting and combining the several different ways of justifying opinions. Sometimes they come to different conclusions.

We can take the question of abortion as an example. We saw in chapter four that Hichem El Arafa highlights general principles and concludes that all abortion is forbidden, because life is sacred. In chapter five we saw that Ahmed Jaballah approached the question differently: he highlights the objectives of shari'a (in this case, the objective of safeguarding procreation) and finds that abortion is forbidden when the fetus becomes viable, but not prior to that point. Both scholars emphasize adapting their general precepts to individual cases, but they face somewhat different practical challenges—challenges that shape, I think, how they approach the Islamic traditions in the first place. Ahmed Jaballah speaks for an organization, the UOIF, and so must be able to answer questions with general rules. He does not have the freedom to treat each case as it comes (unless he speaks with someone in private), so he must arrive at a principle that will sufficiently reflect the idea of "facilitation" championed by the UOIF. By contrast, Hichem El Arafa does not need to issue general opinions (although sometimes he does), but more often consults with individuals, and thus can more easily arrive at a relatively rigid general principle and then tailor his advice to the practical capacities and needs of the individual Muslim who approaches him for advice.

In this chapter we look at a wider range of differences in how scholars and teachers formulate their justifications and how they enter into debates about the relative value of different formulations. Questions that Muslims bring to public debates inevitably raise the issue of whether there should be distinctive Islamic norms for France (and by extension for Europe). In their responses, Islamic public actors engage in two levels of reasoning about Islam in France and Europe. On the first level, the question is what would be best for Muslims living in these non-Muslim lands: How should French Muslims live, work, marry, and sacrifice? On the second level, the issue is about how best to think about questions posed on the first level: Which tools and traditions should we use to reason about such questions? It is on this second level of reasoning, what we can call "meta-reasoning" about Islamic norms, where Islamic public actors in France engage most profoundly—and often most heatedly—with their counterparts in other countries.

I begin with one particular question, namely, whether Muslims may sometimes take out home loans at interest. But the ensuing debates make it clear that responses to this and other questions entail taking positions on a more general issue: Does where you live make a difference in what God expects you to do? Do the duties of Muslims change as they move from, say, Syria to Paris? At this point the debates move up to the meta-level, and at these "meta-moments" issues of methodology and authority suddenly loom large. Do the appropriate tools and modes of reasoning change as you move from a Muslim-majority to a Muslim-minority country? Do Saudi or Syrian scholars retain legitimacy to comment on adaptations made in Paris? As the debates become more sharply located in an Islamic sphere of reference, actors must justify their claims in Islamic terms, but they disagree over *which* Islamic terms are legitimate.

In chapter eight, I flip around the spatial and normative orientation: from debates among Muslims in a *shared* realm of Islamic norms reaching *across* national boundaries, to Muslims and non-Muslims exploring *distinct* realms *within* French national boundaries. Whereas in the first case all actors have a putative commitment to the same overall normative structure, differently interpreted though it may be, in the second case the key issue is precisely *which* normative structure should take precedence: the Islamic or the French—or perhaps some interactive relationship between the two? To illustrate this second kind of debate, I take up questions of marriage and divorce. These inquiries will lead us to ask whether there might not be legal or moral bridges across the two justificatory realms of Islamic norms and French norms. Can concepts such as "contract" or "mutual consent" serve as umbrella concepts under which Islamic practices and French laws and sensibilities find a common home? This possibility remains an intriguing cross-normative parallel to the ideas of shari'a's objectives and may provide an important pathway for a more general convergence across confessional lines in France and Europe.

THINKING ABOUT *RIBÂ*

When French Muslims ask an imam or another religious figure whether, say, they should marry at city hall or work in a bank, they are trying to solve an immediate problem, but they also are asking what is expected of them as Muslims living in Europe. Some Muslims who find it difficult to find a sheep to dedicate at the Feast of Sacrifice wonder whether this ritual expectation could be replaced by giving a gift. Those seeking to buy a house might borrow at interest and then worry that they have contradicted God's will. Those marrying at city hall ask whether that marriage counts as an Islamic marriage as well as a civil one.

These questions arise not because of something essential to Europe but because most European Muslims do not have access to the political, legal, and social institutions that developed over centuries in Muslim-majority societies, from councils of jurists and courts of law to adequate mosques for worship and nearby abattoirs for ritual sacrifice. They wonder whether they should try to establish the same sorts of institutions, applying the same norms, as were present where they or their parents lived, in Algeria, Syria, or Pakistan. Perhaps instead they should seek alternatives. Should they develop new sets of norms for Muslims living as minorities?

Or should they focus on the objectives of those norms and suggest new ways of meeting them that might be valid not only for Europe and North America, but also for lands of long-term Muslim settlement?

These are heady questions, and they bring up matters concerning the very nature of religious authority. Should we value most highly the opinions given by scholars who are firmly anchored in one of the established legal traditions? Or should we turn instead to new Muslim intellectuals in Europe (or for that matter in Pakistan or Indonesia) who emphasize the need to reformulate Islam for new social conditions? As we shall see, many of the claims made by European Muslim teachers and scholars are based not on an established tradition but on the pragmatic argument that following a particular practice will benefit Muslims. To the degree that precise scripture-based norms are either difficult to find or difficult to follow in Europe, pragmatic claims may seem more convincing.

The questions are not entirely new ones, however, in that Muslims long have debated the relationships among ethical and practical judgments, and asked whether the place where one lives determines the nature of one's religious obligations. In other places and at other times the issue has been framed differently. In the fifteenth century, Islamic judges took into account local values and practices to the extent that these did not violate God's commands. In the twentieth and twenty-first, Islamic scholars living in Morocco, Indonesia, and North America ask whether or not cross-cultural differences in gender values justify differences in Islamic law. In India, a country where Muslims are a minority but have longstanding religious institutions, the questions concern how these institutions can fit into a Hindu-majority country under the rule of a secular state. It is thus not unusual for Muslims to consider new norms for life in new social situations.[1]

Let us consider one issue in detail, namely, that of whether or not Muslims may take out loans at interest under certain conditions. Unlike Britain and the United States, France does not yet have Islamic financial institutions, such that French Muslims who require a loan to buy a house consider borrowing from an interest-charging bank.[2] But Islam forbids *ribâ*, which has been taken to imply either a ban on any forms of interest or a ban only on high rates of interest.[3] May Muslims who are planning to reside permanently in Europe take out loans at interest to purchase homes? French Muslim scholars who take positions on this question have to address the issue in Islamic terms and also meet the practical needs of French Muslims. How do they do so?

In the late 1990s, the matter of mortgages was taken up by the European Council for Fatwa and Research, a collection of jurists of various nationalities who mostly now reside in Europe and who are led by Yûsuf al-Qaradâwî.[4] The council, founded in 1997, regularly meets to consider questions brought by individual council members and publishes its opinions (*fatwâs*) on its Web site and in a number of books in Arabic and in European languages. It has ties to ISNA, the Islamic Society of North America, particularly through the Fiqh Council of North America, and in France its members include leaders of the UOIF. The secretary of England's largest Islamic Sharia Council is a member. The European Council is thus part of an international network of scholars engaged in debates about how to think through practical questions facing Muslims in the West

At its very first meeting, held in Dublin in 1997, the council took up the issue of home mortgages, commissioned a report, and at its 1999 meeting issued an opinion or fatwa. The opinion affirmed the prohibition on usury and urged Muslims everywhere to avoid borrowing at interest, but it also said that if Muslims in Europe could not find alternatives, then they could take out a bank mortgage for a first house.

The council's scholars justified their decision in two main ways. First, they drew on past rulings from the Hanafî and Hanbalî legal schools (minority opinions, as it happened) to the effect that while living in non-Muslim countries, Muslims might legitimately make contracts that violated Islamic law. Second, they appealed to the architecture of the objectives of Islamic norms, the *maqâsid ash-sharî'a*. Earlier I explained that in his classic formulation of the maqâsid, the scholar Shâtibî had identified five highest-level objectives of Islam, called the "necessities." He also argued that Muslims work toward meeting these necessities by successfully meeting lower-level "needs" and by making "improvements" that benefit Muslims. In the case at hand, the council argued from necessity to need, citing the Qur'anic texts that

- "He (Allah) has explained to you in detail what is forbidden to you, except under compulsion or necessity";
- "But whosoever is forced by necessity without willful disobedience, nor transgressing due limits; (for him) certainly, your Lord is oft-Forgiving, most merciful."

These quotations give a Qur'anic base to the idea of acting in the face of necessity. The council then extended this reasoning:

Jurists have established that that Hâjah, need, whether for an individual or a group, can be treated in equal terms with Darûrah, extreme necessity. Need is defined as those things which put the Muslim in difficulty if not fulfilled, even if he/she can do without. Extreme necessity, on the other hand, is that which the Muslim cannot manage without. Allah SWT has lifted difficulty as stated in Sura Al-Haj and Al-Ma'idah:
And He has not laid upon you in religion any hardship (22:78).

The concluding scriptural citation added force to the idea that Muslims should respond to mere need or hardship in the same way as they would respond to matters of necessity, for it speaks of "any hardship." The council then made a series of empirical claims: renting a house places Muslims in a state of financial insecurity (a conclusion reinforced by citations from a report from the European Union on immigrant housing); owning a house allows a Muslim to settle in close proximity to a mosque and to modify the house to accommodate religious needs; mortgage payments are equal to or lower than rents. Because Muslims cannot change the institutions that dominate life in their host countries, continued the council, they are not responsible for the existence of an interest-based financial system. If they were forbidden to benefit from banking institutions, then Islam would have weakened them, a result that would contradict the principle that Islam should benefit Muslims.[5]

The ruling did not remove the prohibition of lending at interest but exempted some Muslims living in Europe from the prohibition because of a combination of empirical circumstances, including the high level of rents and the absence of viable alternatives. These circumstances allowed the jurists to apply the principles that necessity allows for exemption in order to relieve a situation that, although perhaps not constituting "necessity," did constitute a hardship. They could then allow Muslims to use otherwise invalid financial instruments when they live in "non-Islamic" countries.

During the early 2000s, more and more Muslims living in France learned of this opinion. Some had heard al-Qaradâwî discuss the matter on television; others had consulted Web sites or heard about it through word of mouth. The issue of bank loans comes up for people in different ways. Those Muslims who can afford to buy a house—and increasing numbers can—must choose between borrowing from a bank at interest and accumulating the money on their own. Other Muslims work in banks and are worried by the religious implications of their work. One CERSI student with whom I spoke frequently worked in a bank in Saint-Denis and told me that such work "is not really compatible with Islam," so he was looking for something else. For those who were not in a position to take out such loans (and who did not work in banks), the ruling nonetheless pointed toward a whole new approach to thinking about Islamic norms in Europe. This possibility excited some and worried others.

The ruling also led to a debate among well-known Islamic scholars around the world, and even some members of the European Council rejected it. It seems to have led the prestigious Cairo institution al-Azhar to issue a fatwa allowing fixed-interest transactions, on grounds that if they were allowed for Muslims in the West, they ought to be allowed for Muslims living elsewhere as well.[6] In response, Muhammad Saʿîd Ramadân al-Bûtî, professor of Islamic law in Damascus, used his December 2002 "monthly word" on his Web site to claim that the sheikh of al-Azhar was merely repeating what the Jews had said to Muhammad, following which God said to Muhammad: "God has permitted trade and forbidden interest (Al-Baqarah 2:275)."[7]

I sought the opinions of Paris-region Islamic scholars on the al-Qaradâwî ruling, and began with Ahmed Jaballah, a jurist on the European Council mentioned earlier. Jaballah explained that the council had decided that Muslims could best provide for their children by moving out of poor neighborhoods and buying houses. "The only way to improve family life is to move out, and the loan helps them do that. Many in the Muslim world objected to the fatwa because it approved interest. They do not understand what social life is like here." This position is consistent with the approach he had sketched out in his classes on jurisprudence, in which he declared acts for which there were no specific Islamic texts to be in a "legal vacuum," permitting Muslims to come up with practical solutions to problems. Najjar, the practicing imam at the Lyon Mosque we met in chapter three, also agreed with the fatwa, in part because "it draws from the Hanafî madhhab, which is better than the others in basing judgments on al-maqâsid al-Qur'an."

But others disagreed, including Hichem El Arafa at CERSI. Shortly after I met Hichem in 2001 he was asked to talk with a group of Muslims studying at universities in Paris. Most, he said, had learned of al-Qaradâwî's fatwa not through the European Council's report but from the scholar's al-Jazira television station broadcasts.

> Everyone has heard about the opinion; if you played "sidewalk microphone" and asked people coming out of a mosque if they had heard of it they would have. So they asked me about it. [JB: And were you opposed?] I was not entirely against it, but I wanted to consider other arguments. I think that it does not lead to creativity in thinking about these issues. For example, the few experiments we do have in Islamic banking, we would not have had them if Muhammad 'Abduh [the important late nineteenth-century Egyptian reformer] had said that you did not need to come up with something new. And experimentation is good, many fail and some succeed and we have new institutions. The problem is difficult, because there is an extreme reticence, hostility, in the society here to new things; if we were to say that an Islamic bank wanted to start operations now in France there would be lots of resistance. One answer is simply to live by the rules in place, French ones.

Hichem himself had bought his house with a bank loan a few years previously.

Dhaou Meskine advanced arguments parallel to Hichem's. "There are too many families in France who live in debt," he said, "and 4 million who have been unable to repay their debts." He went on to explain that there are other, creative ways of obtaining money, such as repaying the seller of the house gradually, perhaps at a higher price, and that he had successfully experimented with such arrangements. Meskine also objected to the very idea of different laws for different places: "Sheikh Qaradâwî says that interest in Europe is acceptable because Europe is not a Muslim land. But laws must be universal: if it is forbidden to steal, or lie, or falsify papers, or to make illegal marriages in Muslim lands, then it is also the case for Muslims living in Europe, in the 'land of treaty.' That is the nature of religion; it is intended to apply everywhere."

Another of the teachers we met earlier, Ahmed Abidi, agreed. In 2003 he told me that when students asked him about the issue,

> I say that, no, you should not borrow money from a bank because there are other ways to buy a house. [JB: Do you know of examples of other ways?] It could be as with the Africans, they do not make much money, but whenever one comes back from Africa he is carrying a lot of goods, and you say, well, he must be rich! But he is not; it is because the community shares their money, and when one is about to leave they all give him money. So one could be inspired by that and share money so one person at a time can buy a house. In other words, there is no necessity. In any case, I heard that after that first fatwa, Qaradâwî was asked the question in another way and said that, no, it was not permitted to do it. You know, his answers depend entirely on the way the question is put to him. The first time it was: "I have to buy a house because if I rent my life is terrible for me and my family," and so he answered yes. The second time it was "I could rent or I could borrow money from a bank to buy; what should I do?" and his answer was that you should rent. Qaradâwî is like that always, he answers in terms of how the question is put. I rent and I see no reason why this is any less satisfactory, paying the rent once a month, than buying over many years to a bank.

Although they all agreed that statements about Islamic norms should be based on sound knowledge of jurisprudence, these scholars advanced socially pragmatic reasons for their views. What would be the social consequences of permitting mortgages or forbidding them? Some hold that bank mortgage gives Muslims the ability to realize their duties to their families, a positive value in Islam. Others counter that retaining the prohibition leads to fruitful experimentation and maintains the moral power of the law. For someone such as Dhaou Meskine, who has lived through years of difficult negotiations with a left-wing local government, many of the problems faced by Muslims come from their not following the rules that are common to Islamic law and French state law. But for all of them, the main issue is how best to help Islam and Muslims, and not how best to interpret the writings of the Hanbalî or Mâlikî school. Their reasoning concerns about what is best for Muslims in France, and more broadly in Europe, and is not "meta-reasoning" about which tools and which sources to use in studying the issue. But this meta-level does emerge in other contexts, as we shall see.

DIFFERENT RULES FOR DIFFERENT LANDS?

Through the UOIF, the French members of the European Council have promoted both this particular fatwa and the broader ways of Islamic reasoning from which it was derived. At its annual gatherings at Le Bourget, where tens of thousands gather to buy Muslim clothes, books, and other products, to hear speakers from Muslim-majority countries, and to spend time in an Islamic ambiance, speakers emphasize the importance of adapting Islam to conditions of life in Europe. In 2006 the vice president of the World Council of Muslim Scholars, Ben Biya (Abdullah Ibn Bayyah), appearing in white robes and turban, used the mortgage fatwa as an example of how to draw on a wide range of sources to make lives easier for Muslims: "We permitted the borrowing of money at interest to buy a house in order that Muslims may have better housing, in order to reduce difficulty. We used a minority opinion to do this."[8] The desired outcome determined the choice of sources.

As Ben Biya continued, he developed a meta-discursive argumentation in support of the UOIF's position on bank interest and on other matters. "When we live in new contexts, we face new social processes, and we must develop facilitation [*taysîr*] based on religion's objectives [*maqâsid*]." He specified three rules for interpreting scripture: first, whenever there is an obstacle, there must be a way to facilitate our way; second, we must alleviate needs or necessity (*darurat*); and third, we must know the objective (*maqsûd*) of a rule. Indeed, these ideas are inextricably linked for the UOIF, because avoiding hardship for Muslims is seen as but one facet of the general objective of doing that which benefits religion.

Ben Biya set out a series of parallels between the statements of great scholars, on the one hand, and the UOIF's rulings on various social matters on the other, inferring from the parallels some general principles that ought to guide judgment. The caliph 'Umar, often mentioned for his willingness to change Islamic norms based on social conditions, ruled that a woman who married and then later converted to Islam but whose husband did not himself convert should not divorce him (even though a Muslim woman should not be married to a non-Muslim man), because preserving marriage was an objective of Islam. The objective trumped the specific rule. Ben Biya paired this case with the European Council's ruling that Muslims should always marry at city hall (even though many Muslims consider civil marriage to have no religious purpose), on grounds that the objective of the act of marrying is to create a contract that binds the husband and wife, and in Europe only the state has the power to enforce that contract. In both cases, that facing 'Umar and the ruling of the UOIF, the rule had to be modified in order to better realize the objective of preserving marriage. He concluded, "Imam Shâfi'î said that studying the maqâsid is difficult but bears sweet fruits. We must study past decisions and jurisprudence [fiqh] but also consider what the final consequences were that the judges had in mind."

A key element in these discussions is the specification of context. Implied by the preeminence of objectives in religious reasoning is the idea that in distinct social circumstances rules might also differ. Ben Biya quoted al-Shâtibî to the effect that decisions should change according to the context and the person. "The very divergence of fatwas is a blessing because it gives greater room for adapting fiqh to changing contexts." The broader issue is as follows: if knowledgeable scholars studied the same texts, using the same methods, and, indeed, often directly learning from each other, why should they differ on important legal questions? Of particular interest is the scholarship of ash-Shâfi'î, the founder of the legal school that bears his name. Imam Shâfi'î was the student of another great scholar and founder of a legal tradition, Imam Mâlik. Since one was the student of the other, how could it be that they differed?

This question comes up frequently in public discussions, such as the discussions on Islam in Europe sponsored for several years in the early 2000s by the publication *La Médina*. I was invited to participate in one such discussion in November 2002, at which one younger man in the audience asked how there could be differences in interpretation in Islam if all Muslims agreed to follow the Qur'an and hadith and if these texts were internally consistent. The moderator, one of *La Médina's* editors, Abdelfattah El Halfaoui, explained:

As you know well, Imam Mâlik was the teacher of Imam Shâfi'î. Imam Mâlik lived in Iraq and Imam Shâfi'î in Egypt. But if you read Imam Shâfi'î there are difference with his teacher, although you would expect them to be of the same opinion. Why? It is because when Imam Shâfi'î lived in Egypt he saw that they had traditions that were different from those in Iraq, Kufra, Saudi Arabia, and so forth, and so he created a new approach, a new *rite*. He said that those people in Iraq, they have their own traditions, and many things, and Imam Mâlik, when he was there, had given responses on the level of fiqh that fit that place, but in Egypt, people were used to different traditions, and so he was obliged to create a new approach. And now the question arises for Muslims in the United States or in Europe, the fact that Muslims are there is something new, and now it is up to the learned people to interpret new laws, new fatwas, according to the tradition. Because the Muslims now in France or in Europe are a minority

community, living with different laws than in Muslim countries, and so we
have to invent our response according to the region in which we live.

The moderator was not a scholar of Islamic law but a well-educated
Muslim involved in debate and publishing, and his response is one that
many Muslims of similar orientation would offer to such a question. The
response respects the legal traditions, and attributes their differences to
the diversity of social conditions: other fields, other fiqhs. Because understanding the scholarship of ash-Shâfiʿî in this way does indeed lead logi-
cally to this general conclusion, scholars and publicists who do not share
this point of view are quick to contradict this version of the distant past,
as we shall see shortly.

In this perspective, the specific claim of European Muslims to be able
to create new norms appears as but one instance of a general approach,
one that some in the UOIF push still further, to mean that opinions developed outside of Europe may be of little relevance to European Muslims.
Shortly after the 2003 American invasion of Iraq, for example, a keynote
speaker at that year's UOIF gathering, Ahmed al Rawi, president of the
Federation of Islamic Organizations in Europe (the originator of the European Council and parent organization of the UOIF), emphasized the
normative specificity of Europe. Speaking in Arabic, he said: "Muslims
living in Europe should not follow fatwas given on this subject in Muslim
countries, because Muslims in Europe have a specific character, which
means that those fatwas are not incumbent upon them."

With Europe and North America in mind, the European Council, and in
particular Yûsuf al-Qaradâwî, have pushed this intuition toward developing a "fiqh for minorities" (fiqh al-qalliyyât), a distinct jurisprudence that
would apply to Muslims living as minorities in non-Muslim societies.[9] Al-
Qaradâwî has constructed a set of interlinked concepts that give content
to the idea of a fiqh for minorities. He speaks of the "fiqh of balances"
(fiqh al-muwânazât) to point to the need to balance minor evils against
greater or longer-term benefits to Muslims. It is this logic that he uses to
justify interest-bearing mortgages as ways for Muslims to improve themselves. Referring to Shâtibî's three-level hierarchy of necessities, needs, and
improvements, he argues that "when interests [masâlih] conflict, a low-
level interest is sacrificed for the sake of a higher-level interest."[10]

This approach also insists that it is the objective that must be kept in
mind and not the specific form, the latter changing with time and place.
In his work addressing the dangers of extremism, al-Qaradâwî criticizes
those who mistake the historically specific form for the objective of revelation. He relates that someone once objected to his argument that a
Muslim woman's dress would normally differ from one time and place
to another, and to buttress his objection the speaker quoted the Qur'anic

verse that Muslim women should "cast their outer garments over their persons [when abroad]. That is most convenient, that they be known [as such] and not molested" (Qur'an 33:59). The man claimed that the verse means that all women should indeed wear "an outer garment." Al-Qaradâwî replied that the Qur'an specified certain forms but that these could change if needs did, and that "the woman's outer garment could be any dress that satisfies the objective expressed in verse 33:59 that Muslim women should be recognized and not molested."[11]

In a different set of arguments, al-Qaradâwî speaks of *fiqh al-wâqi'*, "fiqh of reality." In explaining this idea he emphasizes one sense of the term "fiqh," namely, as "understanding," in order to lend plausibility his method. The fiqh of reality entails bringing knowledge of empirical matters into the normative sphere as matter for reflection, as when the relative rates of rents and mortgage payments were taken as relevant to the normative issue of whether sometimes Muslims may accept bank loans.[12]

Al-Qaradâwî frames these questions and the answers with an old set of ideas about distinct geographical realms: the *dâr al-islâm*, or abode of Islam, versus the *dâr al-harb*, or abode of war. In its classical formulation, the former included the countries ruled under Islamic principles; the latter referred to all other places, where, presumably, Muslims would not be free to worship.[13] Today, many Muslims find discomfort in this way of viewing the world. How is one to define "Muslim societies," the dâr al-Islam? Does one look to the correctness of the government, the piety of the people, or simply the fact that most people living in the country profess Islam as their religion? Is a Muslim-majority country whose government represses its people and prevents the free expression of religious ideas to be considered part of dâr al-Islâm? Conversely, why should countries not governed by Islamic laws but where Muslims are free to worship be considered as belonging to an "abode of war"?

Some Muslims have proposed alternatives. Referring to the protection given to religious minorities by international law, some scholars have proposed *dâr al-ʿahd*, "abode of treaty," the term used by Dhaou Meskine. Others, notably the scholar and lecturer Tariq Ramadan, have proposed *dâr al-daʿwa*, "abode of predication," or *dâr ash-shahâda*, "abode of witness," emphasizing the possibilities open to Muslims in these lands.[14]

But the very idea that Muslim populations living in the two "abodes," however they might be labeled, ought to obey two different sets of norms elicits sharp, negative response from many scholars on grounds that it threatens Islam's universality. Consider the response of Muhammad Saʿîd Ramadân al-Bûtî in June 2001 to this argument, in which he attacked those who call for a fiqh for minorities as part of the "plot aiming at dividing Islam."[15] Al-Bûtî distinguished between the false idea of special dispensations for those Muslims who live in Europe or North America and the valid idea that "whenever there is a hardship exceeding the moral limit, the legal permission which warrants canceling it persists." In other words, the easing of rules due to hardship has nothing to do with where a Muslim lives but rather depends on his or her specific circumstances. He pushes further, however, to recall the idea that if Muslims experience hardship, then they should leave non-Muslim lands:

> On the other hand, if the mere existence of Muslims in the land of disbelief may be considered a source of urgent need which justifies inventing new jurisprudence fitting for the circumstances of the land concerned and those residing in it, then perhaps it is those people whom God denotes when He says: "Indeed, those whom the angels take [in death] while wronging themselves—[the angels] will say, "In what [condition] were you?" They will say, "We were oppressed in the land." They [the angels] will say, "Was not God's earth spacious [enough] for you to emigrate therein?" For those, their refuge is Hell—and evil it is as a destination. (Qur'an, Al-Nisa' 4.97)[16]

Put another way: if you can't stand the heat, get out of the kitchen. Abode differences there may be, but they do not ipso facto relieve Muslims of their obligations to follow scripture.

Others attack the very notion of abodes. In 2001, a course on Islamic economics was offered at Hichem El Arafa's CERSI. The instructor, Khaled, raised the possibility that abodes should dictate which norms one follows, only to dismiss it. But some of his students did not even see the logic of the distinction. After several weeks of hadith study on ribâ, Khaled broached the question: "What should we, Muslims here in France, do?" He answered his own question:

> There are two opinions here. One is that when one is not in *dâr al-islâm* and thus without shari'a laws, then one may loan at interest. Abû Hanîfa delivered a fatwa to this effect, a response to a specific question . But this opinion is not widely followed. The second opinion is more generally followed, that we would like to stay here, in France, and develop roots here, and see what other communities have done. If you find the first fatwa acceptable, [if] you are at peace with it, then you can go ahead and loan with interest. Or you can wait and look for Islamic banks, or perhaps put your savings into an account and give the interest to the poor.

Even though Khaled opposed the Qaradâwî reasoning, a student immediately raised her hand to challenge the very idea of Islamic versus non-Islamic lands, and the implicit claim that Islamic lands followed the shari'a:

> Student: "But does a dâr al-islâm really exist?"
> Khaled: "Well, people in Iran or Sudan would say that it does there."

Student: "But in Saudi Arabia the banks are conventional ones, aren't they?"
Khaled: "Yes, there is a major contradiction here. The first Islamic bank began
in 1963, and it was in Egypt. Only 2–3 years ago did Saudi Arabia approve an
Islamic bank."

A powerful objection to talking of abodes is that it diminishes the universality of Islam. As a founder of the Tawhid group in Lyon, Yamin
Makri, put it, the idea of a fiqh for minorities abandons the "ambition
to the universal, an essential element of Islam" and is equivalent to, in a
society where Muslims are dominated by non-Muslims, seeking a "spiritual minimum wage."[17] I discussed the idea with Hichem El Arafa in
2003: "Sometimes words like this are used over and over again in fatwas,
and then they come to appear as principles without ever being thought
through. When people talk about a fiqh for minorities in Europe they
always do so in the sense of, 'Well, we are a minority, so we have to
adapt to the society around us.' This is the way the UOIF talks, but I
would rather we discuss what Islam could bring to the larger society." In
October 2005 we returned to the topic, and Hichem restated his opposition to this approach to Islamic norms for Europe. The idea of a fiqh of
minorities "closes people in on themselves, and it is not necessary. Look,
Muslims in India have formed a minority for a long time, and they did
not create a whole different structure there. The situation is not that different from that in other countries, say in Tunisia, where we do not have
all that we need for living perfect lives." He recalled that al-Qaradâwî
had argued that because rents were difficult in Europe, Muslims were
compelled to borrow from banks. "Why is the situation different elsewhere?" responded Hichem. "Here, my rent is protected, negotiated for
three years at a time and is renewable. In Tunisia, the owner could throw
you out in a month, and there is not written agreement, so the situation
is hardly better."

Hichem's point was telling, and provides a general justification for objecting to the fatwa on mortgage interest. Because the council had based
their ruling on empirical claims about housing conditions, and anyone
could bring up new empirical evidence, what is to prevent ordinary people from issuing new opinions? Do Islamic norms depend on, and fluctuate with, changing social conditions?

On this issue, the group of younger Muslims who were or are associated with Tariq Ramadan agree. We have already met Karim Azouz in
chapter three, where he discussed the activities of the French Muslims'
Collective. In 2005 he discussed his group's position, which in substance
if not in rhetoric approached that of al-Bûtî: "We talk about the idea of
a fiqh of minorities and we are against it; it makes people think they are
minorities. I do not think that you should say that the rule does not hold

here, that there is an exception for all who live in Europe, for example to buy a house with a bank loan. You could say that the rule holds but the conditions may or may not have been met. Then it would depend on each case, for each Muslim, whether conditions had or had not been met." He also said the al-Qaradâwî fatwa adopted the capitalist logic of investment and that could be contested, "but if that is the goal then it would be more defensible to use a loan to invest in a small business than to buy a house."

CONFRONTATIONS IN THE MOSQUE

These debates are transnational, and often they highlight competing notions of Islamic authority, about who should be able to voice an opinion about Islamic norms. Should it be Muslims living in the society in question, or the most sophisticated scholars of Islamic jurisprudence? These debates concern *how* best to reason through specific issues, which tools and modes of reasoning to apply, thus "meta-reasoning."

Every now and then one finds oneself in a setting where these questions come to the fore, as when I attended an all-afternoon mosque debate in 2002. Each year between 1994 and 2006, the Adda'wa mosque in Paris's nineteenth arrondissement has held panel discussions on a dozen or more Saturday afternoons. (In 2006 the mosque was closed for the construction of a new building.) The mosque's director, Larbi Kechat, presided over the panels, where the assigned topics ranged from the specifically Islamic (jurisprudence, spirituality) to the more broadly social (adoption, AIDS).[18] Among the five to eight panelists was always at least one non-Muslim, but the main draw was one or more speakers from the Middle East, who delivered their remarks in Arabic. A translator provided a short résumé of the Arabic-language presentations, but more than half the audience seemed to understand the modern standard Arabic in which the visitors spoke. (French was translated into Arabic only if a speaker required it.) Each session started after lunch and continued until eight or nine in the evening, with a break for prayers around six o'clock. The events were open, and drew one to two hundred people; a small charge covered the cost of a snack. The audience was invited to deliver questions in writing to the moderator, who would turn to one of the panelists for a response. Sometimes, someone would ask to deliver remarks orally, and a microphone placed on a stand in the seating area allowed that speaker to do so. More often than not these impromptu speakers chose to deliver their remarks in Arabic, and then the translator did as well as he or she could in providing a French summary of these often quite lengthy and usually impassioned speeches.

Larbi Kechat publicly presented these discussions as a dialogue between Muslims and non-Muslims, but they also were debates between traditionally trained scholars of Islam and European Muslims. If the latter described their efforts to adapt to European conditions, the former insisted that Muslims adhere to proper canons of learning and textual interpretation. The visiting scholars had the Islamic credentials and prestige absent among French Islamic scholars, and often they expressed their unhappiness with what they saw as uninformed interpretations of Islam made by self-trained scholars. In such cases they did not so much engage in dialogue as deliver a message. The presence of non-Muslim French speakers on the podium heightened rather than lessened the sense that Islam was centered somewhere else, in the Arabic-speaking world.

After having attended several of these panel discussions in 2001–2, I was invited to participate on a panel titled "Islamic jurisprudence, between rigor and laxity," on April 6, 2002. The main speaker was Dr. Mohamed Tawfik al-Bûti, son and intellectual heir of the more famous Sheikh Mohamed Saʿîd Ramadân al-Bûti, whose opinions we read earlier. Both taught in the Department of Islamic Jurisprudence at the University of Damascus, Syria.

Everyone on the panel made formal remarks, but the session centered on the talk given by al-Bûti, who spoke in Arabic with French translations. Al-Bûti criticized those who said that Islamic law (shariʾa) must be modified to fit the social conditions in different countries, and he had al-Qaradâwî clearly in his sights when he attacked those who would "dilute the rules of shariʾa, and free themselves from its restrictions in the name of integrating into Western societies." There was extensive discussion of these issues on the panel and then questions posed from the floor, but I will examine only the direct give and take between members of the audience and al-Bûti, because they highlight both the substantive issues of Islamic norms in Europe and the issue of who has the right to speak on them.

A medical doctor posed the first question (in Arabic). Dr. Moussa, dean of the faculty of Islamic Studies at Oran, Algeria, argued that we must adapt Islam to a changing world and adopt a "fiqh of reality," the term associated with al-Qaradâwî. He cited, as so many do, the initial revelations of the Qurʾan ("Recite!"), and a hadith of the Prophet Muhammad to the effect that "the entire Qurʾan directs us toward ijtihâd." He mentioned the case of a young woman working as an engineer who was told she had to remove her headscarf at work; she went to him for advice, and he could not resolve the problem. There is no solution to be found in scripture to these questions, said Dr. Moussa. "These are questions from the real world for which we try ijtihâd. . . . It is better that I support a clever young Muslim woman at work than cause her to leave her field." With that Dr. Moussa started to step away from the microphone, but al-

Figure 7.1 Panel at the Adda'wa mosque, 2002, showing Larbi Kechat at right

Bûti shot him a question: "Did you give her a fatwa telling her to remove the hijab?" "No, we told her to wear whatever she could. . . . We have to find a solution, it is better."

The next speaker took al-Bûti's argument farther and blamed scholars such as al-Qaradâwî for weakening Islam. "When Islam was attacked, mainly by the West, they did not succeed in destroying Islamic faith, but they worked hard on another issue, namely, relating religion to life. . . . They started attacking the fixed Islamic rules, and their attack led to a 'fiqh of reality.' We hear these days that some scholars approve of 'making halâl' things such as going without the hijab, borrowing at interest, or eating meat that has not been properly sacrificed."

A woman wearing a long gown with matching headscarf came forward to speak. She was a medical doctor and always wore a scarf. "It would have been easiest if I had taken off the headscarf for university. I had to stop my studies for a year and change towns before I found a situation where I could resume my study covered. . . . When looking for work I received a call from a professor of law, and I said, well, but I wear a scarf, and he said that is perfectly alright, and I have lived what God said." She then talked about how it was not easy to follow that route, and without mentioning his name criticized Dr. Moussa for having encouraged a woman to remove her scarf: "If I have a question about medicine I see a doctor, but when it concerns religion I look for someone who has the competence in that field, but people think they can all say something. . . ."

The moderator then chimed in to agree with this last point, saying in Arabic that only those competent to issue a fatwa should do so. Dr. Moussa had touched a raw nerve in what several saw as too free-wheeling an attitude toward ijtihâd. In his response, al-Bûti summarily dismissed everything that Dr. Moussa had said: "Dr. Moussa spoke. I allow him to talk about profound medical issues, but when he talks about profound matters of the *usûl al-fiqh* [the foundations of jurisprudence], then I do not permit him to talk, because this matter has been discussed thoroughly by scholars."

Al-Bûti clearly had been irked that Dr. Moussa would have dared to issue advice to the young woman faced with the question of covering her head at work. The next speaker from the floor irritated him still further. Hichem, a young student, wanted to return to the role of objectives of shari'a, the maqâsid, as justifications for changing Islamic norms. He said that al-Bûti should recall "the way [the caliph] 'Umar carried out ijtihâd to abrogate the scriptural penalty for theft, even though there is an explicit text. What does that example say about the idea that ijtihâd should be limited, and that we should make circumstances accord with the rules of shari'a, and not the other way around?" The question was a direct challenge to al-Bûti's earlier remarks, and the Syrian scholar took it up.

> I will remind you of my answer concerning al-maqâsid. In fact the maqâsid provide a description of the nature of the Islamic shari'a, not a separate source of rules. . . . There is an illegitimate innovation [*bid'a*] that some follow, called *ijtihâd al-maqâsid* [interpretation based on objectives]. Those people wish to make principles an alternative to the sources of law, and this must be absolutely rejected. . . . The other issue raised was the claim some people make, that Umar abrogated legal penalties [*hudûd*]. He did not abrogate the text but applied it. The penalty for theft has limits and conditions, which include taking other people's money because of urgent need. So, the poor person is not the real thief; it is actually the one who forced this poor person to steal. We may punish the poor man for his deed but not to the extent of applying the legal penalty. And there is a famous rule [to this effect]; I do not want to go into detail, as the matter has been thoroughly discussed.

Not that al-Bûti presented his approach as a literalist one. As he quickly made clear in his same response, the trained scholar, the mujtahîd, *does* consider "the spirit of the text and the conditions under which rules were applied." He then gave examples of scholars in the four Sunni legal schools arriving at different views on the matter of ribâ (specifically, whether you should take the nominal value of gold or silver, or the weight of these substances, in calculating fair exchange). "This is an attempt to use the human mind to extract the reason (*'illa*) for the text. There is nothing called literal translation; there is what is called the right spirit of Islamic shari'a, and the 'illa in the shari'a. Looking at the surface meaning of texts vanished a long time ago because it does not fit with the truth of Islamic law. I think that these are the questions that you asked."

Tawfik Al-Bûti affirmed the position his father had taken earlier in print, namely, that rules derived from scripture remain fixed and universal, and they already contain conditions for their application, and that is what all this talk about objectives and ijtihâd and the caliph 'Umar comes down to. Moreover, we, the scholars of fiqh, have worked all this out, and it behooves you, amateurs in the matter, to read what we have to say and get on with your own business.

THE TRANSNATIONAL ISLAMIC SPHERE

In this criticism of the innovators, al-Bûti is joined by other Muslim scholars teaching at institutions of authority in the Middle East. And it places them squarely against the reasoning pursued by Hichem and for that matter by Larbi Kechat, who frequently draws on the concept of maqâsid in his advice to French Muslims. Indeed, one of Larbi Kechat's goals in shaping the colloquia is to change the opinions of those who occupy authoritative positions in the Muslim world: "By bringing al-Bûti often, I hope that he changes his perspectives, and also that French intellectuals change theirs. One result of these contacts is that he listens."[19]

He mentioned his own trajectory as evidence of the positive effect in Islamic terms that exposure to European society can have:

> For me, coming here [to France] has meant that I am open to all the legal schools. When someone comes to me with a problem, I need to address it in a flexible way, to assess this person's situation. Otherwise I would have remained in the Mâlikî tradition, and it has some difficult aspects. For example, in the Mâlikî tradition it is difficult to combine the prayers, which we need to do in the winter here because the day is so short. And the Mâlikî school requires a woman to have a guardian represent her at marriage, whereas the Hanafî school does not. So I draw on the Hanafî school for that question.

Here, Larbi joins the others we have studied who look for an opinion that will have the desired social effect, rather than reasoning consistently from one legal tradition or school.

Like Hichem El Arafa, Larbi Kechat looks to the condition of the individual when responding to a question:

I try to respond to a question with the conscience of the questioner in mind. Once a man came to me and said that he was driving and the brakes failed, and as a result he killed someone; what should he do? The French legal process already was under way, but he felt that he had to do something in front of God. I said he should fast for two months in a row, but first I sized him up to make sure that he was physically and psychologically capable of doing that; and he was abundantly capable. I urge people to think of the objectives. People with means have started to make the hajj several times, and I tell them that in doing this you are doing it for your own passions, and that there are other things you can do with your wealth: start a school or help the poor or help a student. There is a danger of ritualizing Islam.

These considerations of objectives, conceived of in sociological and psychological terms, underlie Larbi Kechat's own socially pragmatic way of drawing on the traditions of Islamic jurisprudence and his disagreements with a scholar such as al-Bûti: "In matters of fiqh there are areas where al-Bûti and I would disagree, even though we agree in the broad lines. For example, there is the question of what it means if someone says the *talaq* three times at once. This often comes up; a young man came to see me recently asking this question. I draw on Ibn Taymiyyah—he sometimes is rather open in what he says—and he says that it counts as one."[20] Kechat is referring here to the question of whether pronouncing the repudiation three times in succession counts as one instance of divorce, in which case the couple can reconcile easily, or as three instances, in which case the wife must remarry before the husband can bring her back. "And I think about all the single-parent families and the unmarried women," he continued, "and I tell him to try and get back together with his wife, that they are still married. Al-Bûti is stricter on these issues and would probably answer that the man had definitively divorced her [thus, the three times]. Most of the scholars coming from the east are like that, and I talk with them before the seminars and ask them not to go into details about matters of fiqh. If there is a question that comes up to me from the floor (they all are written), I either just hang on to it, or I whisper to the sheikh and say, 'here is how you must answer this.' It is not our point to inflame matters."

I think that it is the commitment to social pragmatism that best describes the commonalities among the set of Islamic scholars and teachers working in France to whom we have listened so far in this book. They may disagree on specific questions and differ in which tools they emphasize in interpreting Islam, but in their justifications they cite both an Islamic norm or text *and* a desired social consequence of their position.

This shared pragmatism places them in opposition to scholars such as the al-Bûtis, for whom the rule, including the conditions already contained in it, is to be applied, not judged against its probable social effects.

But it does not cut off the possibility of dialogue with them. Consider, for example, the remarks made by Sheikh Muhammad Sa'îd Ramadân al-Bûtî at one of Larbi Kechat's sessions, held on June 18, 2005, on the general topic of religions in Europe. As it happened, al-Bûtî senior was the discussant for a presentation I made on the question of how Islamic norms will fit into Europe. He responded at length, with the following remarks on whether or not such components of the Islamic tradition as criminal penalties, polygamy, and the prohibition of interest were valid for Muslims living in Europe:

> The answer is that religious penalties [*hudûd*] can only be applied in *dâr al-islâm*, because they are part of a contract accepted by the whole society for the sake of harmony and peace for everyone; one cannot ask a society that has not signed this contract to apply these penalties. Someone who moves to France, we cannot ask the French state to apply them. And concerning polygamy: it is an authorization, not an obligation, so there is no contradiction with Western societies. In any case, for a man to marry more than one wife, there are stringent rules that are difficult to meet. On usury: a Muslim living in a non-Muslim country is free to avoid the use of usury in banks; this does not contradict his freedom, because he is using his freedom. Nor is there a contradiction when Muslim women use their freedom to wear what they want in accord with their religion. So we always find solutions; there are no contradictions. I rejoice that we share these ideas in a condition of fraternity.

We could read this answer as entirely intransigent. His invocations of freedom did not imply that religious obligations changed, and the reference to religious penalties mentioned only criminal penalties (*hudûd*). But it may be that his reference to the nature of the political contract as shaping obligations represents some degree of the opening hoped for by Larbi Kechat.

But whatever their disagreements, the debates in which these actors and others take part define, by virtue of their justificatory structure, a global, transnational Islamic space. By insisting that arguments remain rooted within a broad "Islamic realm of justification," the Muslims taking part define the space as Islamic, rather than French or European or "modern" or "liberal." They may also take account of norms, laws, and social conditions prevailing in France, but only as elements that are *normatively external but pragmatically internal* to the debates. Participants base their arguments on Islamic forms of reasoning, and their meta-arguments are about preferences among alternative forms of reasoning. They may wish the outcome to have a good fit to current conditions, but they will propose justifications in terms of rules of jurisprudence or the objectives of shari'a. Larbi Kechat, Dhaou Meskine, or Hichem El Arafa may "internalize" French conditions in a pragmatic way, selecting among alternative interpretive pathways so as to end up urging husbands to reconcile with their wives, or allowing Muslims to buy homes from banks—or not allowing such loans, so that Muslims become more financially creative![21] But the interpretive pathways are Islamic ones.

The transnational space that arises from Islamic justifications is global without being either "postnational," in the sense of succeeding earlier events bounded by state boundaries, or "European," in the sense of delimiting themselves to a normatively specific Europe. Nor does it depend on perduring ties to specific places, as often is the case with transnational religious movements.[22] Al-Bûti was not present in Paris as a link to Syria, and he could have been speaking in Jakarta, Lahore, or Chicago (as, indeed, he probably has done) or through the Internet.[23]

As the young French Muslim attends these and other debates and lectures, he or she can follow a thread of reasoning about Islam that combines an emphasis on principles with a general spirit of social pragmatism. The global circulation of these pragmatic ideas, from Qaradâwî and his circle, through diverse European schools and mosques, through the North American ISNA network, and also through much of the Muslim-majority world, makes it possible for the young Muslim man or woman to develop a sense of one globally pursued line of reasoning, available from a wide variety of sources and in a number of different languages. But at the same time he or she would be well aware of sharply opposed Islamic positions, whether from witnessing objections made on French soil or from reading denunciations of Qaradâwî on Web sites (such as that associated with al-Albâni) or in inexpensive books. Many young French Muslims prefer these latter positions; indeed, the director of the Tawhid bookstore in Saint-Denis told me that while for him, "Qaradâwî is our sheikh," his sales reflect different preferences: "The young people prefer al-Albâni to Qaradâwî because he is more straightforward." And while these "straightforward" writers attract one portion of the public, scholars more concerned with the traditions of Islamic jurisprudence (such as al-Bûti, father and son) criticize the French directions at least as severely. That there are Islamic spaces of dialogue and debate by no means leads to a homogenization of Islamic reasoning; these new forms of publicity in fact make it easier for the ordinary Muslim to encounter distinct and opposed forms of Islamic reasoning.

CHAPTER EIGHT

Negotiating across Realms of Justification

ALTHOUGH SOME FRENCH MUSLIMS might carry on deliberations within a transnational Islamic realm of justification, they live in the political space of France. Indeed, many Muslims in France consider their social lives to be mainly governed by French norms, while others, doubtless a much smaller number, might see only Islamic rules as shaping their lives. For those in the middle, those who see both Islamic and French rules as relevant, either because they see them both as legitimate or because they see a practical reason to pay attention to both, life is a bit more complicated. How do they combine or accommodate or broker among these competing sets of norms?

I consider here the case of marriage and divorce, where French laws and Islamic norms set out quite distinct procedures. French law requires that a couple marry at city hall; marriages conducted by religious officials not only have no legal value but are technically illegal if conducted prior to the state wedding. This restriction was intended to emphasize the domination of the Republic over the Church and clearly states the French commitment to the priority of secular marriage and its absolute separation from religious rituals. Although originally passed with priests in mind, in 2008 it was used to levy penalties on two French imams. Religious officials do not have mandates to certify marriages legally, as they do in England and the United States. Divorce requires a civil judge, and may be initiated by either party.

Islam, for its part, focuses on the relationship between the bride and groom. Each must consent to the marriage, and he must give her a token of the marriage, a bridal gift or *mahr*. The function of the mahr varies widely from region to region: it may be merely symbolic (a Qur'an) or it may amount to a substantial sum intended to rest unpaid, giving the wife leverage in case of future disputes.[1] In most Islamic legal traditions the bride must have a male guardian present who agrees to the marriage, and there must be witnesses. Although a religious official may recite verses and the event may take place in a religious setting, these features are not required. A husband may unilaterally divorce his wife by pronouncing the talaq formula; a wife may request that a religious judge dissolve the marriage following Islamic rules.

BETWEEN HALÂL AND THE HÔTEL DE VILLE

Although the basic Islamic rules may seem simple, young Muslims regularly ask local imams for clarification, and often discuss issues related to marriage and divorce on France-centered Islamic Internet sites. Let us follow one exchange of opinions that took place recently on a Web discussion forum. A young Muslim woman introduces herself to readers: she is French, living in Aubervilliers (north of Paris), and of Algerian origin, and anticipating her "religious marriage" in the coming months. She will wed an Algerian man at her mother's home and, wishing to ensure that it conform to religious norms, poses a question on an Internet site about what she should expect.[2]

A French Muslim woman responds, describing her own marriage in Algeria two years earlier, at a time when she was sixteen. She had converted to Islam well before the marriage, in part because of her parents' interest in the religion. She had met the man she would marry when he had visited from Algeria. She describes what she sees as the essence of the religious ceremony: the obligatory presence of her father and of witnesses, the gift from her husband (the *mahr*), and the blessings recited by the imam. She also explains that in Algeria the ceremony is called *les fiançailles*, the engagement, but that in fact it constitutes the Islamic marriage. A few days before writing her response on the internet, she and her husband had married at her local city hall in France. "I had wanted to marry [in civil fashion] right away but unfortunately a law was passed that forbid girls under 18 from marrying even with their father's permission, especially when my husband lives in Algeria and it is difficult for him to come here. The only time he came to my house and the first time I saw him was when I was 15; of course I was not yet ready to marry but 9 months later I was!"[3]

On a different Web site another woman (a French convert) asks how to make sure that her marriage (to an Algerian man) will be *halâl* (permitted). She, too, receives an answer in the form of a personal narrative.[4] Her respondent, a Belgian convert, had tried to marry at the local Islamic center, but the center had refused to marry the couple unless they first married according to Belgian civil law.[5] "That's entirely normal; it is to prevent abuses," she comments. "Some people marry before God and then very quickly forget their promises after sharing their wife's bed." But they had wanted to marry religiously before marrying at city hall, and finally found an imam who would come to their house. The imam explained that her husband was required to give her a gift to make the marriage legal (she had wanted to forgo it), and she received enough "to buy two pairs of fantastic earrings that I wore at our civil ceremony as a symbol." Although parents should give permission for a marriage, she explained, hers were not Muslim, "so the question never arose." Apparently the imam did not raise the issue. They had two Muslim men as witnesses. "By following these steps you won't have a marriage certificate but your union will be Halal."

Others weighed in regarding both cases, giving their experiences and points of view. They all took as a valid premise that marrying in a religious or "halâl" manner was the important thing to do, and that making it official in the eyes of the state was of lesser importance. No one worried too much about the relationship between the two kinds of marriages. Some of the people who joined in on the first discussion did enter into a debate as to whether or not it was worthwhile to make the marriage official at all; several pointed out that you did need help from the French state from time to time and that having the marriage on one's birth certificate helped in that regard, as a practical necessity. In the second discussion, the bride was proud to wear her earrings, the token of her halâl marriage, at the civil ceremony, as a sign, at least to herself, that she already had married in the only way that really mattered. (No one mentioned to her that the absence of a male guardian at her religious marriage could be seen to have invalidated it; that the imam approved of the marriage seems to have satisfied everyone.)

It may seem surprising that in these cases, young Muslims in France would seek advice on fairly complicated matters on Internet discussion forums. After all, a young Muslim living in Aubervilliers—the town of Dhaou Meskine's Islamic day school—has access to the Islamic scholars, mosques, and institutes of higher learning found across the northern Parisian suburbs. The converts to Islam who took part in the exchanges may have been particularly eager to find authoritative responses to their concerns, as converts often are, but in fact they would have been more likely than others to have met regularly with a local imam as part of converting. The choice by these Muslims to seek advice on Internet forums should be seen in terms of the additional value they hoped to find there, rather than as stemming from an absence of information around them. Let me consider for a moment what the attraction of such sites might be.

These open Web forums differ from two other forms of Islamic electronic information that we could call the "electronic text" and the "question-and-answer site." Some of the best-known Islamic Web sites feature articles by noted scholars we have already encountered in earlier chapters, such as al-Bûtî, al-Albâni, or al-Qaradâwî. These sites thus represent different ways to find the same information that one might otherwise find in a bookstore: one-way, authoritative treatises on various topics, sometimes with the advantage of availability in multiple languages. Other French-language Islamic sites are edited by Muslims probably unknown to most of those who happen on the site, but provide clear opinions on a wide range of important topics, from family life to work issues to matters of spirituality.[6] These sites are, then, electronic versions of texts, differing little in form or content from paper versions.

Quite different in their forms are the Islamic sites based on the traditional format of questions and answers. Historically, a religious opinion or fatwa was generated in this way, as a response to a specific question put to a knowledgeable scholar. Some sites feature fatwa sections that are structured in this way, as internal components to broader sites. One of the best-known such sites is islamonline.com, with its links to the European Council for Fatwa and Research and to the Islamic Society of North America (ISNA). The site features an updated fatwa bank, and the ability to post questions and receive answers from recognized Islamic scholars.[7]

These two types of sites both frame what they do as providing definitive answers, sometimes from distant lands, to be accepted and applied. Many young Muslims look for horizontal forms of exchange rather than authoritative replies. They also might wish to explain their particular situation in detail and to have it taken into account, and to encourage others to ask relevant questions, something not possible on the other types of sites. Many Muslims in Europe have made shari'a into a set of individual commitments, and seek to compare opinions with others. The forums are well-suited to this sort of communication and knowledge seeking, and may be attractive for these reasons, even if the participants may not be well versed in religious matters.[8]

The exchange of opinions does not necessarily lead to greater clarity. What does it mean to say a marriage is halâl, as did the participants in the above exchanges? On the Internet and in everyday discussions in France it becomes clear that a grand confusion reigns. Is a marriage halâl if the couple follows the religious steps helpfully outlined by the respondents on the Internet sites mentioned above, regardless of whether they also marry at city hall? Or does the phrase "halâl marriage" indicate that the man and woman have made a binding promise before God and *refuse* to travel to city hall? Or does it mean the opposite: *requiring* that the couple marry in city hall, so that the state may ensure that both parties adhere to their promises? One finds all of these opinions prominently expressed.

Here transnational linguistic borrowings further cloud the question. In Algeria and Morocco, the French term *fiançailles* (engagement), with its sense of constituting a promise to wed, came to be used to refer to the Islamic marriage ritual, the *nikah*, with its witnesses, the consent of the bride's father or other male guardian, and the marriage gift. That it did so was reasonable: in both a French engagement and an Islamic marriage, a promise is made between the two parties, usually with the approval of the parents. The celebration can come later. The North African usage has now been appropriated by couples living in France. For some of them, using these terms may indicate a belief that Islam countenances an engagement, that is, a relationship prior to marriage.[9]

Hence the question posed on another Internet discussion as to whether "halâl marriage" means the same as *fiançailles* as the term is used in Algeria.[10] The respondents have different ideas on this question, but they all agree that the real marriage is the religious one, the halâl. As one person explains, "This halâl is quite simply the marriage before God, after which the couple may consummate the marriage, live together, and so forth, and afterwards if they wish they may carry out the civil marriage. But God considers breaking the halâl as a DIVORCE [caps in original]."[11]

Thinking that the Islamic marriage is akin to the French engagement provides a temporal schema for thinking about marriage in France. It suggests that one should first enter into a contract (halâl marriage for Muslims, *fiançailles* for others), and later on have the celebration at city hall, if one wishes to do so. In this way of looking at things, the Islamic marriage, the nikah, is assimilated not to the church wedding but to the initial act of commitment, as a private arrangement with no state-legal effects. As I mentioned above, this temporal ordering runs counter to the official French model, in which religious ceremonies should follow the civil marriage, but it makes sense if one reads French marriage practices through a North African lens.

The above respondent's reference to divorce, and his apparent need to capitalize the word for emphasis, raises a question much discussed in France among Muslims: how do you *break* a halâl marriage if there was no written marriage contract or certificate? The issue is discussed because it is unclear what recourse is left to a wife whose "halâl husband" abandons her. Many Muslims are concerned about this problem. Although a Muslim husband may divorce his wife on his own, a Muslim wife has no corresponding way of ending the marriage by herself. In countries with Muslim judges, she may ask that the marriage be annulled or the husband be asked to grant a divorce, but France has neither Islamic judges nor Islamic arbitration panels.[12]

Both issues—how to divorce, and the weakness of the halâl bonds— arose in a long Web exchange entitled "Breaking the halâl [marriage]," in which a woman asked how she might divorce when she had married in halâl fashion but not with a civil ceremony.[13] The respondents began to ask for details about her marriage, and troubling facts began to emerge. At her marriage, held in France, she saw no imams (though someone led prayers in an adjoining room); she had no male guardians; and there were no witnesses other than her husband's family members. No marriage gift was exchanged ("but he paid for my dress and rings"); no piece of paper attests to the event.

The responders are nervous, pretty sure that the absence of a guardian and witnesses means she never had properly married even in Islamic terms, and, as she had consummated the marriage (they asked), they were pretty sure that she was not *"dans les règles,"* as they rather delicately put it. One suggested she find "the imam who celebrated the marriage," although there appears to have been no such person; others offered solutions as to how to divorce. "Is it not the case that one or the other of you says three times 'I divorce you'?" asked one reader. This is a group effort; everyone chipping in with their ideas. Several cited books of fiqh; others brought up the amount of the marriage gifts paid by the Prophet. Each drew from the exchange a bit more knowledge of Islamic norms, whether correct or not, thanks to the questioner's unfortunate experience.

At this point someone introduced a discordant note, which moved the discussion off the topic of divorce and back to the issue of the halâl vis-à-vis city hall. "Let me remind participants who are unaware that for the marriage to be valid in Islam, you must have both the halâl and city hall (or a body representing the state). If one or the other is missing, then the marriage is invalid. Islam requires this to avoid the sort of unfortunate event our sister has undergone." A lively debate commenced that left the poor woman's problems behind and continued on for the rest of the day. One participant exclaimed that "city hall does not validate a marriage! . . . If for you, marrying in front of a guy in a bow tie with the red white and blue flag is more important than [marrying] before God, good for you! . . . [The official] does not believe in God and says Muhammad (peace be upon him) is an impostor, and it is *his* signature that will make my marriage halâl? . . . God says in the Qur'an: '*wa kafa billahi shahida*' [and God is sufficient as a witness]."

Some agreed with this view, others argued that civil marriage would have kept the unfortunate young woman from falling into her predicament, because had she married at city hall she now would have a legal means to divorce. One respondent cited a scholar who often writes on the Web sites oumma.com and mejliss.com, Ahmed Elouazzani, to the effect that you must register the marriage with civil authorities to prevent certain young men from failing to fully enter into the obligations of marriage. References were made to other eminent legal scholars (al-Qaradâwî, Ibn Baz) without citations. The argument degenerated into name-calling. The woman who started it all interjected, "So, I've been had. . . ." No one responded; the debate had moved on.

Why the "Halâl" Marriage?

The question of which norms young Muslims should follow when deciding to "marry" has been on the minds of many in France for some time, for reasons poignantly captured in the woman's parting cry, "So, I've been had." Most of the scholars engaged in teaching or preaching are barraged with questions by young Muslim women and men, and most of those questions are about marriage and divorce.

In chapter three we met Najjar Mondher, the imam of the main mosque in Lyon. "In my three years now in Lyon I have come to understand that many people want to marry 'in halâl fashion,' as they say, which means they do not go to city hall. They have the girl's father or a representative, two witnesses, the couple, an imam, and a gift to symbolize the marriage. You know, an imam could be imprisoned for six months for marrying a couple first—but they do it anyway!"

Najjar was particularly adamant about refusing to carry out such marriages. "We refuse to marry someone without a civil marriage. It causes problems when they do this if the couple separates and the husband will not give the wife a divorce. She has nowhere to turn to divorce. [JB: Why do people want to marry this way?] One reason is that they want it to be religious only and don't want to bother with the rest. But also often the man wants to be able to move on to a different woman later. [JB: So why does he not divorce her?] Well, sometimes to punish her. . . ."

Najjar added that the parents in the end acquiesce in these halâl marriages. "The parents might prefer that the couple marry at city hall, but they have no control over them if they are already twenty to twenty-five years old, so they say 'at least marry halâl,' and the couple usually agree to that." Najjar also made more precise the reasons why no one could answer the question posed in the Web site discussion cited earlier, how do you break a halâl marriage if you live in France? If the wife wants to divorce, neither the state nor his office can help her. "The state does not recognize the marriage. I have nothing to recommend, because I am not a judge, so I cannot divorce a couple, apply a *khula* divorce with payment, which would be the wife's right. I tell them that marriage is for life." Najjar's account is a pragmatic one: because France lacks the religious judicial institutions that could apply a religious divorce, a woman should ensure her future ability to free herself from an unsuccessful marriage by marrying in civil fashion. The state not only provides legal force to preserve the marriage, it also provides the mechanism to leave the marriage that, in other societies, might be provided by an Islamic judge.

But Najjar also brought up a reason why some parents, and some imams, recognize, if grudgingly, the value of the halâl-only marriage: at least it places the union in the religious domain. Such was Dhaou Meskine's reasoning. In chapter three I reported that after the prayer service at his mosque in 2006, a man had asked Dhaou if he could marry a woman religiously without undergoing a civil ceremony, and Dhaou said categorically no, that he must not, because what if they were to divorce? "They want to do this because they do not want to have anything to do with the state," he told me afterward. In June 2007 I spoke to his older students and their parents about religion and law. The issue of halâl marriage, or "Fatiha marriage" (so called because the Qur'anic verse al-Fatiha is recited at the wedding) came up. "It is a major problem," said one woman. "In one case I know, the couple had a child, and the father refused to recognize it, and there was nothing the woman could do because they were not married."

Given these remarks, I was surprised when, later on the same day, I asked Dhaou about the problem, and he said, "It is better that people marry young. You should not put too much pressure on the young or they will not follow the correct way. Many in France, Muslim or not, prefer not to marry, because it constrains you and requires that you do this or that, and many prefer just to live in concubinage: both parties have all the same rights that way. Sometimes they have the Fatiha marriage first; that provides a moral constraint, much better than not having that bond. [JB: So there is a good side to only marrying in the mosque?] Yes, it is better than without it." He saw the increase in legal age of marriage, enacted several years ago, from sixteen to eighteen as "preventing Muslim girls from marrying young" and thus contributing to the rise in religious-only marriage—a view substantiated anecdotally by the Web discussion cited above.

Note that Dhaou's approval of the halâl marriage without the civil marriage was only for those who had not reached eighteen. Furthermore, when I mentioned the fear that the woman would be endangered, he replied, "No, they can always register their concubinage." Indeed, French law does allow for a couple to register their status of *concubinage* (roughly equivalent to an American common-law marriage) with a notary, but unless they enter into a civil union (a *pacte civil de solidarité*, PACS), they have difficulty making financial claims on each other if they subsequently decide to dissolve their union.[14] The law has little to say about this situation (or about the private arrangements of couples in general).[15] If a couple of any religion has a religious marriage without a civil marriage, then they are considered to be in concubinage; the religious marriage has no effect, positive or negative, on their legal status.[16]

The French criminal code (article 433-21) does penalize a minister who performs a religious marriage without the couple having previously married according to the law. Until 2008, the statute, originally aimed at Catholic priests trying to subvert the institutions of the Republic, had not been applied to imams. The incidence of halâl marriages became an issue in June 2007, when *Le Monde* published an article on the practice. The newspaper called these marriages "illegal," and noted that no imams yet had been arrested, in part because it was difficult to inspect Islamic marriages because they may be celebrated in private.[17] Someone reading the article, Muslim or not, might have concluded that all young people entering into a halâl marriage had been violating the law and risked six months' imprisonment and and a fine of 7,500 euros.[18] The article was probably motivated by a question posed to the Interior Ministry the previous February by a deputy, who, after claiming that "in most towns" few Muslims marry in civil fashion, urged the minister to remind imams of the law. *Le Monde* did not see fit to publish the response from the ministry, which argued that in Islam marriage is a civil contract, and that if an imam was present it was but "incidental, to deliver a short prayer."[19] If the ministry's view is correct and an Islamic marriage is a civil contract, then it is difficult to see what distinguishes it in the eyes of the law from the celebration of a concubinage, or in what way it violates the law. What probably moved *Le Monde* to mention the problem was less the technical legal question but the worry that those who enter into Islamic marriages do so in order to remain outside the sphere of French society.

One year later, two courts did take action against imams for having illegally celebrated marriages. In June, the criminal court at Orléans sentenced an imam to pay 1,500 euros for having celebrated two marriages of couples not already married legally. The prosecutor may have decided to act because the couples wished to use the religious event to convince immigration authorities that their marriage was sincere and not merely a means to obtain residency papers.[20] In October 2008, an imam at Meaux was placed under examination for a similar offense. Echoing the Internet exchanges we read above, he claimed to have merely "celebrated *fiançailles*" for the couples.[21] He also was accused of embezzling funds, and was party to a dispute between two rival associations.

The French legal status of an Islamic marriage has yet to be settled, but in the space between Islamic and legal marriages, different actors in French public life, Muslims and non-Muslims will continue to construct various versions of how a French Muslim ought to marry. Marriage is not only a technical matter of registration and obligation but a symbol of social and moral order, or *ordre public* (a legal category to which I return below). The divergence or convergence of rules for marriage can be taken as indexing a divergence or convergence of broader moral worlds.

CONVERGENCE I: FROM ISLAM TO THE SECULAR

Indeed, on these and other issues, some Muslims in France and elsewhere in Europe have looked for points of encounter, resemblance, and convergence between Islamic norms and European ones. They criticize as too negative and narrow the Qaradâwî approach we considered in the last chapter—that you may neglect this or that Islamic rule because living in Europe is so difficult—and ask whether Islamic value can be accorded to features of French, and more broadly European, social life.

Should Muslims consider certain French institutions to provide legitimate answers to problems of social life? Perhaps these institutions are
moral and legal equivalents of Islamic institutions. Arguing in this way
requires valuing the general meaning or intent of an Islamic rule over
the social form historically realized in what are considered as "Muslim
countries."

Hichem El Arafa reasoned in this way to explain why Muslims should
consider the civil marriage at city hall to be required on *Islamic* terms:

> Some people think that having to go to city hall and fill out forms is too much
> work, and moreover they consider marriage to be a religious matter—and they
> do so all the more because some Islamic authorities say that marriage is reli-
> gious. They say that the Prophet, in his time, did not have laws about register-
> ing marriage, so it is not necessary for Muslims to do so. But then you can
> say—and this may make you laugh, but there is something to it—that back
> then, the society was composed of tribes, and if someone married he never
> would just leave his spouse because his life would be in danger, everyone knew
> each other then, so there was no need for these regulations. But now it is differ-
> ent. That is reasoning according to the purposes [*maqâsid*] of Scripture.

Marrying in city hall is thus indicated by scripture, because scripture's
passages on marriage have as their purpose to make marriage a stable
contract. Hichem has seen what happens when couples do not have that
contract, and it has led him, like Najjar at Lyon, to refuse all requests to
perform Islamic weddings at a mosque or elsewhere, unless the couple
also marries at city hall. "I refuse, because if they only marry like that,
they do not take it seriously. There are disagreeable things that happen as
a result. In some cases the couple marries in Islamic fashion with an imam
but soon after decide that they are incompatible and they divorce, also
in Islamic fashion [with the husband repudiating his wife with a simple
declaration, the *talaq*]. But if they had married first at city hall then their
agreement [*pacte*] would have been stronger, as it should be in Islam, and
they would have been more likely to stay together."

Hichem thought that it would be possible to make the civil marriage
perform the function of an Islamic marriage. "It ought to be easy to create an event that makes the state marriage also an Islamic one, for it contains almost all of the elements, lacking only the element that the family
must agree to the marriage, so you could have witnesses to the civil marriage, and then the girl's father would meet with the couple and the imam
right after the marriage to announce that he agrees to it." Civil divorce,
however, poses greater hurdles; the long delays involved in obtaining a
divorce lead many couples to become impatient and dispense with what
they consider to be a legal formality, and simply have the husband pronounce the repudiation formula.

Hichem's view of marriage highlights the objectives of scripture and the major elements of Islamic marriage (the contract, the witnesses) and strips away its inessential elements (that it takes place in a mosque, that some words are pronounced in Arabic). This approach does not convince everyone. "Sometimes shocking people can have its place, but here we have to make them understand. I can remember speaking to students about things and having them feel irritated at me. For example, I explained that marriage in Islam was not religious, that a civil marriage was sufficient, and they clearly did not like that. [JB: What did they say?] Some said, 'well, there was no city hall in the Prophet's time, so marrying at city hall is not in accord with Islam.'

"What we need," he added in 2006,

> is to have real statistical studies that count the number of marriages like this, and of them how many had problems and led to divorce, and then document the problems the people had. I hear many of these cases, terrible cases, but do not write them down. Then we need to develop arguments on the marriage that imams—I mean ones with education, not just people who happened to become imams [*imams par circonstance*]—can agree on, and then if they each start telling people they need to be married, not just practice customary marriage—because that is a better term than religious, it is not really religion, the *nikah*—then people might start to follow. But we should work within the tradition, take concepts, such as from Shâtibî, on maqâsid, and work from there to these cases. Here is what Shâtibî says: "If you practice something that is in the tradition and it has negative consequences, causes damages, then you need to rethink whether or not it is legal." But then you have to reason about the particular case, not just cite the general principle, because if you do that some imams might say, "Well, maybe," but they won't change anything. Here is where the sociological study would come in, because then you could see that there are negative consequences, and be more likely to follow this reasoning. Reasoning this way is different from those outside the tradition who instrumentalize the concept of maqâsid.[22]

Indeed, Hichem ties the justification for innovation more explicitly to empirical facts: the more damaging the consequence of avoiding city hall, the more justified is proclaiming civil marriage to be Islamic in nature. Larbi Kechat was willing to go one step further:

> I say that if you marry at the city hall, you have already made an Islamic marriage, because all the conditions for that marriage have been fulfilled: the consent of the two parties is required, and there are two witnesses, and they then can give a ring as the mahr—the mahr can be anything, the recitation of *al-Fatiha*, for example. The ceremony in the mosque is a benediction of the marriage. And also the marriage constrains the two people, so the husband

cannot simply leave, and that meets an Islamic maqâsid, so registering the marriage with the state fulfills a maqâsid.

The Swiss scholar Tariq Ramadan takes a similar position. Ramadan finds al-Qaradâwî's European Council to be unimaginative and trapped in an old style of fiqh, engaging in a juristic bricolage, as he put it, an effort to create a "fiqh lite" without rethinking it in European terms. Ramadan agrees with Meskine that fiqh should be universal, but he would locate the universal dimension at the level of general principles.[23] On marriage, he urges Muslims to recognize that the nature of marriage is a contract. "A civil marriage already is a Muslim marriage, I think, because it is a contract, and that is what a Muslim marriage is." More generally, the European law of contracts corresponds to the Islamic law of contracts, and Muslims are just as obliged to respect contracts with non-Muslims as with Muslims; "that is a universal element of fiqh, valid anywhere. If we take this step, then we can accept much of European law."[24]

This line of reasoning thus begins with the claim that civil marriage fulfills (or easily could fulfill) the conditions for an Islamic marriage because both are, in essence, contracts. But one could accept this equivalence and still prefer to marry only Islamically. The argument in favor of civil marriage over Islam-only marriage must then rest on more than the equivalence of the two practices; in these arguments, it is the positive social consequences of civil marriage that provide its Islamic justification.

This kind of argument has been more fully developed by the director of the Bordeaux Mosque, Tareq Oubrou. Born in 1960 in Morocco, Oubrou, along with many prominent Muslim figures linked to religious concerns, first studied natural sciences—in his case, biology. Oubrou distinguishes between obligatory ritual (*ibâdât*) and social norms (*mu'âmalât*). The former does not change, but the latter may be realized either as law or as ethics, he claims, depending on the political context within which one lives. In a country with Islamic law and social institutions, social norms are realized as law. In countries such as France, where such realization is impossible, Muslims must "ethicize" these norms. He offered an example:

> If a woman comes to me and says, "My husband beats me; do I have the right to ask for a divorce?" then I say: "Yes, divorce him; and when the judge pronounces the divorce you will be divorced, ethically speaking, religiously speaking." So we "ethicize" the Islamic law on divorce: the same values, but we choose the idea from the legal tradition that is more subtle—in this case, for example from the Mâlikî, or another, whichever can best respond to the spirit of the shari'a and also to the society into which Muslims integrate sociologically and anthropologically in French citizenship.[25]

As with al-Qaradâwî and the European Council, Oubrou combines a selection of rulings from legal traditions with a use of the maqâsid. He also joins al-Qaradâwî in advocating a "shari'a for minorities," by which he means the conditions under which Muslims can exist in secularized France, Islam's adaptation to France.[26] Scholars are to provide fatwas that give concrete form to that adaptation, developing forms of shari'a that fit France. Oubrou also argues for a specific methodology: first look to the norms of French culture and the requirements of French law, and then look for the Islamic legal options that offer the best fit with these parameters. In many cases it is the Hanafî or Mâlikî tradition that meets these conditions and the Hanbalî approach (followed in Saudi Arabia) that is the strictest, but Oubrou points out that sometimes this is not the case:

> Sometimes there are zones in Hanbalî law that are more supple than in Hanafî or Mâlikî law, for example on polygamy. Mâlikî law says the husband has to receive the permission of the first wife [to take a second], but the Hanbalî position is by way of the needs of society [*maslaha*], that if the culture is monogamous, then so is the shari'a on this point. I always say, if the first wife accepts the second, then why should I interfere? We accept homosexuality, polyandry, why not a man and a woman? It is scandalous.

Oubrou's argument on this point, couched in the somewhat free-flowing terms of our verbal exchange, makes explicit the socially pragmatic reasoning that, as we have seen, many scholars practice. He seeks to develop an Islamic normative base for a way of life that would be in accord with French social norms and French law. Thus, if the broad society is monogamous, then Islamic norms also must point toward monogamy as the appropriate marital form, and he selects those elements that lead to this conclusion. But he also insists that Islamic norms might on some counts *improve* on French ones. If French men can have mistresses as well as wives, as do many prominent public figures, then would it not be better to legalize these relationships by permitting polygamy?

The Objectives of Halâl Rules for Food

Tareq Oubrou has pursued this same line of reasoning with regard to other questions of fitting Islamic norms to French conditions. Many Muslim living in France find it challenging to find trustworthy sources of halâl meat and to find properly sacrificed meat for the annual Feast of Sacrifice. For meat to be halâl, the animal must have been killed in the appropriate manner, with a swift cut to avoid suffering and a reciting of the Bismillah to emphasize that the life is taken in God's name, and the carcass drained of blood and kept carefully separate from non-halâl foods. For meat to count as the sacrifice performed on the day commemorating Abraham's willingness to sacrifice his son, the animal must be killed after the morning congregational prayer.

To find halâl food, you can look for labels in butcher shops or supermarkets indicating that an inspection service (such as the AVS, discussed in chapter four) guarantees the food's provenance, but how do you know that the beef or chicken really was produced according to halâl specifications? Tareq Oubrou has argued that halâl is more a matter of trust in one's butcher than in carefully verifying each step of the production process. In a widely cited 2000 article, he wrote that one should look to the objectives of the Qur'an: whether or not a Bismillah was pronounced at the moment does not affect the legal status of the meat purchased by a Muslim, he said. One should instead choose one's butcher with his character in mind: does he pray and avoid telling lies?[27] In any case one ought to realize that the Islamic rules were justified by their hygienic rationale: "Why does Islam refuse to eat meat that has not been cleansed of it blood? It is precisely because the blood contains unhealthy germs."[28] In conversations with me in late 2002 he expanded on his reasoning:

Halâl meat? That's different; people confuse the ritual act that is Abraham's sacrifice with an act that is not ritual, there is no "kosherizing" of killing the animal, it is not part of ritual [ibâdât]; it is part of ethics, of mu'âmalât, that the animal be healthy. So the question is how best to kill, and the best way is to cut the transmission between the neurons and the rest of the animal, by cutting the throat, and evacuating the blood immediately; this is the most humane way to kill the animal, as it causes it to lose all feeling, because the oxygen stops.

Secondly, letting out blood rids the animals of germs; I classify it in ethics and do not sacralize it; canonists do not require the pronouncement of the Bismillah at the moment of sacrifice. Of course, people will cite the Qur'an, but you must read the Qur'an; at the time, people sacrificed for idols, so as a reflex, the Qur'an asked them to do it in the name of God. The Prophet himself allowed Â'isha an exemption from this rule. She told him that people had brought them meat and she did not know whether or not they had said the Bismillah or not before killing it, and the Prophet said, you say it before eating. It's really not the end of the world.

But it is sure that if the blood stays in the animal the animal remains forbidden in the ethical sense of the term but not in the ritual sense, because we are in a different register. Even Muslims have taken over categories from the West, because "the rite," "the sacred," did not exist in Arabic thought, the idea of purity and impurity—those are problems exported from a Judeo-Christian register.[29]

Of course, many Muslims object to this reasoning. The *La Médina* article prompted at least one reader to object that (in a letter published in the following issue), "to think in that way is to empty Islam of its meaning, to reduce it to its surface appearance, and to turn aside from the object of all Muslim acts, namely the adoration of God."

Although he disagreed on other points with Tareq Oubrou, Tariq Ramadan has taken similar stands regarding halâl:

> I think that the universal rules have to do with lessening the suffering of the animal, and not with technicalities about how the killing takes place. AVS takes a very strict position, for example forbidding electric stunning and requiring that a Muslim do the killing. That is alright because it means that everyone can agree with them, but only so long as they allow others to have their own positions. For example, in Switzerland we import meat and cannot enforce the same rules. Qaradâwî has said that all meat killed by ahlul kitab ["people of the book," referring to Jews and Christians] is halâl. Saudi Arabia, after all, imports meat from Germany.[30]

In chapter two we discussed the logistical difficulties of getting meat to Muslims who wish to celebrate the Feast of Sacrifice. If one wishes to celebrate the feast day on the day of the congregational prayer, then the sacrifice must take place in the very narrow window between the morning prayer and dinner. For years, municipal authorities and mosque officials have tried various solutions; the difficulties have led many Muslims to reevaluate the importance of the sacrifice. In 2003, Hichem El Arafa told me that he had not sacrificed for several years:

> For one thing the children do not like meat very much. One year we had a lot of meat left over and put in the freezer and it stayed there a year and we had to throw it out. There are two main reasons for the Îd [the feast]. One is to bring the children around you and kill the animal and put away meat to eat, dry it in the sun and it lasts a while. The second is to distribute it to others, especially to people who need it. But here we have enough meat anyway, and it is not clear to whom one could give it. Oh, sometimes I ask among the family to see if there is a relative in Tunisia who needs it, and then I send enough to buy a sheep, about 100 euros now. That makes more sense because they need it.

Increasingly there are calls to think of the Îd as a time to make donations to needy Muslims elsewhere in the world. In 2004, I heard Islamic Aid (Secours Islamique) ask on the radio station Beur FM for Muslims to send Îd money to poor people living in Chechnya and Palestine. This is what the Centre Tawhid bookstore manager, Abdelkadir, does. In 2004 he said, "I don't sacrifice. It's better to send money to Palestine or Chechnya, where people have a greater need. Here we eat meat all the time, so it does not mean anything, but there they don't." He had an Islamic Aid can at the end of the counter for customers' donations.

With so many Muslim public figures not sacrificing, is there a change in the sense of what the Islamic norm indeed is? Certainly many young Muslims look to the sacrifice along with eating halâl foods and fasting as practical and feasible foundations (and perhaps also material signs) of their own religious commitment. When in 2006 I was talking with students at the Institute associated with Dhaou Meskine, a young woman explained that she and others took those courses "to be able to separate religion from tradition, because we had both from our parents." I asked if the "sheep festival" was tradition, and she immediately and emphatically denied that idea (and others showed their agreement): "It is religion, Sunna [the example of the Prophet], and different from incorrect traditions such as when a man says that his wife or daughter cannot leave the house without his permission, traditions that come from maschismo. And many imams have denounced suggestions that Muslims donate instead of sacrifice, saying it is *bid'a* [illegitimate change]."

But others have publicly suggested that over time, the practice will die out. As the Moroccan editor Hakim El Ghisassi, at that time the editor in chief of *La Médina*, explained to me in October 2002, "Most Muslims already have stopped carrying out the sacrifice; they just give money at that time. It is those who do not practice Islam who have a problem; they want their cultural traditions to continue." For those scholars interested in creating new Islamic norms for France, it is important to remind Muslims that performing the sacrifice is a recommended act, not a required one, whereas the ritual prayer performed on the same day is required of all Muslims. Citing the problem of Muslims who neglect the required prayer while carrying out the optional sacrifice, Tareq Oubrou suggested that "[s]acrifice may disappear in the second and third generations. First, the cultural tradition of eating the meat together will disappear, and, second, the way people live, in apartments, make it impossible to carry out the killing of animals. In any case, the practice does not have the importance that Muslims give it. The sacrifice has a symbolic importance, as part of the Muslim tradition, Abraham's sacrifice. It is enough if the imam, or two or three people in the Muslim community, sacrifice. But even if 1 million Muslims do not sacrifice, it's not the end of world, given that it is not an essential rite."[31]

Oubrou's repeated use of "it would not be the end of the world" irritated Hichem El Arafa when I repeated it to him. He commented that Oubrou was correct in saying that sacrificing was not required, but that to dismiss it was hardly sending the correct message to France's Muslims. Hichem: "I think it is better to explain things in a way that people understand rather than just saying something for its shock value. Sometimes shocking people can have its place, but here we have to make them understand."

Convergence II: From French Civil Law toward Islamic Practices

Are these measures taken by Muslims to reinterpret Islamic norms and practices met by any corresponding changes in how French public actors view the requirements of French law? We saw in chapter two that such is the case for matters of halâl meat production and sacrifice, for which the state allows exceptions to slaughtering regulations. But it is with respect to marriage and divorce that questions arise most pointedly about French norms and values.

French legal scholars indeed have been debating what Islamic marriage might mean in French terms. Because Islamic marriage cannot constitute a legal marriage in France, for reasons described earlier, their deliberations concern only marriage and divorces conducted in countries with Islamic legal institutions. Does an Islamic marriage or divorce conducted abroad continue to be valid when one or both of the parties come to France?

Now, generally marriages and divorces conducted in foreign states according to the laws of those states are valid—such is the nature of international private law. The broader area of law is that of "personal status." However, in France, if a judge decides that applying the usual rules for resolving a conflict of laws would produce a solution contrary to French *ordre public*, then the judge may act contrary to those rules.[32]

What, then, is *ordre public*? Although it usually is translated as "public order" (or sometimes, and misleadingly, as "public policy"), the term has quite specific, strongly moral resonances. It refers both to the conditions of social order and to basic values, and it limits the range of laws that a legislator may pass and the decisions that a judge may make. It is one of those basic concepts of a legal system that resist definition precisely because they are expected to provide judges and jurists with the means to translate the values of a society into law, and as these values change, so too do the limits of the law.

With respect to matters that touch on the family, ordre public may be invoked to reject an option or action that otherwise would satisfy legal requirements. These "exceptions due to ordre public" evoke from jurists expressions that reflect the basic moral and emotional level of the objection. Laws or actions are judged to be "odious laws," "shocking to the conscience," or to incite "instinctive repulsion."[33] They may be characteristic of another society, judged to have institutions that offend the morality and values of the French tribunal. And, as a commentator on the role of ordre public in international private law points out, "personal status is the privileged domain for exceptions due to ordre public, because it is there where we are most likely to encounter institutions absolutely opposed to the values of civilization retained by the nation."[34] Finding vivid examples of practices offensive to ordre public in other societies thus not only reveals current French notions about the limits of the morally acceptable but may also be used to render concrete a general sense that France faces a "clash of civilizations" with certain other "civilizations."

It is most notably with respect to Islam that this last function of ordre public emerges, and this use is anchored in France's colonial history, and in particular in the critical role played by legal personal status in sorting out identities in the colonies, protectorates, and French Algeria. Indeed, to avoid essentializing racial or ethnic difference, and thereby to preserve the possibility of assimilating the colonized to civilized France, colonial officials, notably in Algeria, employed terms of "local personal status" to distinguish between North Africans who remained governed by Muslim laws and those who renounced that status for membership in the French legal domain.[35] The opposition between Islamic law and French law thereby came to encode (and in official discourse often substitute for) the opposition between backward and evolved, or between less and more civilized. The dividing lines could be crossed, and colonized subjects could become French nationals and, eventually, French citizens. But they did so by renouncing Islamic family law; for this reason, some Islamic authorities in Algeria declared that crossing this legal line was tantamount to abandoning Islam. Thus, crossing the line between Islamic law and French civil law came to signify for French authorities and jurists the possibility of emancipation through legal change, while maintaining that line came to signify for some Muslims the resistance to colonial domination by nonbelievers.

These legal distinctions, transformed in various ways by succeeding constitutions, associated personal status with degrees of civilization but separated it from domicile. French citizens living permanently in the colonies were governed by French law. Colonial subjects governed by the local legal regime retained that legal status *even if* they entered France. Stepping onto the soil of metropolitan France did not suddenly let them enjoy the benefits of French personal status law any more than it suddenly gave them full French citizenship rights. The bilateral treaties signed by France with each of the former North African possessions at independence in effect prolonged those arrangements.[36]

This historical background may contribute to decisions taken by some French judges and jurists affirming that elements of Islamic marriage and divorce are contrary to French ordre public and thus justify setting aside the usual rules for resolving conflict of laws. These jurists argue that the institutions of unilateral repudiation (*talaq*), on the one hand, and polygamy, on the other, not only are prohibited in France but also violate the French (and European) commitments to the equality of women and men. They would disallow any "effects" produced in France by a talaq divorce or polygamous marriage carried out in another country, even when the marriage or divorce was legal and proper in that country.

Other jurists have pointed out that this position may be logical but that it creates practical problems. If a couple divorces in a country with Islamic tribunals, at which the husband pronounces the talaq, are they then to be considered still married in France? To say so would keep the wife from remarrying were she to reside in or settle in France. That hardly seems to be in the woman's interest. And if a husband married a second wife in a country permitting polygamy and in accord with its rules, and then brought her and their children to France, those children would be denied social welfare benefits because their presence could not be justified under rules of family reunification. Refusing to recognize a polygamous marriage thus would deny those children the rights enjoyed by other children of the same man, and could be held to deny the couple the right to lead a normal family life. Equal rights for all children, and the right to a normal family life, are both enforced by the European Court of Human Rights.[37]

Through the mid-1980s, French court decisions affirmed the general principle found in conflicts of laws rules that if a couple of the same nationality marries, the effects that marriage might have in another country are governed by their own national law. This principle means that a polygamous marriage enacted in a country permitting polygamy is valid in France.[38] The rulings meant that the wives and children of a man legally resident in France were allowed to join him in the name of family reunification and given residency permits. Thousands of women and children did so, coming mainly from Senegal, Mali, and Mauritius.

During the early Mitterrand years, the "right to a difference" reigned, and polygamous marriage practices were looked on as foreign customs to be respected, or at least to be tolerated. With the change in government (Mitterrand's cohabitation with Jacques Chirac as prime minister), and especially during the second term of Charles Pasqua's service as Interior Minister (1993–95), things shifted abruptly, on this as on all questions pertaining to immigration.[39] A 1993 law forbade giving residence permits to second wives.

However, subsequent ministerial directives allowed second wives living in France prior to 1993 to renew their identity cards, and prevented the expulsion of a second wife if she had French children and had been living as a legal resident in France for ten years. These directives required that the maternal units "*décohabitent*," that is, that they live in separate apartments (but did nothing to ensure that such wives, usually not functional in French, could live effectively on their own).[40] In general, local officials and apartment managers adopted a live and let live policy and continue to do so, only intervening if an apartment becomes dangerously over-crowded. From time to time a municipal government decides to enforce the rule on separate apartments, as when in 2003 the city of Mantes-la-Jolie found seventy-five polygamous families in the Val-Fourré housing project and placed each wife in a separate apartment—but on the same floor.[41] But by doing so, the municipality in effect recognized their marital condition.

And indeed, what else could they do? The practical considerations of public policy would seem to require that jurists find a resolution. Officials in fact recognize the "effects" in France of polygamous unions. Women and men need to get on with their lives, and some jurists have sought ways to allow recognition of unilateral repudiation contracted legally in another country, ordre public notwithstanding. To accomplish this end, these judges have employed two instruments already available in the legal literature. Both offer subtle modifications of the ordre public concept. The first distinguishes between institutions or events occurring in France that offend French sensibilities and those that occur elsewhere according to the rules in effect in that country and that later on produce effects in France—for example, because people immigrate. This concept, called "attenuated effect of ordre public," was originally devised to deal with divorces by mutual consent at a time when France disallowed such proceedings. In more recent cases involving Muslims, the device allows a judge to accept that a couple is divorced by talaq or even that a woman is a man's second wife, as long as the marriage and divorce took place else-where and are recognized as valid in that country.[42] The judge may object to the practice in principle and yet not be required to alter everyone's marital status once they cross the French border—a bit like al-Qaradâwî when he affirms the ban on loans at interest but makes a practical excep-tion for European Muslims.

The second conceptual device (borrowed from German and Swiss legal theorists) has been to think in terms of a sliding scale of distance between the objectionable act and France itself. This "distance-relative ordre pub-lic" (ordre public de proximité) is similar to the "attenuation" idea dis-cussed above: it allows a judge to say that if all parties to a polygamous marriage are foreign nationals, then this distance from France allows him or her to recognize the effects produced by the marriage: the second wife and her children may enjoy the same rights as the first wife. But once a French national is involved—and especially if a Frenchwoman is the first wife in a polygamous marriage—then the sociomoral "distance" is shrunk, and the judges do not recognize the second marriage. The same logic applies to talaq divorce: if a Frenchwoman is divorced in that way, then France itself becomes the object of the proceeding, and "the court is shocked," as judges love to say.

The two concepts of attenuation and distance offered judges four advantages over the more blunt-instrument approach of finding polygamy or repudiation ipso facto repugnant. First, judges (and jurists, when they establish *doctrine*) could arrive at reasonable accommodations with practical life: why should a couple who divorce according to Moroccan law be prevented from remarrying if the woman agrees with the procedure?[43] Second, judges could distinguish among the several elements of a proceeding and discover those that could be approved from the standpoint of French notions of ordre public. For example, judges have argued that the problem is "attenuated" if basic principles of fair treatment are observed: if the wife was present at the divorce hearing, presented her case, and received a reasonable compensation, then perhaps "one may find in that repudiation a community of institutions with a French divorce or separation" and accept its effects in France.[44] Third, distinguishing in such a way among acceptable and unacceptable elements might contribute to the evolution of laws in the countries in question toward more gender-equal proceedings, as in the case of the recent modification of Moroccan family laws.[45] Finally, these distinctions would make French authorities seem less hypocritical on a moral plane, at a period in history when increasing numbers of French couples do not marry and a certain number, in particular successive presidents of France, engage in de facto polygamy.[46]

This socially pragmatic reasoning (akin to reasoning from objectives by Muslims) appeared to have convinced a number of judges during the last decade of the twentieth century. Decisions taken by the Court of Cassation in 1999 and 2001 supported this approach, refusing to declare the talaq intrinsically repugnant but looking to the degree to which the wife's interests were guaranteed by the divorce tribunal.[47] Perhaps reflecting the gulf between theory and practice, the masters of *doctrine*, those jurists who write influential comments on decisions, rejected these decisions on grounds that the very institution of talaq was contrary to French and European principles of gender equality and thus of human rights. Influenced by these objections, in February 2004 the same chamber of the Court of Cassation reversed itself and pronounced unilateral repudiation intrinsically contrary to French ordre public and also to the European Convention on Human Rights.[48]

As of 2009, French jurists are debating among themselves about how judges ought to approach Islamic marriages and divorces.[49] Not only is it unclear, and much discussed, what precisely it is that offends ordre public, but jurists must also weigh competing considerations. On the one hand, they would like to allow people who marry or divorce elsewhere to retain that status when they come to France (and the principles of international law dictate such a position). But on the other hand, they would like to use the law to send a message about the kinds of family forms and judicial processes that France sees as fair and gender-friendly.

The debates among scholars of Islam and those among French jurists derive their force mainly from what protagonists see as the consequences of alternative interpretations of legal texts in a French social world that is resolutely plural in its social composition and normative convictions. Under the façades of positive legal unity, on the one hand, and a single divine path for all humans on the other lie the dilemmas of constructing the legal conditions for common life that are capacious enough to "reasonably accommodate" people living in differing conditions and with differing beliefs, yet unitary enough to retain the hope that such a common life is conceivable.

CHAPTER NINE

Islamic Spheres in Republican Space

WE HAVE MOVED from the broadly historical picture of the French Islamic landscape to a closer focus on the mosques, institutes, and schools that populate it, to a still closer-in look at the forms of reasoning and debate that take place among Muslims in these Islamic spaces. We were among Muslims, looking across and outward. In the previous chapter we began to move back from this close focus, and to consider possibilities for convergence across the boundaries of realms of justification. We saw how Muslims invoked socially pragmatic forms of Islamic reasoning to address practical problems, and also how they could provide resources to bridge from Islam toward French legal norms. We were able to make out potential pathways for convergence from the other side as well, from French law toward Islamic institutions of marriage and divorce. These two sets of repertoires bear a closer resemblance than one might think, both drawing on notions of social objectives and legal equivalence. But within each realm we also saw resistance and opposition based, on both sides, on longstanding traditions of jurisprudence.

Now I wish to pull back still further, away from normative and legal reasoning, back through the schools and institutes we examined earlier, out to the broader world of social life and political debates in France. Correct and important though a line of normative reasoning might be, it inevitably takes its social and moral force from a broader, complex field of ideas, values, and emotions and from the experiences and judgments of individuals in their fuller social lives. This requires us to consider the social and moral force of French objections to the sort of Islamic ideas and institutions we have been considering.

Those in France who are worried about Muslims' integration into the Republic usually mention two major problems: first: that some Muslims have remained "communalist" in their tendencies to form Islam-based associations, such as mosques, schools, and neighborhood societies, which prevents them from fully entering the Republican public space, and second, that some Muslims have failed to embrace the requirements of *laïcité* (secularism), because they substitute religious norms and values (or cultural values derived from religion) for secular ones, which keeps them from fully embracing norms of gender equality and religious freedom. The first objection concerns forms of Muslims' sociability; the second concerns their norms and values. Both objections are based on real concerns about social life and national unity, but I will argue that they fail to acknowledge parallels in the pathways toward integration in the Republic between Muslims and other religious groups.[1]

Do Religion-Based Associations Impede Integration?

The criticism of communalism (*communautarisme*) among Muslims evokes a powerful set of political ideas and ideals. French Republicanism promotes the idea that all citizens ought to participate together in public life without being divided by intermediary groups, and toward that end the revolution abolished guilds and corporations, and made it difficult for citizens for form legally recognized associations. In his writings on the new society of the United States, Tocqueville contrasted American reliance on free association with the French reliance on the state.

But a set of contrary ideas created a running counterpoint to the centralizing logic of Republicanism. In the course of the nineteenth century the state gradually permitted certain kinds of corporate bodies to carry out its own interests. The state came to realize that it was better to delegate supervision of bread baking to guilds than to suffer popular discontent at wormy loaves, and that it was better to allow a few recognized labor unions than to suffer wildcat strikes. By 1901, citizens were given the general right to register associations, and the 1905 law on religion was intended to turn churches over to their control. The state saw the advantage of extending this corporatist logic to immigrants as well, who in 1981 were given the same right to form associations, which then could receive aid from the Fund for Social Action (FAS). In effect, the state "subcontracted" immigrant matters to associations organized around cultural or regional identities.[2]

Today, "associative life" thrives in France, with over one million associations registered to promote youth affairs, sports, health, and education, and associations have their own cabinet-level office. The life of associations has become so central to French notions of the good life that the video shown to immigrants during their introduction to French values urges them to join associations, and shows people engaged in sports, dancing, and relaxation.[3] Associations are not supposed to correspond to cultural, ethnic, or religious communities—"association" is a positive term in public discourse, "community" is not—but rather to respond to the shared interests of citizens. But in fact, associations have been the major vehicle for the development of cultural and religious identities in France. Scholars find a "division of social labor" in neighborhoods whereby secular, cultural associations might provide social services and promote identities of origin while religious associations might combine discussions of the Qur'an, sports, and after-school tutoring, and promote identities of shared religion. But both Islamic associations and the cultural ones all frame their activities in universalistic terms, teaching immigrants about how to adapt to life in France, using the French language.[4] Associations involving Muslims, only some of them religious, have come to provide a major set of pathways to integration.

These pathways are hardly specific to Islam. Many religious groups have relied on associative strategies, at least since the legal privatization of religion in 1905. Indeed, during the second half of the twentieth century, established religious traditions—Catholic, Jewish, and mainstream Protestant—experienced a decline in attendance at regular rituals but a flourishing of religion-based associations. Catholic youth movements, benefiting from state aid, grew steadily in numbers in both urban and rural areas after 1945. They have had strong links to trade unions since the interwar years, despite shifts in ideological commitments.[5] Catholic and Protestant youth organizations played active roles in the major political and cultural movements that traversed the country, and in particular the antiwar and student movements from the early 1950s through the 1970s. Evangelical associations have expanded: for example, the Catholic evangelical Jeunesse Mariale, which recruits young people from parishes and religious school, holds meetings and summer camps and attracts young people who wish to work to help others, for example in development projects or in work with the handicapped.[6] While maintaining its Catholic basis, an association such as the French Sports and Cultural Federation is able to integrate tens of thousands of Muslims and other non-Christians because of its emphasis on sports and artistic activities.[7] And of course, in much of small-town France churches still organize much of daily social life for Catholics, with church bells signaling the passage of time and church graveyards replete with freshly changed flowers.

As they became more closely integrated into the Republic, Catholic social and political networks grew in public support. When the Debré law of 1959 gave a massive infusion of money to the Catholic schools by paying for teachers, it transformed teaching at these schools from emphasizing Catholic doctrine to following the national curriculum. The religious schools thereafter become much more broadly attractive and hence more socially powerful. By 1981, they were able to block the Socialist government's attempt to dissolve them into the national educational structure, and they have continued to recruit an ever-growing proportion of French children, increasing numbers of whom are not practicing Catholics.

Successive waves of Jewish immigrants from Eastern Europe and from North Africa relied on mutual aid associations to build and rebuild communities in France. In the early twentieth century, the Consistory, the national federation created by Napoleon as a privileged interlocutor with the state, declared Jewish schools to be better at assimilating Jewish children to France than public schools, precisely because they provided religious foundations for assimilation.[8] But immigrants also formed their own (non-Consistory) schools and, by the interwar years, their own ethnic and religious associations.[9] Rebuilding the community after the German occupation and the deportations was organized in part by the CRIF (Conseil Représentatif des Juifs de France, Representative Council of French Jews), formed in 1944, working alongside Zionist groups and cultural associations. New Jewish immigrants from North Africa formed associations that were more religious in character than the CRIF and gave a higher public profile to Jewish foods and to Orthodox Jewish men and women.[10] As with Catholics, attendance at Jewish religious ceremonies has declined in the past quarter-century, but attendance at Jewish schools has risen sharply: by 1986 there were eighty-eight Jewish schools in France, mainly in the Paris region.

Despite their strikingly different histories, Catholics and Jews were integrated into Republican space through their associations, and successful integration has not meant a diminution of religion-based associative life. Is it different for Muslims? What sort of orientations do young Muslims receive as they move through religion-based associations? And are they compatible with being a French citizen?

Return to School

Each of the institutions we have considered in this book provides Islamic spaces that incorporate a sense of moral distance from French mainstream society while providing signposts about how to engage in French civic life. They come into play at different stages in a French Muslim's life.

In chapter six, we looked at the Islamic day school La Réussite in Aubervilliers. The school takes children who have completed state primary schools and teaches them the national curriculum within a space marked as Islamic.[11] Judging from their examination results, it teaches them well, in large part because of the small class sizes and the overall emphasis on success. But we also saw that the pupils learn to maintain an ethical distance from the French pedagogical program. In biology, they learn how to understand evolution, but also how to treat the assumption of a single origin for life as a working hypothesis, unnecessary for mastering the science and perhaps, in the long run, to be proven false. In civics class, they learn about the social habits of mainstream French people, who cohabit outside of marriage, and welcome gay and lesbian unions, but also that those are things that *those* people do, not the habits of "*chez nous.*" In religion class, they learn the basic practices of Islam but also the importance of being good neighbors and thereby being good citizens. In other words, they learn to retain the distinctive commitments of their own religion and to engage fully in civic life.

As we saw earlier, Islamic day schools (three were operating by 2009) have been criticized for their supposed "communalism," even though they are identical in admissions policy and curriculum to the widely used Catholic schools. Efforts to found the school in Lyon were so strongly opposed by the director of the area academy and on such weak grounds that he was forced to resign. The national education hierarchy has continued to block recognition of the Success School despite the (belated) support of the prefect and mayor.

There are reasons to argue that in France, a Muslim child would benefit psychologically from attending an Islamic school even more than might a Catholic who attended a Catholic school, given the multiple instances in everyday life in which a Muslim child would be likely to be criticized for his faith. Most of the Islamic character of the school comes not from its curriculum but from the fact that acting publicly as a Muslim—wearing a headscarf, praying at the prescribed times, fasting during Ramadan—is normal in that space. In a public school, even breaking the fast is considered to contravene norms of laïcité.[12]

What, if anything, can we say about whether and how education in this type of religious private school prepares pupils for civic engagement? First, we should note that the Islamic private schools, along with nearly all French Catholic and Jewish schools, teach a precisely prescribed French state curriculum, limit religious teaching to one elective hour per week, and admit students of any religion. At least since the Debré law of 1959, French educational policy treats these schools as forming "normal" and critical parts of the state educational system, with little curricular difference from secular schools. Many parents treat them the same way, more as private schools of high quality than as confessional schools.[13]

In these respects, French religious schools are closer to French secular schools than to English or U.S. religious schools. Britain finances faith schools that have a good deal of curricular latitude and that may and do restrict admission to certified followers of a particular faith. The United States does not finance religious schools, but it permits a wide range of private schools to operate on a faith basis as substitutes for public schools. Many of these schools resemble more closely the French Catholic schools of the immediate postwar period, which taught religious doctrine as part of the regular curriculum. Many of the Anglo-American critics of religious schools in general take as an assumption that such schools teach their subjects in a way that is fundamentally different from that experienced in a public school, and that, in particular, habits essential to civic engagement, such as critical reasoning and mutual respect, are subordinated to obedience and responsibility.[14]

Now, even if these assumptions do not hold for Islamic schools (or other religious schools) in France, can we criticize such schools for their Islamic ambiance? Given that attachment to a religious community and to a set of religious commitments is strengthened through daily exposure to remarks by teachers, extracurricular activities, and the manifest religious orientations of other pupils, does that strengthening come at the expense of a commitment to national civic principles and the national community? Such are the criticisms levied by some state officials.

Let me suggest that something a bit more complex is involved, namely, that the pupil learns both how to maintain a critical distance between her or his moral commitments and the norms and values of the wider society, and how to participate in that society according to its norms. We already looked at how a La Réussite teacher gave a lesson about neighborliness in religion class. The civic values of mutual respect, reciprocity, and toleration for others were taught from the example of the Prophet Muhammad, just as the sayings of Jesus about reciprocity and toleration provide a Christian basis for teaching the same values. Are these ways of teaching these values inferior to a purely secular way of doing so? Political theorists are divided on this point: some say that the society should welcome it when religious groups find their own reasons for affirming central civic values (what I have been calling "convergent reasoning"), while others argue that society is better off if everyone, when push comes to shove, is likely to fall back on the same basic reasons.[15]

But if we take as given the existence of diverse communities of religious and other strongly held moral beliefs in a society, then surely we should welcome their efforts to converge on a set of civic principles, diverse though the starting points might be. It seems to me that the French private school arrangement—public funding providing the incentive for religious schools to open up to the national curriculum, inspections, and a potentially multireligious clientele—is superior on these particular dimensions of civic education than are the British or U.S. arrangements. The French arrangement provides the greatest degree of pedagogical and civic standardization within a framework that accepts schools with a religious ambiance.

After graduating from high school, a French Muslim pupil might enter university and at the same time seek to continue studying Islam at an institute such as Hichem El Arafa's CERSI. Here, too, he or she would find an Islamic space, but one that adds a scientific focus on religious knowledge that does not intersect in any major way with university studies. The student learns to think of Islamic knowledge as a set of disciplines that demand linguistic and textual study. Hichem and other such teachers intend this pedagogy as a kind of spiritual inoculation against the Salafi approaches. Islam is again normalized in these spaces. Those students who attend other sorts of Islamic-ambience institutes, such as the training institutes described in chapter five, also enter an Islamic social space, where religious references and practices are considered to be a normal part of the "associative life," even though the manifest instructional content is technical.

A National Islamic Sphere at Le Bourget

These young Muslims might also attend debates at mosques or, more likely, spend a day or two at the annual Salon du Bourget, sponsored by the UOIF Islamic federation and held in three former airport hangers at Le Bourget, north of Paris. Thousands of Muslims attend. By 2006, after the debates on headscarves, the 2005 riots, and the increasing electoral presence of Muslims, the press and mainstream politicians had begun to pay attention to what takes place at Le Bourget. Simultaneous telecasting has meant that many Muslims in the Gulf states and North Africa also follow events at the gathering.[16]

Figure 9.1 Stands at the Salon du Bourget, 2006

From wandering through the stands, taking in lectures, and enjoying food and music, the young Muslim visiting the Salon would learn that he or she lived in a multidimensional Islamic world. Let me underscore three of those dimensions. First, visitors experience the spiritual and liturgical dimensions of that world, their Islamic religion in a narrow sense. Visitors find travel services for the pilgrimage to Mecca, carpets with compasses indicating the direction of Mecca, Muslim toothbrushes (the small *mishwak* sticks), gowns, sandals, and perfumes modeled after the Prophet's lifestyle, and hundreds of bookstore shelves offering sacred texts, manuals on prayer, and works of theology and spirituality.[17] The drinks of choice are Mecca Cola and Muslim Up. Inspirational speakers from throughout the Muslim world draw the largest crowds. The mainstream print media covers only the political aspects of the gathering—in 2001, the concerns with Palestine; in 2003, Nicolas Sarkozy's speech that launched the anti-scarf frenzy; in 2006, how Muslims would vote in the next elections. But visitors flock to the more spiritually oriented speakers.

The spiritual, emotional dimension of the Salon supports its second dimension, awareness of the global humanitarian and political plights of Muslims. In 2001, the humanitarian agency Islamic Aid (Secours Islamique) had several stands together in a row; one of them was a Chechen refugee tent containing a simple cooking pot on a tripod and decorated with photos of battles and suffering. Three other stands had been set up by exiles, featuring respectively the repression of political freedoms in Tunisia, killings in Algeria, and the persecutions of the Moroccan Islamic figure Sheikh Abdessalam Yassine, with video clips of police attacking Moroccan demonstrators on International Human Rights Day. Stands proclaiming the troubles Muslim face in these three countries of the Maghreb are present every year. (Although Muslims from other regions attend the gathering, at least as of 2006 there have been few references in the stands to West Africa or to Turkey.)

Most of the Muslims strolling among the stands live in France, however, not in a Chechen camp or in Palestine, and the social reality of their lives in France forms the third dimension of this Islamic space. Visitors encounter people asking for help in building a mosque, either at stands featuring architectural diagrams or from men and women walking through the buildings and outside crying out "*fisabilillah*," "work for the sake of God," and holding sacks into which you were invited to toss a few coins. By 2006, I could visit six stands presenting plans to build Islamic private secondary schools. Most of the higher institutes offering Islamic study had booths. Each year, Hichem El Arafa has set up a stand for CERSI; in 2003 he told me that the gathering "has become the agora for the Muslims in France, and so we must have a presence here, so people know of us."[18] People listen to speeches about what it means to be a young Muslim in France or in Europe, and younger speakers such as Hassan Iquissien and Farid Abdelkrim are more likely to urge their listeners to engage broad social issues than to talk about worship or religious norms. In 2006 Abdelkrim asked the audience, "How many of you are willing to give up the television for reading: no, you have become a second television, repeating what you hear. I suggest a fast of one month without television, a detox!"—an exhortation greeted with much applause. Young men and women wander freely, and one bookstore owner estimated that "60 percent of the young people who come here do so to get married, and the others already found a spouse here."[19]

Of course, the global and political can also become part of this third dimension of Islam, the social life of Muslims in France. In 2003 the stand about Abdessalam Yassine's combats in Morocco had been replaced by one belonging to representatives of his movement in France, called Participation et Spiritualité Musulmane, at which an enthusiastic young woman described to me their talks and summer camps, all inspired by Yassine's teachings and often featuring his daughter, Nadia Yassine. (Overall, men and women are equally present as presenters and as visitors, although the vast majority of the speakers are men.) What had been a set of demands for freedom in Morocco now was a set of possibilities in France.

Although much remained constant over this period, there was a palpable shift in mood and message from 2001 to 2006 concerning the relationship of Muslims to the broader society. Although Muslims still felt under attack in 2006, and were quick to talk about it, they were more likely to represent themselves as builders than as victims. More of the stands than in prior years showed them frenetically engaged in creating new schools and mosques, publishing new books, and offering new services, from halâl certification to medical advice to a financial instrument that would avoid paying interest. The triple threat of the attacks on September 11, 2001, the 2003 invasion of Iraq, and the passage of the 2004 law against Islamic scarves in schools had galvanized Muslims into more social action than before.[20]

At Le Bourget, a Muslim will find an impressive array of services, which give a rather capacious sense of what one might mean by being Muslim in France: sources of spiritual renewal and normative education, ways of helping other Muslims throughout the world but also throughout France, clothing and other goods—all of it Islamic in one way or another. In coming years one may start to find Islamic banking services (as one finds throughout the corresponding North American event, the national gathering of ISNA), or a greater array of social services, and these will extend and expand ways one can retain an Islamic orientation within the political space of France. The normative references here are Islamic, not French or European, but the kinds of engagement promoted—building schools and houses of worship, caring for those in need abroad—surely are basic to French ideas of being an active citizen.

When French commentators denounce Muslims for forming their own socioreligious worlds, and thus practicing "communalism," they fail to acknowledge that citizens can draw religious and moral inspiration from their associative lives in order to better enter into broader social and political activities. That Catholics, Protestants, Jews, and others have done so does not arouse great concern today; these activities have become part of the taken-for-granted background to French social life.[21] That Muslims do so is new, and it worries those in France who fear that French Muslims will place their global religious allegiances above their French Republican ones. In a deeper historical context, this fear is not novel. Catholics and Jews, in particular, have felt such accusations, and not only in France. These accusations move us from considering forms of sociability to considering anxieties generated about the norms and values expressed by some French Muslims.

ON PRIORITIES AND VALUES

This second kind of criticism turns on two claims. The first is that some French Muslims have an insufficient commitment to secularism, because they place religious commands above national or secularist ones. As a remedy, some propose that Muslims explicitly affirm the primacy of Republican-secularist principles over religious ones—a demand notably not made of Catholics. The second claim is that some French Muslims have not completely assimilated French values because they have retained pieces of their "cultures of origin" that are at odds with the dominant values of France. I examine each in turn.

The Primacy of Secularism

I began this book noting that Muslims are often the most effective critics of Islam, and such is the case in France. Those French Muslim authors whose works and opinions appear in the mainstream press and on television programs argue for an Islam that is clearly encompassed by Republican principles. They vary somewhat in their emphases—an Enlightenment Islam, the glory of past Islamic civilizations, the spiritual value of prayer, or a liberal Islam of individual choice.[22] But they converge in critiquing Muslims who engage in what I have called "convergence reasoning," or working from Islamic principles toward Republican ones. Their criticism resembles that made of religious education: even if you could reach

French ideas by reasoning from Islamic principles, you would fail to start on the same page as more secular-minded French citizens, who make principles of human rights, gender equality, and religious freedom their shared and *sole* foundation for evaluating religious ideas and practices.

A 2000 debate over apostasy turned on this question of legitimate starting points. A Muslim's freedom to leave Islam arises frequently in discussions about Islam and human rights and is far from a simple or settled matter. Some argue that, whereas you are free to choose your religion, once you are a Muslim you may not renounce Islam. Penalties for so doing were revealed to Muhammad and made known by him to his followers. Others quote the well-known Qur'anic verse that asserts there is "no compulsion in religion" (Qur'an 2:256), and interpret Muhammad's statements and actions as coming from a time when leaving the community was tantamount to treason, conditions that no longer apply today. Islamic public actors often try to avoid the issue; the 1981 and 1990 Islamic declarations on human rights make all rights subject to shari'a, without making explicit the implications of that proviso.

The issue arose in France because, through the late 1990s, the Ministry of the Interior had been working with several Muslim groups to develop a text regarding the main lines of Islam in France; the process was called "the Consultation," and it eventually led to the creation of the national French Islamic Council. A clause affirming the right to change one's religion had been included in an early draft and then withdrawn at the insistence of one of the participating groups. In January 2000, two Islamic intellectuals sharply criticized the government's willingness to withdraw the freedom-to-change clause; the authors were Leïla Babès, professor of sociology of religions at Lille, and Michel Renard, co-editor with Said Branine of the Islamic review *Islam de France*.[23] Championing the cause of the "law in common" against "communitarian law," they argued that Muslims in France must declare themselves fully for liberty of conscience, which implies the right to change religions. They suggested that leaving the matter unspecified opened the door to those interpretations of Islamic law that prescribe the death penalty for such an action.[24] Babès and Renard even criticized the government for its use of the Arabic term al-'istishâra ("consultation") to refer to the process. They charged that this usage implies "that the principle of consultation required a specifically Islamic legitimation to be accepted," a move they saw as dangerously opening the door to Islamic law. In other words, Islam ought to become part of the Republic entirely on Republican terms, without an attempt to rationalize the merger on Islamic grounds.

A number of intellectuals wrote in response. One pointed out that the Catholic Church had never acknowledged the right to divorce, yet Catholics in France are perfectly well integrated into the Republic; why could not the same tacit acceptance of divergence among religions (and vis-à-vis nonreligious positions) be extended to Muslims?[25] The broader issue was whether there could be two distinct sets of values coexisting in French public policy. Babès and Renard argued that to admit the Qur'an, or even an Arabic phrase, into public policy discussions was to deny the universality of Republican values and threaten the unity of French society. In other writings, Babès advocates an "interior Islam" of faith, one that would neither embrace Islamic law nor consider French Muslims to be an ethnic group.[26]

To underscore the differences in normative starting points, Babès published a dialogue with the Bordeaux scholar Tareq Oubrou entitled *Loi d'Allah, loi des hommes* (God's Law, Humans' Law)."[27] In the book, Oubrou argues that Muslims can arrive at broadly ethical positions from Islamic starting points (as we saw him do in chapter eight) and further, that Muslims are obliged to remain within the tenets of Islam, because once you accept the truth of Revelation, "there are inevitable consequences for your behavior."[28] For Babès, the issues are "simple and fundamental: freedom (of conscience and expression), the rights of men and women, and equality"; Islamic norms flatly contravene these principles. They frame the issue raised in the book's title in starkly different ways, Babès asking citizens to choose between the two sources of law, Oubrou asking citizens to reconcile them.

The mainstream setting ensured that Oubrou would lose the debate. Effectively the senior editor of this book by a mainstream publisher (Albin Michel), Babès sets the agenda and Oubrou remains on the defensive: the question is never, "Do your ideas, Mme Babès, conform to God's words?" but rather "Do your ideas, M Oubrou, conform to the demands of freedom and equality?" Oubrou must deliver apologetics. Yes, some Muslims believe this or that, but look, the Caliph 'Umar did not cut off hands, and many of us now think that scripture must be adapted to new times and places. His most effective argument—that a position on shari'a that starts outside Islam, such as that presented by Babès, will not help matters because it will not convince Muslims—can be effectively dismissed by her as tantamount to accepting a "scandalous" position that would execute an apostate and stone an adulteress.[29]

In the French mainstream, any argument that starts from scripture is highly vulnerable to a counterargument that starts from universal values. Muslim spokespersons for the universalist position, such as Babès, are particularly effective because they can then assure readers that they are religious persons, following an Islam of faith and morals that does not seek to replace Republican laws with sacred Law but that rests in its proper sphere, that of private relationships between individuals and God.

"Assimilation Defects"

More recently, critics of Muslims have pursued them into the private realm, claiming to see in their everyday behavior signs of insufficient replacement of older (Arabic, Islamic, African) values with new French ones. One emblematic and influential statement of this theory was the 2002 book, *The Lost Territories of the Republic*, which denounced "Arab Muslim culture" for encouraging school children to refuse integration into the Republic.[30] Focusing on deep-seated values obviates responding to the point that Muslims in France now work within a publicly secularist context. Muslim political demands are for the even-handed application of *French* laws (on schooling, religious freedom, houses of worship) and not for the development of shari'a-based laws.[31] But if Muslims appear to be accepting the explicit rules of the game, they can nonetheless be scrutinized for their embrace of French values. Even Muslims who were born in France, speak French, hold mainstream jobs (and so cannot easily be said to be "communalist"), and give typically French answers to poll-takers might nonetheless be harboring radical differences in fundamental commitments, which would then emerge through singular, revealing events.[32]

Let us consider four recent controversies. The oldest is the long series of debates over Islamic headscarves, which occupied public attention between late 1989 and early 2004. During this period, if a Muslim girl covered her head while in school she violated no law, but some in France thought that the insistence on wearing these scarves showed politically un-Republican commitments and contradicted the equality of men and women. Critics also argued that the scarves introduced unwelcome divisions into classrooms (and more generally into French society) and put pressure on other Muslim girls to cover their hair. The series of reports, speeches, and media coverage led to the 2004 law banning "religious signs" from public schools, and to efforts to keep headscarves out of other areas of public service such as hospitals and city halls.[33]

Second, as described in chapter eight, in June 2007 some politicians complained that Muslims were marrying in religious fashion without marrying formally at city hall. No action was taken at the time, because the couples themselves violated no laws. But the complaints stemmed from a worry that younger Muslims were avoiding state institutions because they did not fully accept the norms and values associated with being a French citizen. A year later, as we saw earlier, two imams were prosecuted on the still controversial grounds that they had "celebrated" religious marriages.

Third, in April 2008, a court in Lille accepted a husband's argument that their marriage should be annulled on grounds that his wife had lied concerning "an essential quality of the person," to use the language of the Civil Code, in this case her virginity. His wife did not contest the request. It also happened that the parties were Muslims (he a convert), but this fact did not figure in the court's public reasoning. At the time, the case drew little attention, and the minister of justice, Rachida Dati, supported the court's decision on grounds that it was legally correct, allowed the woman to continue with her life, and in other cases could protect women from unwanted marriages. But by June the case had attracted wider attention, and many public actors attacked the decision for giving legal backing to a retrograde value, that women should avoid premarital sex.[34] Mme Dati changed her mind, and the decision eventually was overturned.

Finally, in June 2008, the French State Council (Conseil d'État) refused to grant French nationality to a woman from Morocco on the grounds that her religious practices had led her to hold values that ran counter to the equality of men and women and caused her to suffer from insufficient assimilation to become a French citizen: she had an "assimilation defect" (*défaut d'assimilation*). The woman had married a French convert to Islam who had requested that she wear a full face covering (called a *burqa* by the court). She was reported to stay at home and to have insufficient knowledge of the right to vote and the basics of laïcité. She had met the formal conditions for citizenship, having waited the required period of time after marriage before requesting naturalization. The couple had three children.

Now, these four cases regard a variety of legal and social issues, but all received public attention because they concerned the status of women in Islam. It is also worth noting what they did *not* involve. Two recurrent French fears often are mentioned in discussions of Islam and integration but do not adequately explain the level of anxiety and outrage generated in these cases: rampant "multiculturalism," and religious incursion into public, political space.

First, despite the frequent French attacks on "multiculturalism," supposedly associated with the Mitterrand era, the four cases mentioned here did not involve requests for special rights.[35] In none of the cases did a Muslim ask for special legal treatment or any measure of cultural recognition by the state. Scarf-wearing girls were in full compliance with the law; that is why the legislature changed the law. Nothing compels Muslims or Catholics or atheists to marry at city hall; they may live together as unmarried partners in France, and increasing numbers do so.[36] The marriage annulment in Lille was deemed perfectly correct in legal terms by the minister of justice as well as by the judges of the courts in question before it raised alarms in the media. No law forbids wearing a face covering. In all these cases, Muslims wished to be treated as was everyone else;

it was French politicians who insisted they had to be treated as a separate category of persons.

Nor was protecting secular public space a major source of passion in these four cases. Surely, one might object, that was what the headscarf case was about! Indeed, when President Chirac came out in support of a law on religious signs, he defined secularity (*laïcité*) as "the neutrality of the public space," and one can find an insistence on removing religious signs from public space recurring in the history of French secularity enforcement, starting from the 1905 law prohibiting posting religious signs in public space.[37] Moreover, a commonly shared repugnance to build new religious signs in public surely lies behind strong opposition to minarets.[38] And yet at the same time that pressure was building for the antiscarf law, Nicolas Sarkozy (as Minister of the Interior) began a campaign to "bring the Muslims out of the basements" by helping them to construct public, visible mosques. Some mayors also began to work with Islamic associations to find land for new mosques, often in highly central, visible locations. Indeed, some of these mayors insist that these new buildings be open to the public, including the non-Muslim public, as are churches.[39] It seems, then, that during the headscarf fervor period, French policy was to make *more* public the worship of Muslims, not less so. And we should keep in mind that the State Council had consistently found that scarf-wearing girls were not violating norms of secularity in schools.

The major objections raised to scarves in schools were twofold: first, that the scarves introduced political divisions into the classroom, and second, that they stood for religious claims that women are inferior to men.[40] As the primary incubator of the citizenry, the classroom should treat pupils as mere citizens, who have left their particularities outside the school. When French politicians, beginning with the prime minister, denounced the scarves as political signs, they were providing a justification for excluding them from schools. Moreover, as signs of gender inequality, they could be condemned in *any* setting, public or private. Notice the way in which one of France's key theorists of citizenship, the sociologist Dominique Schnapper, makes clear that it is not enough that people keep cultural or religious specificities in the background: such features must be compatible with French values, and they must not become the basis for political identities:

> If the specific cultural features of particular groups are compatible with the requirements of living together [*la vie commune*], citizens and regular residents have the right to cultivate these features in their private lives and in social life, on the condition that they respect the rules of public order [*l'ordre public*]. . . . But at the same time, these specific features should not become the basis for a specific *political* identity, recognized as such in public space.[41]

The scarf-wearing girls were allowing features of their lives to become the basis for a political identity, and, to make matters worse, they were implicitly advocating values that were incompatible with *la vie commune* and did not correspond to the sociomoral conception of French ordre public. When in 2008 nationality was denied to the Moroccan woman wearing a face covering, State Minister Fadela Amara brought back this argument when she declared that "the headscarf and the burqa are the same. I am against wearing the headscarf, which is not a religious sign but, like the burqa, a sign of women's oppression."[42] Most of those criticizing the Lille marriage annulment complained that introducing virginity as a criterion for marriage was anathema to contemporary values of gender equality; some of them also argued that the annulment improperly introduced religious values into a secular tribunal. The behaviors by Muslims were not criticized because they were public; they were criticized because they were inconsistent with French principles of the equality of women and men.

Commentators on wearing scarves, obtaining citizenship while in a burqa, and accepting a lie about virginity as reason for annulment made a second sort of argument as well. They reasoned that if the state acquiesced in these and other Islamic practices, it would encourage such socially undesirable practices as pressuring schoolgirls to wear scarves, pressuring wives to wear burqas, and encouraging Muslim families to have their nonvirgin daughters' hymens repaired. Of course, each of these arguments rests on a very specific set of assumptions that one might question: For whom do headscarves symbolize oppression? How do we know? What evidence is there of a causal link between scarves and bullying? Is denying citizenship really the best way to repair an "assimilation defect" on the part of a married mother living permanently on French territory?[43]

But I wish less to debate the arguments than to point out the direction they chart: toward a systematic critique of the values associated with some Muslims. The burqa decision "shows that the legal system is more and more likely to pronounce on value conflicts posed by Islam to the society," said the former director of the Religions Bureau in the Interior Ministry.[44] Indeed, the burqa case rests entirely on value conflict—or value pluralism, depending on one's philosophy—because it concerned someone who stayed in her own private space and could not have been said to impose religion on others or to have constructed a public, political identity.

In a similar fashion, the husband asked for the marriage annulment on grounds that his wife had lied about what he thought to be an essential quality, that is, her virginity. His argument fit with the way jurists have interpreted the relevant passage of the Civil Code, namely, that it is the parties to the marriage who define what counts as an "essential quality" of their persons. The marriage is a contract, and one of the parties to the contract must not conceal something that the other would consider to be essential to it. The set of such qualities is a private matter, and not a matter for public policy.[45] Only about eighty annulments are granted each year, and this case resembled others from recent years, when a husband lied to his wife about his impotence, his homosexuality, or the positive result on an AIDS test, or when one party married only to obtain a financial advantage or legal residence—and in all cases annulments were granted. Most jurists supported the court's decision to annul in the Lille case as well, on the ground that such decisions rest not on the values revealed in the case but on the "freedom of consent" that underlies a marriage.[46]

But the public reaction by politicians and public (non-Muslim) intellectuals was almost entirely on the other side, and was accompanied by strong emotions. Fifty French deputies to the European Parliament signed a protest against these "fundamentalists in their archaic struggle"; the leader of an association that fights violence against women said the decision was a "fatwa against women's freedom."[47] One of President Sarkozy's close advisors urged ending the practice of annulment entirely—apparently, as one editor pointed out, forgetting that most annulments in fact come at the request of state officials trying to eliminate fraudulent marriages.[48] Most of these commentators systematically misrecognized the court's logic, claiming that France was championing a virginity test for brides and thereby siding with Muslim fundamentalists.[49]

Although the newspaper *Le Figaro* noted with relief that "Muslim litigants have lost on most of the legal fronts opened in recent years," including complaints about workplace discrimination against scarf-wearing women, requests for separate women's hours at pools, or demands for access to women doctors at hospitals, these cases reflect a growing French impatience with conceptions of gender that are seen as contravening those prevailing in France.[50] They also indicate a growing worry about the assimilability of Islam, particularly on this issue, and for some they recall the struggle against the Catholic Church over contraception and abortion, and the long debate over whether colonized peoples, and in particular Algerians, could be assimilated into France. These cases fit into preexisting frames of thinking in which religion opposes women's rights, and Muslims cannot easily become French.

One can side with mainstream French opinion that women and men should have the same rights, and yet wonder at the brittleness and anger exhibited at requests made by women (Jewish as well as Muslim) for a few hours at a pool with a little less *mixité* than usual, requests that in the 1990s were accepted by some municipal leaders—including Lille's Socialist mayor Martine Aubry—but that now have become politically difficult to sustain. New lawsuits threaten to roll back the progress already made in building proper urban mosques. The once acceptable "reasonable accommodations" of Moroccan divorce procedures are now categorically dismissed on grounds that the entire regime of Islamic divorce is offensive to ordre public. Citizenship is denied someone because her *private* behavior shows she is not really French in her values.

We are, I think, witnessing a tightening of the value-screws, a stronger rejection of pluralism in the name of national integration. But value pluralism in associational life, in religious circles, and in the family, is precisely what allowed France to "integrate" Catholics, Protestants, and Jews into the Republic—to preserve a heritage and a set of religious beliefs (including decidedly non-gender-equal ones) in social life, and on the basis of that associational base, to embrace—very gradually, in the case of the Church—the principles of public, political life in the Republic.

Changing people's religious beliefs or general values is not the task of laïcité, which only asks that when people enter public, political life, they conform to certain accepted rules of the game.[51] France does not ask the Catholic bishops (or individual Catholics) to publicly acknowledge the value of choosing abortion or using contraception, because France knows that value pluralism does not weaken political engagement.

Nor does engaging in Islamic associational life lead Muslims to take leave of the Republic. In Aubervilliers, from where did the leader of the UMP slate (Sarkozy's party) get his start? In Dhaou Meskine's Islamic school! Fayçal Menia worked outward from Islamic associational activities, to campaigning for a new mosque, to fielding an electoral slate to advance the mosque's cause, to joining the municipal government. Integration begins at home, with the values of home.

TOWARD A PRAGMATICS OF CONVERGENCE

Recent French political rhetoric is not promoting a convergence with Islamic norms and ideas. When Fadela Amara says that headscarves are just the same as burqas because all these coverings stand for the oppression of women, she comes close to saying that an entire class of Islamic forms of reasoning are by their very nature beyond the pale of a common life in France, and that the choices made by women to wear such garments are inadmissible, presumed to reflect unacceptable coercion or a "defect of assimilation." This form of "block thinking" substitutes generalizations across a category of people for an inquiry into the motives of particular individuals.[52]

We have seen the roots of an alternative in the socially pragmatic styles of reasoning advocated by some in France. These forms of reasoning are not "multicultural"; rather, they extend and adapt established French legal and moral categories to include Muslims. For years, some French civil servants have seen it as a requirement of the legal and moral norm of equity that Muslims, like Christians and Jews, be able to worship in decent surroundings, be able to find food that meets their religious requirements, and be able to organize their everyday lives in ways that satisfy their conceptions of piety. Until Parliament passed the law of March 15, 2004, the State Council had consistently upheld the right of Muslim girls to wear headscarves, on the ground that those girls considered that form of dress to be part of their religious life in society. Despite continued opposition from the Far Right, some mayors continue to help Islamic associations build mosques, and some prefects continue to find creative ways to get enough properly sacrificed meat to Muslims on the Day of Sacrifice. Some jurists continue to argue that in some cases, marriages and divorces conducted in Islamic courts in other countries meet the substantive criteria of French public order and so ought to be recognized in France. Most jurists continue to argue that private arrangements that happen to involve Muslims—entering into an Islamic marriage but not a civil one, making promises to each other as a condition for a marriage—are just as legally acceptable as are arrangements made by others in France, such as those involved in concubinage. In each case, these acts of reasoning are wholly within the Republican realm of justification, on the terms of French norms and laws.

These examples of pragmatic reasoning make use of accepted French social forms—legally registered associations, divorce by mutual consent, private agreements—to legitimate institutions that may be innovative in specific form (mosques, outdoor abattoirs, talaq divorce) but that legally and morally extend to Muslims those rights already secured by others in France. Properly understood, laïcité guarantees that the state will manage religions in an even-handed way, such that Muslims, too, can carry out religious obligations and can take advantage of the possibilities offered by French law without suffering religious-based discrimination. At stake in each case are substantively equal rights, not special group rights.

For most of this book we have concentrated on convergence from the other direction: socially pragmatic forms of reasoning within the Islamic tradition. Many Islamic public actors have developed forms of Islamic reasoning that make use of accepted Islamic categories—the legal traditions, the *maqâsid ash-sharî'a*, the contractual nature of marriage—to legitimate practices that may be innovative in their specific form (French-language sermons, home loans at interest, civil marriage taken as already Islamic) but that extend to French Muslims the guarantees and the benefits already enjoyed by fellow Muslims living in societies with a broader range of Islamic institutions. Debated though these innovations may be—and they are strongly contested by many scholars—they are made within the Islamic realm of justification and not on the basis of extra-Islamic norms.

These extensions and convergences set out the empirical outline of a positive answer to the question, Can Islam be French? The challenge for each side involves broader acceptance of pluralism and pragmatism, but in quite different ways. French Muslims find themselves debating and deliberating in a transnational realm of Islamic justification, where they are hard-pressed to provide sophisticated Islamic foundations for their views. As we saw, some prominent French Muslim actors justify their interpretations on the grounds that they will have positive social consequences. Even when they offer textual support for their argument, the formulation of the argument is motivated by the desired social outcome, and this motivation is one basis for the criticism they receive.[53] Can these scholars, or their next generation, develop arguments with more fully developed historical and juridical bases? If they can, they and their colleagues elsewhere in Europe and North American might muster broader global support for their efforts to develop new, innovative Islamic institutions.

Conversely, France's challenge is to find ways to theorize—in law, politics, and social life—the actual social situation of value-pluralism. Might the makers of French public opinion discover that a shared objective, that of joining in a "common life" in Republican political space, can be reached along more than one pathway? Treating Muslims' pathways as similar to those once followed by Catholics and Jews might make the projects of Dhaou Meskine, Hichem El Arafa, or Larbi Kechat seem less like exotic, or dangerous, imports and more like new entries in the long-running story of the Republic. If dominant ways of thinking about laïcité and about integration shift away from an ideal of value-monism and toward an ideal of shared respect for a common legal and political framework, then that discovery might be made.

Notes

1. Pew Global Attitudes Project (2006). When asked to choose between religion and nationality as their primary identity, 42 percent of them said French first, Muslim second. By contrast, only 7 percent of British Muslims and 3 percent of Spanish Muslims put nationality first.

2. My visit was in October 2006.

3. Bowen (2007).

4. I do not know who first uttered this phrase, but I have heard it many times in the speeches of Tariq Ramadan.

5. I have set out the political-theoretic issues in an earlier work on Islamic Indonesia (Bowen 2003); the contrast here is to the later writings of John Rawls (especially Rawls 1999). My ethnographic-analytic focus on how actors reason given the constraints of a specific field, or "realm of justification," rather than a normative focus on whether their reasons are acceptable in liberal-democratic societies distinguishes this approach from most work developed in the wake of Rawls's writings but is neither contradictory to nor inconsistent with it.

6. Boltanski and Thévenot (2006) distinguish six such "worlds" of justification, of which the "civic" closely resembles idealized forms of Republicanism and the "inspired" concerns aesthetics, not religion. A more ethnographic and inductive approach, and thus closer to what I try to do here, comes from Lamont and Thévenot (2000), who begin with the Boltanski and Thévenot classification, but then highlight French-American contrasts in dominant modes of justifying specific policy measures. Both approaches differ from the cognate scheme advanced earlier by Michael Walzer (1983), in that Walzer bases his distinction of "spheres of justice" both on values, such as "hard work," and on institutional domains, such as "office." All these lines of inquiry are indebted to Max Weber's efforts to analyze ideas of status and worth, but recent work seems to have slighted Weber's perceptive analyses of religious goods, such as salvation, as constitutive of hierarchies. Even Walzer, much of whose career has concerned salvation and religious certainty, gives only a few pages to the subject (1983: 243–48), and Boltanski and Thévenot's scheme seems to leave out religion entirely; Lamont, however, has insisted on the importance of morality as a criterion of worth. Finally, I refer to the idea of "social fields" developed by Pierre Bourdieu, for example in the case of "religious field" (1971), but I find the fields treated in this book to be better seen as unstable outcomes of historical compromises than fixed spaces structured by diverse sorts of capital. Specific Islamic initiatives reawaken the anxieties and resentments generated by those compromises, as in the case of Islamic private schools or Islamic marriages. For a different application of Bourdieu's theory to the French Islamic case, see Peter (2006).

7. On the issues of Republicanism, associations, and religious life, see Gauchet (1985, 1998) and Rosanvallon (2004, 2006); on the specific legal history of French secularism, see Boyer (2004).

8. I can only indicate something of the range of excellent, recent studies of gender and Islam by pointing to a few titles: on contemporary legal reform and women's rights, Welchman (2007); on scripture, Ahmed (1993), Ali (2006), and Wadud (2006); for a historical study of judicial practice and fatwas, Tucker (1998); for an ethnographic analysis of gender and agency in religious practice, Mahmood (2005); and on Indonesian judicial practices and reforms, my own study (Bowen 2003).

9. These comparative remarks concern Western Europe. We must remember that parts of southeastern Europe have been mainly Muslim for centuries, as have areas of Russia; see my overview of the broader Western European Muslim world in Bowen (2008a), and see Caruso (2007), Cesari (2004), and Rath et al. (1999).

10. Ansari (2004); Lewis (2002).

11. For example, Frégosi (2006); Venel (2004); and see the discussion in chapter two. The first work along these lines was Gaspard and Khosrokhavar (1995), which must be seen as an important political response to a far-right denunciation of scarf-wearing, as well as a pioneering academic work.

12. The classic in this genre is Tribalat (1995); see also Tribalat, Simon, and Riandey (1996).

13. Cesari (1998); Souilamas (2000); Venel (2004). See Khosrokhavar (2004) on prison life. Other studies have had different aims. Kepel (1991) is a detailed historical and political account of Islamic institutions and practices in France; Roy (1999, 2002) has pursued an inquiry into the global nature of Islam in France and elsewhere.

14. Roy (1999, 2007). See also Gauchet (1998) and my discussion in Bowen (2007: 182–96).

15. The 2001 report by the High Council on Integration followed earlier scholars in estimating the number of Muslims at slightly over 4 million, but insisted that the number of people "of Muslim religion" would be closer to 1 million, the rest being "of Muslim culture" (Haut Conseil 2001: 36–39). They based their estimate of the number of people of "Muslim religion" on surveys concerning how often Muslims pray in mosques. Because the census is not allowed to gather data on "faith," figures in France always have to settle for official data on immigration and naturalization, and surveys on religious practices.

16. A number of younger European scholars also seek to understand French Islamic understandings of religion, including Alexandre Caeiro (2004, 2006), Frank Peter (2006), and Amel Boubekeur (2004). I draw on the work of many other colleagues as well, cited elsewhere in this book.

17. For recent discussions of the ideas of general interest and public good, see Opwijs (2007) and Zaman (2004).

CHAPTER TWO: FASHIONING THE FRENCH ISLAMIC LANDSCAPE

1. On the history of immigration in France, see Dewitte (2003), Feldblum (1998), Hargreaves (1995), Viet (1998), and Weil (1991); on the contrast between France and Britain on ideas about and laws regulating immigration, see Favell (2001). On the history of secularism, see Baubérot (2004); on anti-Semitism,

Wieviorka (2007); on the contemporary legacies of colonialism, Blanchard, Bancel, and Lemaire (2005).

2. On national identity, see Lebovics (1992) and Noiriel (1995). The debates in 2007 over the inclusion of the phrase "national identity" in a new ministry remind us how contentious this notion is for its echoes of Vichy-era anti-Semitism, particularly when, as in the case of the new ministry, it is linked to immigration (Weil 2008).

3. For overviews and analyses of France's "Islamic politics" in colonized territories, see three recent volumes: Bancel, Blanchard, and Vergès (2003), Le Pautrement (2003), and Luizard (2006).

4. Jewish residents of Algeria eventually were declared to be French citizens, but Muslims had to renounce their Islamic civil or personal status in order to apply for French citizenship. Adopting citizenship came to be thought of by many as giving up Islam; see Stora (2004) and Shepard (2006).

5. On Algerian migrations and post-independence demographics, see J. Simon (2002) and Stora (1992).

6. On these separate immigration streams, see the essays in Dewitte (1999), and see Dewitte (2003) for an overview.

7. I explore these contrasts in Bowen (2008a). Briefly, the sources of difference vary for each country: Britain's South Asian Muslims are divided into many competing factions by their schools of origin, Germany's Turkish Muslims mainly by the division between state-run and Millî Görüs mosques, and those in the Netherlands and other northern countries by the wide range of countries of origin.

8. Sargent and Larchanché-Kim (2006); see also Timera (1996).

9. For an analysis of the recent attention to "blacks" as a socioracial category in France, see Ndiaye (2007).

10. Petek (1998).

11. Petek (1998); Kastoryano (1986); see also Amiraux (2001) on Turkish leaders in Germany.

12. Héran, Filhon, and Deprez (2002).

13. Godard and Taussig (2007: 27)

14. Godard and Taussig (2007: 25). The situation is complicated by different state language policies and by differences in education and generation: French is an official language in Mali or Senegal, but recent emigrants from rural regions of those countries may never have attended school; Algerians' competence in French varies by shifting educational policies, and so on.

15. These percentages are 45 percent of Tunisians, 37 percent of those who were born in Algeria or Morocco, 26 percent of those from Turkey, 39 percent of Senegalese, and 21 percent of those from Mali (Borrel 2006). We may also analyze the numbers of new arrivals to France who do not have French residency papers (and who a fortiori are not French nationals). In 2003, of those who signed the new "contract of welcome and integration," which requires language lessons and civics lessons in return for residence and the eventual possibility of naturalization, 29 percent were Algerians, 17 percent Moroccans, 7 percent Tunisians, and 6 percent Turks.

16. Each HLM is run by one or more private or public companies, or is jointly owned by residents, and benefits from state funding by way of a tax levied on

businesses. Today there are almost 300 HLM state offices, which bring together local governments, state officials, and private companies to provide funds and supervise day-to-day operations. There also are private HLM companies that work in parallel with the public offices and receive subsidized loans (as do the inhabitants). Today nearly 5 million people live in just over 2 million HLM units; see Barou (2002) and Tellier (2007). For a moving account of the slums in which many immigrants lived prior to finding decent lodgings, see Sayad (1995); on Tunisian workers' spaces, see G. Simon (1979).

17. Lepoutre (1997: 42).

18. Cited in Laurence and Vaisse (2006: 36). These figures do not include children of immigrants.

19. Meurs, Pailhé, and Simon (2005). See Maurin (2004) and, on schools, Bowen (2008b).

20. See Bromberger (2006) for a personal account of Clichy-sous-Bois.

21. About three-quarters of legal immigrants arrive in France today through claims of marriage or family ties, most often when a French citizen reaches back to a country of origin to find a spouse (*Le Monde*, January 4, 2006).

22. This common identity was reinforced by the tendency of others in France to assimilate all North Africans to the category of "Arabs" or *Maghrébin* (from the Arabic word for West, also used for Morocco, on the western edge of the Muslim world). Anthropologist David Lepoutre noted for the Quatre-Mille projects near Paris that young people use the categories of "Arabs," "Blacks," or "French"—today in their current slang forms of *Rebeu, Renoi,* and *Céfran* (Lepoutre 2001: 79–106).

23. Students from North Africa had formed associations at least since 1907, and continuing on to the present, but it was only in the 1960s that workers began to do so. These associations tended to either be organized by or on behalf of origin countries, such as the Friends of Algerians in Europe, or as a vehicle to oppose regimes in the home countries. See Silverstein (2004) and Wihtol de Wenden and Leveau (2000).

24. Sayad (1999) gives a moving sociological account of the immigrant's plight; Boubeker (2003) and Hajjat (2005) do so for the *beur* generation. See Chattou and Belbah (2001) on the meaning of citizenship for Moroccan immigrants.

25. Cited in Godard and Taussig (2007: 420). See the essays in Boubeker and Hajjat (2008) on these new movements.

26. *Le Monde*, May 24, 2005.

27. Tariq Ramadan is the grandson of Hassan al-Banna, the founder of the Muslim Brotherhood in Egypt. A prolific author and lecturer, he has argued for a European Islam that preserves its ties to the Islamic tradition and also cultivates practices of European citizenship. He often is the target of accusations of "double-talk" because he does speak both to Islamic audiences and to broad-based European ones.

28. On these associations, see Wihtol de Wenden and Leveau (2000).

29. In an avowed effort to drive Muslims out of his town, the mayor of Charvieu-Chavagneux, in the Isère region, tore down buildings used for prayer by the local Islamic association in August 1989. Two years later he demanded they leave another set of buildings loaned to them by the regional government (*Le Monde*, August 17, 1991).

30. On the positions and anxieties surrounding the series of "headscarf af-fairs," up to the passage of a law in March 2004, see Bowen (2007); the reference is to an article signed by several of France's leading left-leaning intellectuals in *Le Nouvel Observateur* at the moment of the first "headscarf affair" in 1989.

31. Among them are Cesari (1994, 1998), Guénif-Souilamas (2000), Gas-pard and Khosrokhavar (1995), Tietze (2002), Venel (1999, 2004), and Weibel (2002).

32. Venel (1999: 71).

33. Souilamas (2000: 184–94).

34. Cesari (1998).

35. But see the important corrective to this claim by Alexandre Caeiro (2006), who emphasizes the ties connecting European institutions of *ifta* (the giving of fatwas) to older Islamic practices. For an overview of the problem of Islamic au-thority in Europe, see Caruso (2007).

36. Tunisians play a preponderant role as teachers, in part because actions taken by the Bourguiba government against Islamic-oriented parties and move-ments led many Islamic scholars to leave the country.

37. Examples of teachers developing this dual track are Tareq Oubrou in Bor-deaux, Ahmed Jaballah and Hichem El Arafa in Saint-Denis, and Dhaou Meskine in Aubervilliers, all mentioned below.

38. The term "Salafi" can be used to convey multiple meanings. The term refers to the "pious ancestors" who followed the Prophet Muhammad and is invoked as part of diverse calls to return to older, more religious ideas and practices. In the late nineteenth century and early twentieth century it was adopted by modern-ist thinkers such as Muhammad 'Abduh, who wished to return to the original sources to introduce a new spirit into Islam. Its current use to indicate literalist or radical Muslim thinkers is more often than not imposed from without: many of those labeled Salafi in Europe would choose to call themselves *ahlul hadîth*, "those who follow the hadith." Most observers of European Islam distinguish be-tween a Salafism oriented toward da'wa, "predication," and one, far less numeri-cally important, oriented toward armed struggle; see Roy (1994, 2002). Salafists in the first sense often refer to such scholars as the hadith specialist Nâsir al-Dîn al-Albâni, and the Saudi Grand Mufti Abdelaziz Ibn Baz, both of whom died in 1999, and al-'Uthaymîn (d. 2001); many of their works are available in French translations in Islamic bookstores in France. For competing French accounts of the issues, see Kepel (2004) and Burgat (1995).

39. Galembert (1994, 2005); Kepel (1991).

40. On the "application" of the 1905 law and the development of Islamic as-sociations in Algeria, as well as the eventual challenge to French governance of Islam, see Bozzo (2006), Achi (2006), and Shepard (2006).

41. These peaks came in 1989, when fear of the Ayatollah Khomeini came at a time of disillusion with the grand political projects of the preceding decades; in the mid-1990s, when some on the French Left sought to link growing politi-cal violence in Algeria and its spillover into France to the growing expression of Islamic beliefs; and again starting in 2001, when a series of government reports described malfunctioning schools and a growing lack of contact between the ethnic France and the children of immigrants, and the attacks of September 11

raised domestic fears of Islamic violence; see Bowen (2007). On the chronology of security-related events, see Bowen (2009).

42. For a comprehensive examination of these efforts, see Laurence and Vaisse (2006).

43. Sarkozy gave the two vice-presidential positions to leaders of the two other large mosque networks. The National Federation of French Muslims (Fédération Nationale des Musulmans de France, FNMF), formed in 1985, was associated with Morocco and most of its affiliated mosques were led by Moroccan imams; since the creation of the Islamic Council, however, the Moroccan association has split into two groups, with challengers winning seats in the 2008 elections and a Moroccan, Mohammed Moussaoui, chosen as the new Islamic Council president. The UOIF was mentioned above. Several other organizations have been represented in the Islamic Council: the two largest associations of Turkish mosques, the proselytizing Tablighi Jama'at organization, and an association of Muslims from West Africa and other French overseas departments and territories.

44. On the state's role in regulating Islam and on the hostage crisis, see Bowen (2007: 34–62, 145–46).

45. Zeghal (2006).

46. *Le Monde*, July 6, 2007.

47. See Brisebarre (1998) for some of these efforts.

48. *Libération*, Febuary 11, 2003; *Le Monde*, February 11, 2003.

49. Renard (1999) discusses this history.

50. Kepel (1991: 145–59); Pitti (2008).

51. The body originally had the modifier "Algerian" added to it name; this word was dropped in 1963.

52. I follow the major outlines provided by Kepel (1991: 125–68) for this period; on the use of these spaces by the workers, see Diop and Michalak (1996).

53. Galembert (1994).

54. See the case described by Kepel (1991: 161–68).

55. See Frégosi (2006: 44 et passim).

56. For more on the legal dimensions of these collaborations, see Bowen (2007: 39–48).

57. In Toulouse, for example, in 1999 an imam appointed by the Algerian government to the mosque at Empalot became the leader of the association formed to work with the city to build a new mosque. Others, especially younger, French-born students, disputed his leadership. Their standard-bearer became Mamadou Daffé, who had come from Mali to pursue a doctorate in biology at Toulouse and a postdoctoral fellowship in the United States before taking a position at the CNRS in Toulouse, and who presides at the al-Houceine mosque next to Toulouse-Le-Mirail University. The division was not only along generational lines but also pitted Algerians against those from Morocco and elsewhere. "It is always like that," he told me in 2001. The division stalled the mosque project for years, although by 2005 construction had begun on land provided by the city. Similar rivalries among Muslim associations have stalled other projects to build mosques, even when the city administration had committed funds, most notably in Strasbourg and Marseille.

58. I draw on the analysis in Maussen (2009).

59. Bowen (2007).

60. *Le Monde*, July 7, 2006, July 17, 2007.

61. Godard and Taussig (2007: 130).

CHAPTER THREE: MOSQUES FACING OUTWARD

1. Frégosi (2006) provides a sophisticated analysis of mosques in some regions of contemporary France, Maussen (2005) an overview of studies on mosques and imams in Europe; see also Maussen (2009) for a detailed history of public policy on mosques in the Netherlands and France. Cesari (1994) provides a detailed account of Marseille mosques and other Islamic institutions; Ternisien (2002) includes some interesting aperçus on mosques as part of a broader survey. For a look at new Islamic spaces in Europe and North America, including mosques, see the essays in Metcalf (1996b).

2. *Le Figaro*, March 21, 2005, quoting the Interior Ministry.

3. *Le Monde*, November 16, 2006.

4. *Le Monde*, November 3, 2005. The upper Clichy mosque was run by young people affiliated with the FNMF, a rival organization to Boubakeur's Paris Mosque within the CFCM, and they did not want the Paris Mosque to appear to be speaking for Muslims.

5. On the UOIF Web site: http://www.uoif-online.com/modules.php?op=mod load&name=News&file=article&sid=414, accessed July 7, 2007.

6. Oumma.com, November 7, 2005.

7. See the interview with Yamin Makri in Boubeker and Hajjat (2008: 217–24).

8. This asymmetry had given rise to petty rivalries with the other associations, such that the coalition ceased their activities for one year to let things cool down. Indeed, when Fouad Imarraine opened an all-day seminar sponsored by the coalition in May 2001, he began by declaring that the association "has no goal of federating or uniting" (my fieldnotes).

9. See also Frégosi (1998).

10. *Le Monde*, February 8, 2002. No similar study has been undertaken since 2001, but the secret police, who plant informants in mosques throughout the country, reported about forty mosques under "Salafi" control by early 2005, a term used in those circles to refer to teachings close to those of Saudi religious leaders; these figures suggest that at least some sermons took on a more political tone (*Le Monde*, February 22, 2005). It should be noted that after 2001, sermons were much more likely to be policed than before, and that few revelations of radical sermons have surfaced in the ever-vigilant mass media.

11. Cesari (2005).

12. Later on in our conversation I asked him about his ideas on an "Islam de France," and he reacted negatively to the phrase: "When people say that, they mean something 'moderate,' such as Dalil Boubekeur." I reminded him that he had used the phrase, and he said yes, he was talking about how most people use it.

13. On this tension in French political history, see Rosanvallon (2004, 2006). Karim invited me to speak about Islam in the United States to the 2005 annual

gathering. But a few days before the gathering he called me, embarrassed, to say they had circulated the program, and the speaker they had invited from Senegal had refused to come if there was an American on the program, and they already had paid for his plane ticket, so that they had to "disinvite" me.

14. See the interview with Boualam Azahoum on DiverCité, and with Salah Amokrane on les Motivé-e-s, in Boubeker and Hajjat (2008: 201–6, 265–71).

15. This section is based on interviews with mosque personnel conducted in April, 2006; see also Frégosi (2006: 302–5).

16. *Le Monde*, October 13, 2006.

17. Knowledge of usûl al-fiqh is generally acknowledged as particularly deficient, not only in France, and at the same time necessary for the project of rethinking jurisprudence.

18. The imam of Roubaix, Imam Kerzazi, was jailed in 1997 for the death of a girl he was exorcising (*L'Express*, November 9, 2006). The Abbe Bellot, exorcist in Paris, said that many Muslims come to see him because they figure that on Catholic territory he would be more effective against jinn than Muslims would be. On Bellot, see *Le Monde*, December 31, 1995.

19. Najjar specified the action called a "khula" divorce, or an action taken by the wife in which she offers payment, sometimes the value of the marriage gift, the *mahr*, in return for the husband's willingness to acquiesce to the divorce. I return to the problems with extralegal marriages in chapter eight.

20. Here the references are to Ibn Baz (d. 1999) and al-'Uthaymîn (d. 2001), Saudi grand muftis, and probably to Shaykh 'Arabî al-Tabbân.

21. Godard and Taussig (2007: 104); Galembert (2005).

22. Direche-Slimani and Le Houérou (2002: 103–18).

23. Comoro Muslims followed the Shâfi'î tradition, in contrast to the majority of North Africans, who are Mâlikî followers, and to the Hanafî followers in the Middle East and South Asia.

24. This description is taken from Direche-Slimani and Le Houérou (2002: 103–39).

25. This section draws from Bava (2003, 2004); see also Ebin (1996).

26. In this respect the practices of this and other Sufi groups resemble those pursed by the networks of some Shi'ite groups; see Blank (2001) for a case study.

27. Bava (2003: 161).

28. Soares (2004); on a different West African case, the Soninké, see Timera (1996).

29. Frégosi (2006: 63).

30. Comité de coordination des Musulmans Turcs de France, CCMTF.

31. Caymaz (2002: 216).

32. Frégosi (2006: 58).

33. Frégosi (2006: 80–81).

34. Two other major categories of imams have been mentioned only briefly: those affiliated with the Tablighi Jama'at and those labeled "Salafi."

35. "Congregationalism" as an analytical term tends to include two dimensions: organizing along voluntary membership lines of governance, and the provision of community services. Immigrant communities in the United States tend to adopt some form of this model; see Ebaugh (2003).

CHAPTER FOUR: SHAPING KNOWLEDGE TO FRANCE

1. Many sophisticated books of fiqh are also arranged by topics and provide rules, and I discuss an example from Qaradâwî below. By rule-book I mean an approach that frames learning in terms of simply following rules.

2. On the Tablighi Jama'at, see Metcalf (1996a).

3. The center has changed names several times as well. I first knew it in 2001 as the IEIP, Institut d'Études Islamiques de Paris, or Paris Institute of Islamic Studies.

4. In 2006, each sequence cost 460 euros per year. There is also a four-month intensive Arabic course for those who already have some knowledge of the language.

5. In the early 2000s the last-mentioned course was based on a reading of a French edition of the twelfth-century theologian al-Ghazzâlî's Revival of the Religious Sciences.

6. See chapter two, n. 38, on the polysemy of the term "Salafi."

7. On the development of scholarship about and uses of the hadith, see Brown (1996) and Graham (1993).

8. Qur'an 2:225. Many Muslims consider reciting this verse to bring more merit than any other verse.

9. Al-Qaradâwî (1995:17).The book relies heavily on the Riyâd al-Sâlihîn of the seventh-century scholar Imam Nawawi. On al-Qaradâwî, see Feldman (2007) and Mariani (2003); see also Zaman (2006).

10. Al-Qaradâwî (2001, 2002).

11. On the Egyptian Renewal movement to which Hichem is attuned, see Baker (2003). On the broader field of religious education in Cairo, see Zeghal (1996, 2006).

12. Despite Hichem's many criticisms of the Saudi approach to knowledge, the center receives funding from Saudi sources, as do many other Islamic institutions in France. One day in class in 2001, Hichem entered accompanied by a bearded, tall man, whom he introduced as the representative of the Saudi embassy in charge of looking at what is being done for Islamic education in France. He spoke only Arabic. Hichem later told me that they like to control things, keep tabs on what is being done everywhere. This aid makes Hichem visibly nervous, and in truth, it is unclear that the Saudis exert any efforts to control what is taught. No other teachers have ever accused him of being influenced by this aid.

13. Abû Ishâq al-Shâtibî (d. 1388) grew up in Granada; most references are to his work al-Muwâfaqât; see Masud (1977) and al-Raysuni (2005). Shâtibî's approach was one among several distinct efforts to place the concept of welfare (maslaha) within the broader framework of Islamic legal reasoning; see Opwijs (2007). The continuing interest in Shâtibî can be seen on the Internet, where, for example, as of late 2008, the Web site www.islamonline.net had nine fatwas in its fatwa bank that cited Shâtibî. On the question of whether these forms of reasoning are ultimately able to advance jurisprudential reasoning, see the arguments set out in Hallaq (1997). On relationships between objectives, principles, and the "cause" ('illah) of a verse, see Kamali (2008: 126–36).

14. Ibn Ashur (1879–1973) studied at al-Zaytuna in Tunis and in 1932 was named Sheikh al-Islam. Among his works is Maqâsid al-Shari'ah al-Islâmiyyah,

available in translation (Ibn Ashur 2006). On al-Fâsî, see Johnston (2007). The Qaradâwî quote is from Zaman (2004: 135).

CHAPTER FIVE: DIFFERENTIATING SCHOOLS

1. Note how he casts the presentation of fiqh in the past by making the analogy to equivalents "today."

2. The students were doing their best to understand precisely what to do; one told me later, "I take the classes to add to what I understand about my religion, not with the idea of teaching or being an imam."

3. Here he is probably referring to al-Bûtî's criticisms of maqâsid reasoning; see chapter seven.

4. Note the same emphasis made by the UOIF, described in chapter seven.

5. Bourdieu (1971); cf. Peter (2006).

CHAPTER SIX: CAN AN ISLAMIC SCHOOL BE REPUBLICAN?

1. Some 98 percent of all private schools under state contract are Catholic, and in 2000, 40 percent of families used Catholic schools; the number is doubtless higher by 2009 (Troger 2001). Two other Islamic day schools had begun teaching in metropolitan France by late 2008: one in Lille, sponsored by the UOIF, and a second in Lyon, around which sufficient controversy reigned to cause the resignation of the director of the regional school academy (the governing body for schools). The relative success of the Lille school has confirmed the suspicions of some that those who play the state's game (in this case, by joining the Islamic Council) are more likely to be rewarded.

2. Dhaou continued to make unfavorable comparisons with the Rose Luxembourg school, noting after the Success School's first year that only one pupil failed to achieve the average grade (and he did achieve it the following year), whereas only 15 percent of the public school's pupils did.

3. By 2002, of the 913 children who had ever taken a class or gone on a summer camp, most came from Seine-Saint-Denis, and most of those, 508, had declared their nationality as Tunisian, followed by French at 313, and far smaller numbers for other nationalities.

4. *SaphirNews*, November 7, 2005.

5. At the following year's examination, one girl did not pass. When she arrived at the designated site for the examination, a public school in the eastern Paris suburb of Montreuil, she was told to take off her headscarf before entering the classroom; Dhaou claimed this incident distracted her. She retook the examination later that year and passed.

6. Fayçal's slate gained only 8 percent of the second round vote, but that was enough to get him and the next candidate elected to the local council.

7. *Libération*, June 21, 2006; *Le Figaro*, July 5, 2006.

8. *Le Monde*, November 11, 2006; *Le Figaro*, November 2, 2006.

CHAPTER SEVEN: SHOULD THERE BE AN ISLAM FOR EUROPE?

1. See Hallaq (1997), Johansen (1999), Powers (2001), and the essays on ifta' in Masud, Messick, and Powers (1996); on the German case, see Rohe (2004).

2. As of 2006 I knew of one institution that would accompany a Muslim to a bank to propose an arrangement whereby the bank would buy the house and the client would repay at a slightly higher price but without interest.

3. See Saeed (1996) for a review of the varying Islamic approaches to the idea of ribâ.

4. The fatwa discussed here appears on the council's Web site in the list of resolutions taken at the 1999 session: http://www.fioe.org/ask_the_scholar/fourth%20statement.htm. On the council's history and the mortgage fatwa, see Caeiro (2004).

5. In the paper prepared for the deliberations, a member of the council, al-Arabi Bichri, drew on the analysis of ribâ made by the legal scholar 'Abd al-Razzâq Sanhûrî and concluded that for some types of ribâ, demonstrating mere needs (hâja) sufficed to authorize an exception. He also proposed that a loan at fixed interest, perhaps limited to a rate of 7 percent, could be considered equivalent to an installment sale (Caeiro 2004: 353–54).

6. Caeiro (2004: 374).

7. See the site http://www.bouti.net/en/article.php?PHPSESSID=c9153546701 ed7fb35b22f45a728f9ed&id=349, accessed November 9, 2007.

8. Ben Biya's speech was translated from the podium. All quotations are from my notes from the French translation, though I also noted the key Arabic terms he and others used. Beyond these general pronouncements, the UOIF's own fatwa body, the Dar al-Fatwa, has made use of the possibility of issuing individual fatwas to extend the boundaries of the community fatwa on interest. In 2006, a member of the Dar al-Fatwa, Ounis Qourqah, told me that on the previous day he had spoken with someone he had known for ten years and who had a good idea to open a business. "I told him that it was permissible to take out a bank loan for that purpose because his situation was an emergency [darurat]." A general fatwa to that effect would also be in the interest of the Muslim community in general, he continued, but the European Council does not want to consider that question: "it is too difficult, touches so many people."

9. Al-Qaradâwî has achieved recognition for his advocacy of the "middle way" (wasatiyya, juste milieu). Born in 1926 in Egypt, al-Qaradâwî studied and taught at al-Azhar before moving to Qatar, where he created a faculty of shari'a. Today he publishes his thoughts in books and (since 1997) on his Web site and through his contributions to the television station al-Jazira; he also heads the committee responsible for the site Islam On-line. The idea of a fiqh for minorities may have originated in the mid-1990s with the Iraqi scholar Taha Jabir al-Alwani, who directs the School of Islamic and Social Sciences in Leesburg, Virginia, near Washington, D.C., and whose book, *Towards a Fiqh for Minorities: Some Basic Reflections*, appeared in Arabic in 2000 and in English in 2003.

10. Al-Qaradâwî (2002: 19); see Feldman (2007).

11. Al-Qaradâwî (1991: 113).

12. Al-Qaradâwî (2002).

13. On the early modern Hanafî position, see Abou El Fadl (1994: 173–74).

14. Ramadan (2002).

15. See http://www.bouti.net/en/article.php?PHPSESSID=c9153546701ed7fb3 5b22f45a728f9ed&id=336, accessed November 9, 2007.

16. See also al-Bûtî (2001). In the passage quoted, I have altered the English slightly for readability.

17. A "*SMIC spirituel*" (Makri 2005).

18. Work began on a new mosque and Islamic cultural center in September 2008, but sufficient funds had been raised only to cover the cost of building the foundation.

19. The visits may have had more of an effect on the father; see below.

20. Taqi ad-Din Ahmad ibn Taymiyyah (1263–1328) followed the teachings of Ibn Hanbal and often is considered to be a relatively strict interpreter of Islam, but some of his specific opinions, such as this one on divorce, are cited by those seeking to adapt Islam to European conditions. That it is Ibn Taymiyyah whom they cite may add additional rhetorical force to their efforts.

21. Islamic public actors may also strategically invoke French and European norms, as when some scholars argued that girls should be allowed to wear head-scarves to school because of the European convention on human rights; see Soysal (2002), although unlike her, I do not see a change in the structure of justifications within the Islamic realm.

22. Werbner (2003)

23. See Mariani (2006).

CHAPTER EIGHT: NEGOTIATING ACROSS REALMS OF JUSTIFICATION

1. As an example of the diverse potential social functions of norms surround-ing mahr, consider the contrast between Indonesian gifts, which are usually low in value and play a smaller role after the wedding, with those in much of South Asia and Iran, which may be very high and play a critical role in subsequent bargain-ing. See Mir-Hosseini (2001) for examples of how in contemporary Iran, a high mahr gives the bride leverage with respect to divorce and child custody.

2. The site le-mariage.com; it specializes in these questions of marriage for Mus-lims. The specific discussion was at http://www.le-mariage.com/speak/messages/ 66/5301.html?samedi7avril200722h28, last accessed June 14, 2007.

3. Since 2006 a woman must be eighteen to contract a marriage in France. This example is complicated by the fact that they appear to have legally married in Algeria, and that marriage could have been recognized in France but for her age.

4. The general-purpose French-language Yahoo site http://fr.answers.yahoo .com/question/index?qid=20070620102458AAApehHZ, accessed June 24, 2007.

5. Belgium has requirements regarding marriage similar to those in force in France.

6. An example is maison-islam.com, which focuses on religious questions; other sites, such as oumma.com and saphirnews.com, include such articles among other types of news, opinions, and general information.

7. On the question-and-answer format across Islamic history, see the essays in Masud, Messick, and Powers (1996).

8. On the interrelationships of authority and individualization on the Islamic Internet, see Roy (2002: 165–83).

9. For the Moroccans living in France interviewed by a team of sociologists in the mid-1990s, *les fiançailles* meant a promise to marry and not a simple "trial run" between a man and a woman, and this reflected the usage in Morocco itself, where the promise opened a period of negotiations about the terms of marriage (Rude-Antoine et al. 1998). In France the term seems to have come to mean, for some, the "trial run," or something like an engagement, which does not figure in mainstream Islamic understandings of Islam. See Boubekeur (2004: 116–22) on varying ideas of marriage and *fiançailles* in France.

10. The question began a thread about halâl marriage, on a site devoted to women's issues, http://forum.aufeminin.com/forum/f341/__f1286_f341-Fiancaille -ou-et-mariage-halal.html, accessed June 24, 2007.

11. Respondents disagreed sharply, however, as to whether or not Islam recognized an engagement. Some denied this claim vehemently, while others argued the opposite, on grounds that men had long promised their daughters to other men, and is this not engagement? See, for example, the long account at http://www .sajidine.com/fiq/mariage/fiancaille.htm, accessed June 24, 2007.

12. Some French imams will assure a woman who has divorced in civil fashion that she also is now free to remarry in the eyes of God, but there are no clear and agreed-on procedures or doctrines to this effect.

13. On the site http://www.bladi.net/forum/61455-rompre-hallal/index4.html, accessed June 24, 2007.

14. A condition clarified in the law no 99-944 of November 15, 1999.

15. See, on this point, Bénabent (1996: 28).

16. See Hafiz and Devers (2005: 261).

17. *Le Monde*, June 8, 2007.

18. Indeed, one blogger on a Muslim site expressed horrified surprise that fellow Muslims had been running this risk, which of course does not exist for the parties to the marriage under any interpretation of this law; see http://www.islamie .com/des-jeunes-musulmans-veulent-saffranchir-du-mariage-civil-t36601.html?s =2eb252d405907c0d9595c400ad8bf266&p=333054#post333054, accessed June 26, 2007.

19. See the ministerial response to the question posed by the UMP deputy Étienne Mourrut, published in the *Journal Officiel*, August 5, 2007, p. 4319.

20. *Le Nouvel Observateur*, June 23, 2008.

21. *Le Parisien*, October 21, 2008.

22. He mentioned the author Malik Chebel as someone who did just that in referring to Islam but not reasoning from Islamic principles.

23. See Ramadan (1998) for his most extensive analysis of the heritage of Islam.

24. Interview, Saint-Denis, May 2, 2001.

25. Interview, Bordeaux, November 12, 2002.

26. Oubrou (2004).

27. Note the parallel with the procedures for evaluating reports of the Prophet's deeds and statements, discussed in chapter four.

28.Oubrou (2000: 43).

29. Interview, Bordeaux, November 12, 2002. Oubrou made the same argument in his extended debate with Leïla Babès, in Babès and Oubrou (2002: 328).

30. Interview, Saint-Denis, May 2001.

31. Interview, Bordeaux, November 12, 2002.

32. For an informed overview by one of the major commentators on these issues, who now sits on the Court of Cassation, see Monéger (2005).

33. See Libchaber (1996: 65).

34. Libchaber (1996: 69).

35. On the history of these categories in Algeria, see Shepard (2006).

36. The bilateral treaties also were consistent with the general principles of personal status within French interpretations of international private law, following which individuals carry their family status with them as they travel from one country to another; the relevant body of laws is that of the country in which they have citizenship. If they married or divorced in their own country following the rules of that country, they remained married or divorced when they traveled to France. If a conflict were to arise over that marriage or divorce while the couple happened to be in France and the husband or wife took the matter to court, the French judge would follow the legal rules that defined valid marriage and divorce in the country where the marriage or divorce took place, even if they conflicted with France's own rules. This basic tenet of the conflict-of-laws doctrine corresponds to common sense, in that one does not want marriages to become alternately valid and invalid as couples cross borders and laws change.

37. On these dilemmas and for an up-to-date review of the debate, see the analysis by Hugues Fulchiron (2006). Article 8 (right to lead a normal family life) of the European Convention on the Protection of Human Rights and Fundamental Freedoms is invoked to challenge expulsions of family members, but what counts as the "normal family life" to which all have a right remains under dispute.

38. In its *Bendeddouche* decision of 1980, the Court of Cassation ruled that a polygamous marriage could have effects in France, as did the *Montcho* decision taken by the Council of State the same year, which prevented a prefect from deporting a second wife and her children on grounds that the polygamous marriage went counter to ordre public.

39. On the history of immigration laws in France, see Feldblum (1999) and Weil (1991).

40. Alaux (2001); on some of the consequences for West African women in polygamous situations, see Sargent and Cordell (2003).

41. Lahouri (2004).

42. See Libchaber (1996: 72) and especially Begdache (2002: 140–52) and Monéger (2005: 54–55).

43. See especially Fulchiron (2006) on this point.

44. Libchaber (1996: 74).

45. Several Belgian lawyers have begun to reason in this way regarding the future evolution of the Morocccan code (France Blanmailland, personal communication, Brussels, July 15, 2008).

46. By 2000, more and more couples were avoiding marriage entirely, and 40 percent of children born in France each year were born to an unmarried couple,

according to the National Institute of Demographic Studies (INED), at http://
www.ined.fr/fichier/t_telechargement/3705/telechargement_fichier_fr_fiche4.pdf,
accessed June 26, 2007. See also INED (n.d.). On the tendencies toward de facto
polygamy by successive French presidents, see Deloire and Dubois (2006).

47. Several law professors expressed their acceptance, if not enthusiasm, for
this solution to me as late as 2008.

48. Fulchiron (2006).

49. For an example, see the debates on talaq in the special issue of the *Revue
internationale de droit comparé*, no. 1, 2006.

CHAPTER NINE: ISLAMIC SPHERES IN REPUBLICAN SPACE

1. On charges of "communalism" (*communautarisme*), see Bowen (2007: 155–
81); on "insufficient secularism," Bowen (2007: 183–207) and Roy (2007); on the
question of values, particularly regarding gender equality, Bowen (2007: 208–41)
and Scott (2007: 151–74).

2. See Rosanvallon (2004) on the first point; Kastoryano (2002) on the second
and especially at p. 101. In this section I draw extensively on Kastoryano (2002)
and Wihtol de Wenden and Leveau (2000).

3. The figures for associations are taken from the government Web site, http://
www.associations.gouv.fr, accessed August 8, 2008.

4. Kastoryano (2002: 107–12).

5. Kastoryano (2002: 98–104.

6. Tippett-Spirtou (2000: 76–77).

7. Cholvy (1999: 360–68); Pelletier (2002).

8. Hyman (1998: 114–35).

9. Hyman (1998: 142–44).

10. Benbassa (1999: 179–99).

11. Many of these pupils will have studied some Arabic and the basics of Islam
at a mosque or perhaps at La Réussite while of primary-school age.

12. See Bowen (2007).

13. See Beattie (2000).

14. See the cogent analysis of the issues, made with British and U.S. schools
in mind, by MacMullen (2007). On Islamic education in Britain, see Mandaville
(2006).

15. See Galston (2002) for the former position and MacMullen (2007) for the
latter among Anglo-American theorists.

16. Indeed, in both 2005 and 2006 the telecast was the most widely viewed
among all French on-line broadcasts. I attended the gatherings held in 2001,
2003, and 2006.

17. The bookstalls, each with its own orientation, provide a subtly shifting
map of the range of Islamic tendencies that fit under the UOIF's umbrella. Lyon-
based *Tawhid* features books it publishes, and in particular those written by
Tariq, Hani, and Said Ramadan. *Sana* publishes works by authors associated
with Saudi "Wahhabi" tendencies, such as Ibn Baz and al-Albâni. The Left Bank
store *al-Bourraq* emphasizes Sufis and more "scholarly" works, while *Arrissala*

publishes translations of Arabic-language religious books. By 2006, the Tawhid store had left the Salon, a sign of the break between the Lyon-based Collectif des Musulmans, whose leading light had been Tariq Ramadan, and the UOIF. A new magazine, *Generations*, now appeared, with a less expensive stand to the side of the hall, and translations of the Egyptian preacher Amr Khaled appeared alongside Saudi authors in several stands.

18. He and his associates kept busy answering questions from would-be students; they exhibited a set of pie charts showing where their students lived (mainly in Seine-Saint-Denis), how they had evaluated the courses (very positively), and whether they had found satisfactory employment afterward (75 percent had).

19. In other words, the UOIF performs the same function as the upper-class Catholic social networking events, the *rallyes*!

20. About thirty French Islamic associations had stands along the side of the main hall in 2006. These included seventeen groups seeking help to build mosques, four that appealed for humanitarian aid, two (La Réussite and Savoirs Utiles) soliciting new pupils for their schools, one for the Women's League, three for children's or students' associations, a booth for the arts, the one for *Generations*, and one for the sign language Muslims, "Give Me a Sign."

21. During the lively contest for the office of Grand Rabbin de France, for example, it was reported that one candidate, Gilles Bernheim, who won the contest, was accused by many in "the community" of "speaking too frequently with Christians." These comments did not elicit the kind of attacks that one would have heard if comparable comments had been made by Muslims (*Le Monde*, June 25, 2008).

22. This framing no doubt explains why a much larger percentage of French citizens find no conflict between Islam and modern society than is the case for other Europeans or North Americans. The best exemplar of the "Enlightenment Islam" perspective is Malik Chebel, featured regularly on talk shows and in the mainstream weeklies, whose book on 27 propositions to reform Islam led to criticism from some Muslims that he was "setting himself up as God by inventing a religion" (see the discussion on the Islamic site www.mejliss.com, May 5, 2006). A "liberal Islam" promotes the rights of "individual ijtihâd" and shows up on the mainstream shelves particularly through the writings of Dounia Bouzar (2004).

23. *Islam de France*, one of the more intellectual efforts within the Islamic public sphere, began life in January 1997 as a magazine, and that September transformed itself into a booklike quarterly review. Michel Renard, a French convert, and Saïd Branine, French of Algerian parents, were the editors. In 2000, Branine developed a Web version of the review, which eventually succeeded the print publication as allahouakbar.com and then oumma.com.

24. *Libération*, June 26, 2000. In a later version of this letter that was published in *Islam de France* (8:47–51, 2000), they make their suggestion of dire consequences more specific by referring to the killing of Mahmoud Mohammed Taha in the Sudan and the forced divorce and exile of Nasr Abou Zeid by an Egyptian court, both on grounds of apostasy.

25. Allahouakbar.com, July 5, 2000. See the response to their critics by Babès and Renard in *Islam de France* (8:64–66, 2000).

26. Babès (1997: 147–97) but see especially Babès (2000).

27. Babès and Oubrou (2002). Tariq Ramadan has told me that initially Babès proposed to write the book with him, but that after starting work with her he declined to continue.

28. Babès and Oubrou (2002: 23, 34).

29. Babès and Oubrou (2002: 82–85).

30. Brenner (2002); *Libération*, December 17, 2003. President Chirac cited *The Lost Territories* publicly during 2003, and the book is said to have had a strong influence on his decision to advocate a law against scarves in schools, passed in early 2004.

31. See Roy (2007).

32. Studies on values in France tend to affirm similarities between Muslims and others, but, as with most French studies trying to say something about a religious category, they run up against the problem of defining religious "identity" and the absence of data based on religious affiliation or preference. See, nonetheless, Brouard and Tiberj (2005), which samples "persons of immigration origins" from Africa and Turkey, a category that oddly mixes three generations of respondents and requires further analysis to discern religious orientation. They find the greatest difference in expressed values in responses to questions about premarital sex, an issue explored in this section.

33. Bowen (2007) is an account of the processes leading up to the law and an analysis of why such pressures grew during this period; the analyses in a special issue of the review *Droit et Société* (2008) provide invaluable insider accounts of the debates.

34. I do not take up here the question of the meanings and social roles attached to virginity among different Muslim men and women; Boubekeur (2004: 68–71) points to the insistence on the part of many young Muslim women on making the issue a matter between husband and wife.

35. In political theory, "multiculturalism" usually refers to two broad types of projects: those that would grant some degree of legal autonomy or special legal rights to members of certain groups, and those that would grant a degree of public recognition to efforts by groups to build their own institutions and identities; see Kymlicka's (1995) normative distinction between demands for self-government and those for polyethnic expression, and subsequent efforts to contrast "strong" and "weak" forms of multiculturalism, as in Shachar (2001). French theoretical discussions invariably refer to Anglo-American theorists; see, for example, Mesure and Renaut (1999) and Wivieorka (1996).

36. Whether or not the imam who participated in the nikah ceremony violated the law is, as I have mentioned, a question for continued legal debate.

37. This law was the same one that ended the official, public status of the churches. Exception was made in the law for religious buildings, funeral monuments or graves, and museums, and said that local or state rules would govern the ringing of church bells. In effect, the law leaves a great deal of discretion in the hands of local officials, and one hears church bells as much in parts of southern France as in Italy, though not in Republican Paris.

38. Muslim leaders have understood this repugnance and often keep even new mosque buildings out of public view. During 2003–4, I followed the building of a mosque in Bagnolet, a city bordering Paris on the east. The mosque is located

in a commercial park in the middle of a low-rent HLM complex, and from the outside it looks like any storefront, with a sign identifying it as the Olive of Peace Cultural Center. Inside, however, the visitor finds a large prayer room with carved pillars, rooms for Arabic classes, and proper facilities for ablutions. When the municipality learned that prayers were being held in a commercial park building, the director found himself in the middle of a zoning dispute. His own reticence to showcase the building as a mosque came from years of battling the antireligious mayor of a nearby community over the right to construct a new mosque.

39. I have been following this process in Bobigny, where the relevant municipal councilor has insisted on this public character. "It is a public building for a religion, not a meeting place for a sect," he explained to me in 2006.

40. See my lengthy exposition of this argument in Bowen (2007), and see Scott (2007) for a related set of claims.

41. The quotation is on p. 80 of the English edition of Schnapper's *Community of Citizens* (1998), but I have retranslated it from the French original.

42. *Le Figaro*, July 16, 2008.

43. See Olivier Roy's remarks to this effect in *Le Monde*, July 14, 2008.

44. Didier Leschi, quoted in *Le Monde*, July 11, 2008.

45. See Hugues Fulchiron's (2008) analysis to this effect.

46. *Le Point*, September 15, 2008; *Le Monde*, June 6, 2008.

47. *Le Monde*, June 6, 2008. The president of Ni Putes Ni Soumises made the second statement in *Le Monde*, May 31, 2008.

48. *Le Point*, June 5, 2008.

49. In September 2008, the state's attorney at nearby Douai, in consultation with the wife's lawyer and in order to "protect the interests of society," recommended that the marriage annulment be upheld but that some other grounds be sought that would not be contrary to ordre public, such as non-consummation. As some of the many public commentaries pointed out, the upshot was to annul for the original reasons but then to find another public justification that would not offend people (*Libération*, September 22, 2008).

50. *Le Figaro*, June 12, 2008.

51. Here I agree with the argument developed recently by Olivier Roy (2007). Is it ironic that French objections often target expressions of modesty, such as avoiding premarital sex, covering oneself, or remaining at home?

52. See Gaonkar and Taylor (2006).

53. See here Hallaq's (1997) trenchant critique of these modes of reasoning, and Masud's (2001) more hopeful assessment.

Bibliography

Abou El Fadl, Khaled. 1994. "Islamic Law and Muslim Minorities: The Juristic Discourse on Muslim Minorities from the Second/Eighth to the Eleventh/Seventeenth Centuries." *Islamic Law and Society* 1 (2): 143–87.

Achi, Raberh. 2006. "Les apories d'une projection républicaine en situation coloniale: La dépolitisation de la séparation du culte musulman et de l'État en Algérie." In *Le choc colonial et l'Islam: Les politiques religieuses des puissances coloniales en terres d'islam*, ed. Pierre-Jean Luizard, 237–52. Paris: La Découverte.

Ahmed, Leila. 1993. *Women and Gender in Islam: Historical Roots of a Modern Debate*. New Haven, CT: Yale University Press.

Alaux, Jean-Pierre. 2001. "À la rue sous prétexte de polygamie." *Plein Droit*, no. 51.

Ali, Kecia. 2006. *Sexual Ethics and Islam: Feminist Reflections on Qur'an, Hadith, and Jurisprudence*. Oxford: Oneworld Publications.

al-Alwani, Taha Jabir. 2003. *Towards a Fiqh for Minorities: Some Basic Reflections*. London: International Institute of Islamic Thought.

Amiraux, Valérie. 2001. *Acteurs de l'Islam entre Allemagne et Turquie. Parcours militants et expériences religieuses*. Paris: L'Harmattan.

Ansari, Hayuman. 2004. *The Infidel Within: Muslims in Britain since 1800*. London: Hurst & Co.

Babès, Leïla. 1997. *L'Islam positif: La religion des jeunes Musulmans de France*. Paris: Éditions de l'Atelier.

———. 2000. *L'Islam intérieur: Passion et désenchantement*. Paris: Éditions Al Bouraq.

Babès, Leïla, and Tareq Oubrou. 2002. *Loi d'Allah, loi des hommes: Liberté, égalité et femmes en Islam*. Paris: Albin Michel.

Baker, Raymond William. 2003. *Islam without Fear: Egypt and the New Islamists*. Cambridge, MA: Harvard University Press.

Bancel, Nicolas, Pascal Blanchard, and Françoise Vergès. 2003. *La République coloniale: Essai sur une utopie*. Paris: Albin Michel.

Barou, Jacques. 2002. *L'Habitat des immigrés et de leurs familles*. Paris: La Documentation Française.

Baubérot, Jean. 2004. *Laïcité 1905–2005: Entre passion et raison*. Paris: Éditions du Seuil.

Bava, Sophie. 2003. "Les Cheikh-s mourides itinérants et l'espace de la ziyâra à Marseille." *Anthropologie et Société* 27 (1): 149–66.

———. 2004. "Le dahira urbain: Lieu de pouvoir du mouridisme." *Les annales de la recherche urbaine*, no. 96, *Urbanités et liens religieux*, pp. 135–43.

Beattie, Nicholas. 2000. "Yeast in the Dough? Catholic Schooling in France, 1981–95." In *Catholicism, Politics and Society in Twentieth-Century France*, ed. Kay Chadwick, 197–218. Liverpool: Liverpool University Press.

Begdache, Roula el-Husseini. 2002. *Le Droit international privé français et la repudiation Islamique*. Paris: L.G.D.J.

Bénabent, Alain. 1996. "L'Ordre public en droit de la famille." In *L'Ordre public à la fin du XXème siècle*, ed. Thierry Revet. Paris: Dalloz.

Benbassa, Esther. 1999. *The Jews of France* (orig. French 1997). Princeton, NJ: Princeton University Press.

Blanchard, Pascal, Nicolas Bancel, and Sandrine Lemaire, eds. 2005. *La fracture coloniale: La société française au prisme de l'héritage colonial*. Paris: La Découverte.

Blank, Jonah. 2001. *Mullahs on the Mainframe*. Chicago: University of Chicago Press.

Boltanski, Luc, and Laurent Thévenot. 2006. *On Justification: Economies of Worth* (orig. French 1991). Princeton, NJ: Princeton University Press.

Borrel, Catherine. 2006. "Enquêtes annuelles de recensement 2004 et 2005." Insee Première no. 1098, août 2006, http://www.insee.fr/fr/ffc/ipweb/ip1098/ip1098 .html, accessed July 5, 2007.

Boubeker, Ahmed. 2003. *Les mondes de l'ethnicité*. Paris: Balland.

Boubeker, Ahmed, and Abdellali Hajjat, eds. 2008. *Histoire politique des immigrations (post)coloniales: France, 1920–2008*. Paris: Éditions Amsterdam.

Boubekeur, Amel. 2004. *Le voile de la mariée: Jeunes musulmanes, voile, et projet matrimoniale en France*. Paris: L'Harmattan.

Bourdieu, Pierre. 1971. "Genèse et structure du champ religieux." *Revue Française de Sociologie* 12 (3): 2995–334.

Bouzar, Dounia. 2004. *"Monsieur Islam" n'existe pas: Pour une déislamisation des débats*. Paris: Hachette.

Bowen, John R. 2003. *Islam, Law and Equality in Indonesia: An Anthropology of Public Reasoning*. Cambridge: Cambridge University Press.

———. 2007. *Why the French Don't Like Headscarves: Islam, the State, and Public Space*. Princeton, NJ: Princeton University Press.

———. 2008a. "Europe." In *The Muslim World*, ed. Andrew Rippin, 118–30. London: Routledge.

———. 2008b. "Republican Ironies: Equality and Identities in French Schools." In *Just Schools: Pursuing Equality in Societies of Difference*, ed. Martha Minow, Richard A. Shweder, and Hazel Rose Markus, 204–24. New York: Russell Sage Foundation.

———. 2009. "Recognizing Islam in France after 9/11." *Journal of Ethnic and Migration Studies*.

Boyer, Alain. 2004. *1905: La séparation églises-état: De la guerre au dialogue*. Paris: Éditions Cana.

Bozzo, Anna. 2006. "Islam et citoyenneté en Algérie sous la IIIe République: Logiques d'émancipation et contradictions coloniales (l'exemple des lois de 1901 et 1905)." In *Le choc colonial et l'islam: Les politiques religieuses des puissances coloniales en terres d'islam*, ed. Pierre-Jean Luizard, 197–222. Paris: La Découverte.

Brenner, Emmanuel, ed. 2002. *Les territoires perdus de la république*. Paris: Mille et Une Nuits.

Brisebarre, Anne-Marie. 1998. "L''Ayd al-Kabir en France." In *Le Fête du Mouton: Un sacrifice musulman sans l'espace urbain*, ed. Anne-Marie Brisebarre, 43–188. Paris: CNRS Éditions.

Bromberger, Dominique. 2006. *Clichy-sous-Bois: Vallée des anges*. Paris: Arléa.

Brouard, Sylvain, and Vincent Tiberj. 2005. *Français commes les autres? Enquête sur les citoyens d'origine maghrébine, africaine et turque*. Paris: Presses de la Foundation Nationale de Sciences Politiques.

Brown, Daniel. 1996. *Rethinking Tradition in Modern Islamic Thought*. Cambridge: Cambridge University Press.

Burgat, François. 1995. *L'islamisme au Maghreb*. Paris: Payot.

al-Bûtî, Mohammad Saʿîd Ramadân. 2001. "La confluence de la 'jurisprudence des minorités' et le fractionnnement de l'islam n'est nullement une coïncidence," at http://www.islamophile.org/spip/article.php3?id_article=107.

Caeiro, Alexandre. 2004. "The Shifting Moral Universes of the Islamic Tradition of Iftāʾ: A Diachronic Study of Four Adab al-Fatwā Manuals." *Muslim World* 96 (4): 661–85.

———. 2006. "The Social Construction of Sharîʿa: Bank Interest, Home Purchase, and Islamic Norms in the West." *Die Welt des Islams* 44 (3): 351–75.

Caruso, Antonella. 2007. "Au Nom de l'Islam . . . : Quel dialogue avec les minorités musulmanes en Europe?" Paris: Institut Montaigne.

Caymaz, Birol. 2002. *Les mouvements islamiques Turcs à Paris*. Paris: L'Harmattan.

Cesari, Jocelyne. 1994. *Etre musulman en France: Associations, militants et mosquées*. Paris: Karthala.

———. 1998. *Musulmans et républicains: Les jeunes, l'Islam et la France*. Brussels: Editions Complexe.

———. 2004. *L'Islam á l'épreuve de l'occident*. Paris: Découverte.

———. 2005. "Mosques in French Cities: Towards the End of a Conflict?" *Journal of Ethnic and Migration Studies* 31 (6): 1025–43.

Chattou, Zoubir, and Mustapha Belbah. 2001. *Sujet et citoyen: Evolutions, enjeux et significations de l'acquisition de la nationalité française par des Marocains en France*. Paris: Ministère de l'Emploi et de la Solidarité.

Cholvy, Gérard. 1999. *Histoire des organisations et mouvements chrétiens de jeunesse en France, XIXe –XXe siècle*. Paris: Éditions du Cerf.

Deloire, Christophe, and Christophe Dubois. 2006. *Sexus politicus*. Paris: Albin Michel.

Dewitte, Philippe, ed. 1999. *Immigration et integration: L'état des saviors*. Paris: La Découverte.

———. 2003. *Deux siècles d'immigration en France*. Paris: La Documentation Française.

Diop, Moustapha, and Laurence Michalak. 1996. "'Refuge' and 'Prison': Islam, Ethnicity, and the Adaptation of Space in Workers' Housing in France." In *Making Muslim Space in North America and Europe*, ed. Barbara Daly Metcalf, 74–91. Berkeley and Los Angeles: University of California Press.

Direche-Slimani, Karima, and Fabienne Le Houérou. 2002. *Les Comoriens à Marseille: D'une mémoire à l'autre*. Paris: Éditions Autrement.

Ebaugh, Helen Rose Fuchs. 2003. "Religion and the New Immigrants." In *Handbook of the Sociology of Religion*, ed. M. Dillon, 225–39. New York: Cambridge University Press.

Ebin, Victoria. 1996. "Making Room versus Creating Space: The Construction of Spatial Categories by Itinerant Mouride Traders." In *Making Muslim Space in North America and Europe*, ed. Barbara Daly Metcalf, 92–109. Berkeley and Los Angeles: University of California Press.

Favell, Adrian. 2001. *Philosophies of Integration: Immigration and the Idea of Citizenship in France and Britain*, 2nd ed. Houndmills, UK: Palgrave.

Feldblum, Miriam. 1998. *Reconstructing Citizenship: The Politics of Nationality Reform and Immigration in Contemporary France*. Albany: State University of New York Press.

Feldman, Noah. 2007. "Shari'a and Islamic Democracy in the Age of al-Jazeera." In *Shari'a: Islamic Law in the Contemporary Context*, ed. Abbas Amanat and Frank Griffel, 104–19. Stanford, CA: Stanford University Press.

Felouzis, Georges, Françoise Liot, and Joëlle Perroton. 2005. *L'apartheid scolaire: Enquête sur la ségrégation ethnique dans les collèges*. Paris: Éditions du Seuil.

Frégosi, Franck. 1998. "Les filières nationales de formation des imams en France." In *La formation des cadres religieux musulmans en France*, ed. Franck Frégosi, 101–39. Paris: L'Harmattan.

———. 2006. *L'Exercice du culte musulman en France: Lieux de prière et d'inhumation*. Paris: La Documentation Française.

Fulchiron, Hugues. 2006. "'Ne répudiez point . . .': Pour une interpretation raisonée des arrêts du 17 février 2004." *Revue internationale de droit compare* 1: 7–26).

———. 2008. "De la virginité dans le marriage." Le Blog Dalloz (dalloz.fr), June 2, 2008.

Galembert, Claire de. 1994. "L'exclu et le rival: L'Eglise catholique et les musulmans en France." In *Exils et Royaume: Les appartenances au monde arabo-musulman aujourd'hui*, ed. Gilles Kepel, 365–84. Paris: Presses de la Fondation Nationale des Sciences Politiques.

———. 2005. "The City's 'Nod of Approval' for the Mantes-la-Jolie Mosque Project: Mistaken Traces of Recognition." *Journal of Ethnic and Migration Studies* 31 (6): 1141–59.

———, ed. 2008. *Le voile en procès*. Special issue of *Droit et Société*, no. 68.

Galston, William. 2002. *Liberal Pluralism: The Implications of Value Pluralism for Political Theory and Practice*. Cambridge: Cambridge University Press.

Gaonkar, Dilip, and Charles Taylor. 2006. "Block Thinking and Internal Criticism." *Public Culture* 18 (3): 453–55.

Gaspard, Françoise, and Farhad Khosrokhavar. 1995. *Le foulard et la République*. Paris: La Découverte.

Gauchet, Marcel. 1985. *Le désenchantement du monde: Une histoire politique de la religion*. Paris: Gallimard.

———. 1998. *La religion dans la démocratie: Parcours de la laïcité*. Paris: Gallimard.

Godard, Bernard, and Sylvie Taussig. 2007. *Les musulmans en France, courants, institutions, communautés: Un état des lieux*. Paris: Robert Laffont.

Graham, William. 1993. "Traditionalism in Islam: An Essay in Interpretation." *Journal of Interdisciplinary History* 23 (3): 495–522.

Guénif-Souilamas, Nacira. 2000. *Des Beurettes aux descendantes d'immigrants nord-africains*. Paris: Bernard Grasset.

Hafiz, Chems-eddine, and Gilles Devers. 2005. *Droit et religion musulmane*. Paris: Dalloz.

Hajjat, Abdellali. 2005. *Immigration postcoloniale et mémoire*. Paris: L'Harmattan.

Hallaq, Wael B. 1997. *A History of Islamic Legal Theories: An Introduction to Sunnî usûl al-fiqh*. Cambridge: Cambridge University Press.

Hargreaves, Alec G. 1995. *Immigration, "Race" and Ethnicity in Contemporary France*. London: Routledge.

Haut Conseil à l'Integration. 2001. *L'Islam dans la République*. Paris: La Documentation Française.

Héran, Françoise, Alexandra Filhon, and Christine Deprez. 2001. "A dynamique des langues de France au fil du XXème siècle." *Opulations & Sociétés* 376 (February): 1–4.

Hyman, Paula E. 1998. *The Jews of Modern France*. Berkeley and Los Angeles: University of California Press.

Ibn Ashur, Muhammad al-Tahir. 2006. *Treatise on Maqâsid al-Sharî'a*, trans. Mohamed el-Tahir el-Mesawi (orig. Arabic 1946). London: International Institute of Islamic Thought.

IFOP. 2001. "L'Islam en France et les reactions aux attentats du 11 septembre 2001." Paris: Institut Français de l'Opinion Publique.

INED. n.d. *Genre et population, France 2000*. Paris: INED.

al-Jazaïri, Abubaker Jaber. 2001 *La voie du Musulman* (trans. of Minhaj al-Muslîm). Paris: Maison d'Ennour.

Johansen, Baber. 1999. "The Muslim Fiqh as a Sacred Law: Religion, Law, and Ethics in a Normative System." In *Contingency in a Sacred Law: Legal and Ethical Norms in the Muslim Fiqh*, ed. Baber Johansen. Leiden: Brill.

Johnston, David L. 2007. "'Allâl al-Fâsî: Shari'a as Blueprint for Righteous Global Citizenship?" In *Shari'a: Islamic Law in the Contemporary Context*, ed. Abbas Amanat and Frank Griffel, 83–103. Stanford: Stanford University Press.

Kamali, Mohammad Hashim. 2008. *Shari'ah Law: An Introduction*. Oxford: Oneworld.

Kastoryano, Riva. 1986. *Être Turc en France: Réflexions sur familles et communauté*. Paris: L'Harmattan.

———. 2002. *Negotiating Identities: States and Immigrants in France and Germany*. Princeton, NJ: Princeton University Press.

Kepel, Gilles. 1991. *Les banlieues de l'Islam: Naissance d'une religion en France*. Paris: Éditions du Seuil.

———. 2004. *The War for Muslim Minds: Islam and the West*. Cambridge, MA: Belknap Press of Harvard University Press.

Khosrokhavar, Farhad. 1997. *L'Islam des jeunes*. Paris: Flammarion.

———. 2004. *L'Islam dans les prisons*. Paris: Balland.

Kymlicka, Will. 1995. *Multicultural Citizenship: A Liberal Theory of Minority Rights*. Oxford: Clarendon Press.

Lahouri, Besma. 2004. "Polygamie: Cet interdit qui a le droit de cite." *L'Express*, January 15, 2004.

Lamont, Michèle, and Laurent Thévenot, eds. 2000. *Rethinking Comparative Cultural Sociology: Repertoires of Evaluation in France and the United States*. Cambridge: Cambridge University Press.

Laurence, Jonathan, and Justin Vaisse. 2006. *Integrating Islam: Political and Religious Challenges in Contemporary France*. Washington, DC: Brookings Institution Press.

Le Pautrement, Pascal. 2003. *Le politique musulmane de la France au XXème siècle*. Paris: Maisonneuve et Larose.

Lebovics, Herman. 1992. *True France: The Wars over Cultural Identity, 1900–1945*. Ithaca, NY: Cornell University Press.

Lepoutre, David. 2001. *Cœur de banlieue: Codes, rites, et langages* (first published 1997). Paris: Odile Jacob.

Lewis, Phillip. 2002. *Islamic Britain: Religion, Politics, and Identity among British Muslims*, 2nd ed. London: I. B. Tauris.

Libchaber, Rémy. 1996. "L'Exception d'ordre public en droit international privé." In *L'Ordre public à la fin du XXème siècle*, ed. Thierry Revet, 65–81. Paris: Dalloz.

Luizard, Pierre-Jean. 2006. *Le Choc Colonial et l'Islam: Les politiques religieuses des puissances coloniales en terres d'islam*. Paris: La Découverte.

MacMullen, Ian. 2007. *Faith in Schools? Autonomy, Citizenship, and Religious Education in the Liberal State*. Princeton, NJ: Princeton University Press.

Mahmood, Saba. 2005. *Politics of Piety: The Islamic Revival and the Feminist Subject*. Princeton, NJ: Princeton University Press.

Makri, Yamin. 2005. "Du sense et de la cohérence," www.oumma.com, May 27, 2005; accessed November 9, 2007.

Mandaville, Peter. 2006. "Islamic Education in Britain: Approaches to Religious Knowledge in a Pluralistic Society." In *Schooling Islam*, ed. Robert W. Hefner and Muhammad Qasim Zaman, 224–41. Princeton, NJ: Princeton University Press.

Mariani, Ermete. 2003. "Yussuf al-Qardawi: pouvoir électronique, financier et symbolique." In *Mondialisation et nouveaux medias dans l'espace arabe*, ed. Frank Mermer, 195–204. Paris: Maisonneuve et Larose.

——— 2006. "Les oulémas syriens à la recherché d'une audience virtuelle." In *La société de l'information au Proche-Orient: Internet en Syrie et au Liban*, ed. Yves Gonzalez-Quijano and Christophe Varin, 93–115: Beirut: Presses de l'Université Saint-Joseph.

Masud, Muhammad Khalid. 1977. *Islamic Legal Philosophy: A Study of Abu Ishaq al- Shatibi's Life and Thought*. Islamabad: Islamic Research Institute.

———. 2001. *Muslim Jurists' Quest for the Normative Basis of Sharî'a*. Leiden: ISIM Occasional Papers.

Masud, Muhammad Khalid, Brinkley Messick, and David S. Powers, eds. 1996. *Islamic Legal Interpretation: Muftis and Their Fatwas*. Cambridge, MA: Harvard University Press.

Maurin, Éric. 2004. *Le ghetto français*. Paris: Éditions du Seuil et La République des Idées.

Maussen, Marcel. 2005. "Making Muslim Presence Meaningful: Studies on Islam and Mosques in Western Europe." Working Paper 05/03. Amsterdam: Amsterdam School for Social Science Research.

———. 2007. "Islamic Presence and Mosque Establishment in France: Colonialism, Arrangements for Guestworkers and Citizenship." *Journal of Ethnic and Migration Studies* 33 (6): 981–1002.

———. 2009. "Constructing Mosques: The Governance of Islam in France and the Netherlands." Ph.D. dissertation, University of Amsterdam.

Mesure, Sylvie, and Alain Renaut. 1999. *Alter ego: Les paradoxes de l'identité démocratique*. Paris: Flammarion.

Metcalf, Barbara Daly. 1996a. "New Medinas: The Tablighi Jama'at in America and Europe." In *Making Muslim Space in North America and Europe*, ed. Barbara Daly Metcalf, 110–27. Berkeley and Los Angeles: University of California Press.

———, ed. 1996b. *Making Muslim Space in North America and Europe*. Berkeley and Los Angeles: University of California Press.

Meurs, Dominique, Ariane Pailhé, and Patrick Simon. 2005. *Mobilité intergénérationelle et persistence des inégalités*. Paris: INED, Documents de Travail 130.

Mir-Hosseini, Ziba. 2001. *Marriage on Trial: A Study of Islamic Family Law*, rev. ed. London: I.B. Tauris.

Monéger, Françoise. 2005. *Droit international privé*, 3rd ed. Paris: LexisNexis.

Ndiaye, Pap. 2007. *La condition noire: Essai sur une minorité française*. Paris: Calmann-Lévy.

Noiriel, Gérard. 1995. *The French Melting Pot* (orig. French 1988). Minneapolis: University of Minnesota Press.

Opwijs, Felicitas. 2007. "Islamic Law and Legal Change: The Concept of Maslaha in Classical and Contemporary Islamic Legal Theory." In *Shari'a: Islamic Law in the Contemporary Context*, ed. Abbas Amanat and Frank Griffel, 62–82. Stanford: Stanford University Press.

Oubrou, Tareq. 2000. "Le 'minimum islamique' pour l'abbatage ritual en France." *La Médina* 5:42–43.

———. 2004. "La sharî'a de minorité: Réflexions pour une intégration légale de l'islam." In *Lectures contemporaines du droit islamique: Europe et monde arabe*, ed. Franck Frégosi, 205–30. Strasbourg: Presses Universitaires de Strasbourg.

Pelletier, Denis. 2002. *La Crise Catholique: Religion, société, politique en France (1965–1978)*. Paris: Payot.

Petek, Gaye. 1998. "Les ressortissants Turcs en France et l'évolution de leur projet migratoire." *Hommes et Migrations* 1212 (March–April): 14–23.

Peter, Frank. 2006. "Leading the Community of the Middle Way: A Study of the Muslim Field in France." *Muslim World*, 707–36.

Pew Global Attitudes Project. 2006. *The Great Divide: How Westerners and Muslims View Each Other*. Available: http://pewglobal.org/reports/display .php?ReportID=253.

Pitti, Laure. 2008. "'Travailleurs de France, voilà votre nom': Les mobilisations des ouvriers étrangers dans les usines et les foyers durant les années 1970." In *Histoire politique des immigrations (post)coloniales: France, 1920–2008*, ed. Ahmed Boubeker and Abdellali Hajjat, 95–111. Paris: Éditions Amsterdam.

Powers, David S. 2001. *Law, Society, and Culture in the Maghrib, 1300–1500.* Cambridge: Cambridge University Press.

al-Qaradâwî, Yûsuf. 1991. *Islamic Awakening between Rejection and Extremism* (orig. Arabic 1982), 2nd ed. London: Zain International.

———. 1995. *Le Licite et l'Illicite en Islam* (trans. of *Al-halâl wa al-harâm fî Islam*). Paris: Al-Qalam.

———. 2001. *Fî Fiqh al-aqalliyât al-muslima: Hayât al-muslimîn wasat almudjtma'ât al-ukhrâ.* Cairo: Dâr al-Churûq.

———. 2002. *Priorities of the Islamic movement: The Coming Phase* (orig. Arabic 1990). Swansea, UK: Awakening Publications.

Ramadan, Tariq. 1998. *Aux Sources du Renouveau Musulman.* Paris: Bayard Éditions.

———. 2002. *Dâr ash-shahâda: L'Occident, espace du témoignage.* Lyon: Tawhid.

Rath, Jan, Rinus Penninx, Kees Groenendijk, and Astrid Meyer. 1999. "The Politics of Recognizing Religious Diversity in Europe: Social Reactions to the Institutionalization of Islam in the Netherlands, Belgium and Great Britain." *Netherlands Journal of Social Sciences* 35 (1): 53–68.

Rawls, John. 1999. "The Idea of Public Reason Revisited." In *The Law of Peoples*, 131–80. Cambridge, MA: Harvard University Press.

al-Raysuni, Ahmad. 2005. *Imam al-Shâtibî's Theory of the Higher Objectives and Intents of Islamic Law.* London: International Institute of Islamic Thought.

Renard, Michel. 1999. "France, terre des mosquées?" *Hommes et Migrations* 1220: 30–41.

Rohe, Matthias. 2004. "The formation of a European Shari'a." In *Muslims in Europe: From the Margin to the Center*, ed. Jamal Malik, 161–84. Münster: Lit Verlag.

Rosanvallon, Pierre. 2004. *Le modèle politique français.* Paris: Éditions du Seuil.

———. 2006. *La contre-démocratie: La politique à l'âge de la défiance.* Paris: Éditions du Seuil.

Roy, Olivier. 1994. *The Failure of Political Islam* (orig. French 1992). Cambridge, MA: Harvard University Press.

———. 1999. *Vers un islam européen.* Paris: Esprit.

———. 2002. *L'islam mondialisé.* Paris: Éditions du Seuil.

———. 2007. *Secularism Confronts Islam* (orig. French 2005). New York: Columbia University Press.

Rude-Antoine, Edwige, coordinator. 1998. *L'Étranger en France, face au regard du droit.* Paris: Unité de Recherche Migrations et Société (URMIS), unpublished report.

Saeed, Abdullah. 1996. *Islamic Banking and Interest: A Study of the Prohibition of Riba and Its Contemporary Interpretation.* Leiden: Brill.

Sargent, Carolyn, and Dennis Cordell. 2003. "Polygamy, Disrupted Reproduction, and the State: Malian Migrants in Paris, France." *Social Science and Medicine* 56 (9): 1961–72.

Sargent, Carolyn F., and Stéphanie Larchanché-Kim. 2006. "Liminal Lives: Immigration Status, Gender, and the Construction of Identities among Malian Migrants in Paris." *American Behavioral Scientist* 50 (1): 9–26

Sayad, Abdelmalek. 1995. *Un Nanterre algérien, terre de bidonvilles*. Paris: Éditions Autrement.

———. 1999. *La double absence*. Paris: Éditions du Seuil.

Schnapper, Dominique. 1998. *Community of Citizens: On the Modern Idea of Nationality* (orig. French 1994), trans. Séverine Rosée. New Brunswick, NJ: Transaction Publishers.

Scott, Joan. 2007. *The Politics of the Veil*. Princeton, NJ: Princeton University Press.

Shachar, Ayelet. 2001. *Multicultural Jurisdictions: Cultural Differences and Women's Rights*. Cambridge: Cambridge University Press.

Shepard, Todd. 2006. *The Invention of Decolonization: The Algerian War and the Remaking of France*. Ithaca, NY: Cornell University Press.

Silverstein, Paul A. 2004. *Algeria in France: Transpolitics, Race, and Nation*. Bloomington: Indiana University Press.

Simon, G. 1979. *L'Espace des travailleurs Tunisiens en France*. Poitiers: Université de Poitiers.

Simon, Jacques, ed. 2002. *L'immigration algérienne en France, de 1962 à nos jours*. Paris: L'Harmattan.

Soares, Benjamin F. 2004. "An African Muslim Saint and His Followers in France." *Journal of Ethnic and Migration Studies* 30 (5): 913–27.

Souilamas, Nacira Guénif. 2000. *Des "beurettes" aux descendantes d'immigrants nord-africains*. Paris: Grasset.

Soysal, Y. N. 2002. "Citizenship and Identity: Living in Diasporas in Postwar Europe?" In *The Postnational Self*, ed. U. Hedetoft and M. Hjort, 137–51. Minneapolis: University of Minnesota Press.

Stora, Benjamin. 1992. *Ils venaient d'Algérie: L'immigration algérienne en France, 1912–1992*. Paris: Fayard.

———. 2004. *Histoire de l'Algérie coloniale (1830–1954)*. Paris: La Découverte.

Tellier, Thibault. 2007. *Le Temps des HLM, 1945–1975: La saga urbaine des Trent Glorieuses*. Paris: Éditions Autrement.

Ternisien, Xavier. 2002. *La France des mosquées*. Paris: Albin Michel.

Tietze, Nikola. 2002. *Jeunes musulmans de France et d'Allemagne: Les constructions subjectives de l'identité*. Paris: L'Harmattan.

Timera, Mahamet. 1996. *Les Soninké en France: D'une histoire à l'autre*. Paris: Karthala.

Tippett-Spirtou, Sandy. 2000. *French Catholicism: Church, State and Society in a Changing Era*. Houndmills, UK: Macmillan.

Tribalat, Michèle. 1995. *Faire France: Une grande enquête sur les immigrés et leurs enfants*. Paris: La Découverte.

Tribalat, Michèle, Patrick Simon, and Benoît Riandey. 1996. *De l'immigration à l'assimilation: Enquête sur les populations d'origine étrangère en France*. Paris: La Découverte.

Troger, Vincent. 2001. *L'École*. Paris: Le Cavalier Bleu.

Tucker, Judith E. 1998. *In the House of the Law: Gender and Islamic Law in Ottoman Syria and Palestine*. Berkeley and Los Angeles: University of California Press.

Venel, Nancy. 1999. *Musulmanes francaises: Des pratiquantes voilées à l'université*. Paris: L'Harmattan.

———. 2004. *Musulmans et citoyens*. Paris: Presses Universitaires de France.

Viet, Vincent. 1998. *La France immigrée*. Paris: Fayard.

Wadud, Amina. 2006. *Inside the Gender Jihad: Women's Reform in Islam*. Oxford: Oneworld Publications.

Walzer, Michael. 1983. *Spheres of Justice: A Defence of Pluralism and Equality*. Oxford: Basil Blackwell.

Weibel, Nadine B. 2002. *Par-delà le voile: Femmes d'islam en Europe*. Brussels: Éditions Complexe.

Weil, Patrick. 1991. *La France et ses étrangers: L'aventure d'une politique de l'immigration de 1938 à nos jours*, 2nd ed. Paris: Gallimard.

———. 2008. *Liberté, Égalité, Discriminations: L' "Identité Nationale" au regard de l'histoire*. Paris: Grasset.

Welchman, Lynn. 2007. *Women and Muslim Family Laws in Arab States: A Comparative Overview of Textual Development and Advocacy*. Amsterdam: Amsterdam University Press.

Werbner, P. S. 2003. *Pilgrims of Love: Anthropology of a Global Sufi Cult*. London: Hurst.

Wieviorka, Michel, ed. 1996. *Une société fragmentée? Le multiculturalisme en débat*. Paris: La Découverte.

———. 2007. *The Lure of Anti-Semitism: Hatred of Jews in Present-Day France* (orig. French 2005), trans. Kristin Couper Lobel and Anna Declerck. Leiden: Brill.

Wihtol de Wenden, Catherine, and Rémy Leveau. 2000. *Le Beurgeoisie: Les trois ages de la vie associative issue de l'immigration*. Paris: CNRS Éditions.

Zaman, Muhammad Qasim. 2002. *The Ulama in Contemporary Islam*. Princeton, NJ: Princeton University Press.

———. 2004. "The 'Ulama of Contemporary Islam and Their Conception of the Common Good." In *Public Islam and the Common Good*, ed. Armando Salvatore and Dale F. Eickelman, 129–55. Leiden: Brill.

———. 2006. "Epilogue: Competing Conceptions of Religious Education." In *Schooling Islam*, ed. Robert W. Hefner and Muhammad Qasim Zaman, 107–30. Princeton, NJ: Princeton University Press.

Zeghal, Malika. 1996. *Gardiens de l'Islam: Les oulémas d'al-Azhar dans l'Egypte contemporaine*. Paris: Presses de Sciences-Po.

———. 2006. "The 'Recentering' of Religious Knowledge and Discourse: The Case of al-Azhar in Twentieth-Century Egypt." In *Schooling Islam*, ed. Robert W. Hefner and Muhammad Qasim Zaman, 107–30. Princeton, NJ: Princeton University Press.

Index

'Abduh, Muhammad, 65, 100, 141, 203n38
Abidi, Ahmed, 86, 92–95, 104, 142
Abortion, 83–84, 135–36
Adda'wa. *See* Mosques
Adoption, 93–94
Advanced Institute in Islamic Sciences (ISSI), 95–105
Africans: North, 16–21, 31–33; West, 11–12, 17–18, 59–60. *See also* Algerians; *Maghrébins;* Moroccans; Tunisians
Â'isha (wife of the Prophet Muhammad), 76, 97, 170
al-Albâni, Muhammad Nâsir al-Dîn, 73, 77–78, 156, 159, 203n38, 213n17
Algeria, 15–18, 25–26; colonial divisions in, 174, 201n4, 203n40; marriage in, 158, 160–61, 210n3; and Paris Mosque, 25–26; war in, 16, 19, 21, 30
Algerians: identity of, 22–23, 105; as imams, 54, 88, 204n57; and immigration to France, 16–18, 26, 201n15; in mosques, 33, 38, 52, 61, 204n57
Arafa, Hichem El, 67–68; at CERSI, 50, 66–87, 92–95, 113, 184, 207n12; on objectives of Qur'an, 81–84, 90, 135–36, 166–68, 171–72; on fiqh of minorities, 141, 148
Arabic language, 17, 55, 72; use of in debates, 149–52; instruction in 31, 55, 69, 85–89, 93, 95–98, 102, 105–7, 112–115, 207n4, 213n11; at Islamic secondary schools, 118, 120–21, 124
ibn Ashur, Muhammad al-Tahir, 56, 65, 82–83, 88, 100, 207n14
Associations, 31–33, 49–51, 179–85; Catholic, 181; Jewish, 181–82
Aubervilliers, 111, 117
AVS (À Votre Service), 45–46, 49, 170–71
al-Azhar University, 27, 140–41, 209n9
Azouz, Karim, 49–51, 57, 148–49, 205n13

Babès, Leïla, 189–90
Banking, 83, 88, 138–43, 146–49, 155–56, 187, 209n2, 209n8. See also *Ribâ*

ibn Bayyah, Abdullah (Ben Biya), 143–44
ibn Baz, Abdelaziz, 56, 73–74, 77, 79, 162, 203n38, 206n20, 213n17
Bekri, Abdelkrim, 88–89
Berber languages, 17, 21, 33, 59
Beur, 21–22
Bid'a, 56, 77, 152, 172
Boltanski and Thévenot, 199n6
Boubakeur, Dalil, 26, 43, 88, 205n12
Boulâbi, Abdurraouf, 100, 103
Bourdieu, Pierre, 108–9, 199n6
Bourget, Salon du, 143, 185–88
Britain, contrast with France, 9, 33
al-Bûtî, Muhammad Sa'îd Ramadân, 93, 140–41, 146, 148, 155–56, 208n3
al-Bûti, Mohamed Tawfik, 150–56

Catholic Church: and associations, 181–82, 214n19; and Islam, 30; and the Republic, 7, 110, 164, 188–89, 195–96; and schools, 110, 116–18, 181, 183, 208n1
Center of Studies and Research on Islam (CERSI). *See* Arafa, Hichem El
Citizenship, 3, 5, 7, 9, 21, 30, 110, 180, 182–83, 191–92, 201n4, 202nn24 and 27, 212n36; in Algeria, 25, 174
Civil unions, 119–20, 164
Clichy-sous-Bois, 20, 37–43, 202n20
Collective of French Muslims, 44–51
Colonialism, 25–26, 30, 33, 174
Communalism, 111, 116, 179–88, 191, 213n1

Daffé, Mamadou, 43, 48, 204n57
Damascus, University of, 92–93, 141, 150
Dâr al-islâm, 146–47, 155
Discrimination, 19–20
Divorce: in French civil law, 173–77, 197, 212n36; Islamic, 41, 55–56, 79–81, 102–4, 143, 154, 157–58, 161–63, 166–68, 206n19, 210n20, 211n12

Ethnicity: in associations, 21, 180; and housing, 20–21; in Islam, 3, 58–62